W9-AHR-773

TREASURES OF
Colorado

Colorado State Capitol in Denver

by William Faubion
and Dale Campbell

MORGAN & CHASE PUBLISHING INC.

a part of the Morgan & Chase Treasure Series
www.treasuresof.com

© 2008 Morgan & Chase Publishing, Inc. All rights reserved.
No portion of this book may be reproduced or utilized in any
form, or by any electronic, mechanical or other means without
the prior written permission of the publisher.

Morgan & Chase Publishing, Inc.
531 Parsons Drive, Medford, Oregon 97501
(888) 557-9328
www.treasuresof.com

Printed and bound by Taylor Specialty Books–Dallas TX
First edition 2008
ISBN: 978-1-933989-26-6

THE
TREASURE
SERIES

I gratefully acknowledge the contributions
of the many people involved in the writing and production of this book.
Their tireless dedication to this endeavour has been inspirational.
–Damon Neal, Publisher

The Morgan & Chase Publishing Home Team

Operations Department:
V.P. of Operations–Cindy Tilley Faubion
Travel Writer Liaison–Anne Boydston
Shipping & Receiving–Virginia Arias
Customer Service Relations–Elizabeth Taylor, Vikki West
IT Engineer–Ray Ackerman
Receptionist–Samara Sharp

Production Department:
Office Manager–Sue Buda
Editor/Writer–Robyn Sutherland
House Writer–Prairie Smallwood
Proof Editor–Clarice Rodriguez
Photo Coordinator–Wendy L. Gay
Photo Editor–Mary Murdock
Graphic Design Team–C.S. Rowan, Jesse Gifford, Jacob Kristof

Administrative Department:
CFO–Emily Wilkie
Accounting Assistants–David Grundvig, Tiffany Myers
Website Designer–Molly Bermea
Website Software Developer–Ben Ford

Contributing Writers:
Mary Beth Lee, Trent Bakich, Scott Woodward, Catherine Perez, Dusty Alexander, Jeanie Erwin,
Jennifer Buckner, Kait Fairchild, Karuna Glomb, Kate Zdrojewski, Laura Young, Marek Alday, Mary Knepp,
Nancy McClain, Paul Hadella, Sandy McLain, Sarah Brown, Todd Wels, Tamara Cornett

Special Recognition to:
Casey Faubion, April Higginbotham, Gregory Scott, Megan Glomb, Eric Molinsky, Marie Manson,
William M. Evans, Heather Allen, Gene Mitts

While we have made every effort to ensure that the information contained in this book is accurate at the time of publishing, neither the authors nor Morgan & Chase Publishing shall have any liability to any person or entity with respect to any loss or damage caused or alleged to be caused directly or indirectly by use or inclusion of the information contained in this book. Trademarked names appear throughout this book. Rather than list the names and entities that own the trademarks or insert a trademark symbol with each mention of a trademarked name, we state that we are using the names only for editorial purposes and to the benefit of the trademark owner with no intention of infringing upon that trademark. All trademarks or service marks are the property of their respective owners.

This book is dedicated to Colorado's most amazing resource,
the people who live there.

Foreword

Welcome to the *Treasures of Colorado*. This book is a resource that can guide you to some of the most inviting places in Colorado, a state filled with rich history and rugged natural beauty. From the awe-inspiring Rocky Mountains to the high deserts of Mesa County, Colorado offers stunning views of a diverse landscape. From west to east, the state consists of desert-like basins, windswept plateaus, alpine mountains and the grasslands of the Great Plains. Colorado is known for its natural splendor and its intelligent and imaginative people. They've created some of the finest resorts, galleries, shopping, recreational opportunities and cuisine to be found anywhere in the world.

While visiting Colorado, you should partake in its fascinating cultural heritage and take a moment to experience the interesting and moving events throughout the state. People will love to spend the weekend in Denver, also known as the Mile-High City, where they can attend a play, stroll through the Denver Art Museum or experience a one-of-a-kind performance in the Red Rocks Amphitheatre. Colorado also has an abundance of natural beauty. The Continental Divide stretches through the heart of Colorado, encompassing nearly every peak along the Rocky Mountains. Whether they're photographing the wildflower bloom in Estes Park, exploring the trailheads of Pike's Peak or trying the exhilarating slopes of Vail, outdoor enthusiasts will enjoy an endless supply of winter and summer adventures.

In preparing the *Treasures of Colorado*, we talked to literally thousands of business people about their products and their passion for excellence. We walked the Continental Divide Trail and marveled at the magnificent peaks of the Rockies. We visited community theatres and attractions such as wildlife refuges and museums, and enjoyed many types of family entertainment. All this information was compiled so that you can find the best places in Colorado to eat, shop, play, explore, learn and relax. We hope the *Treasures of Colorado* will entice you to travel through this enchanting state, meet its charming people and explore its many wonders.

—Cindy Tilley Faubion

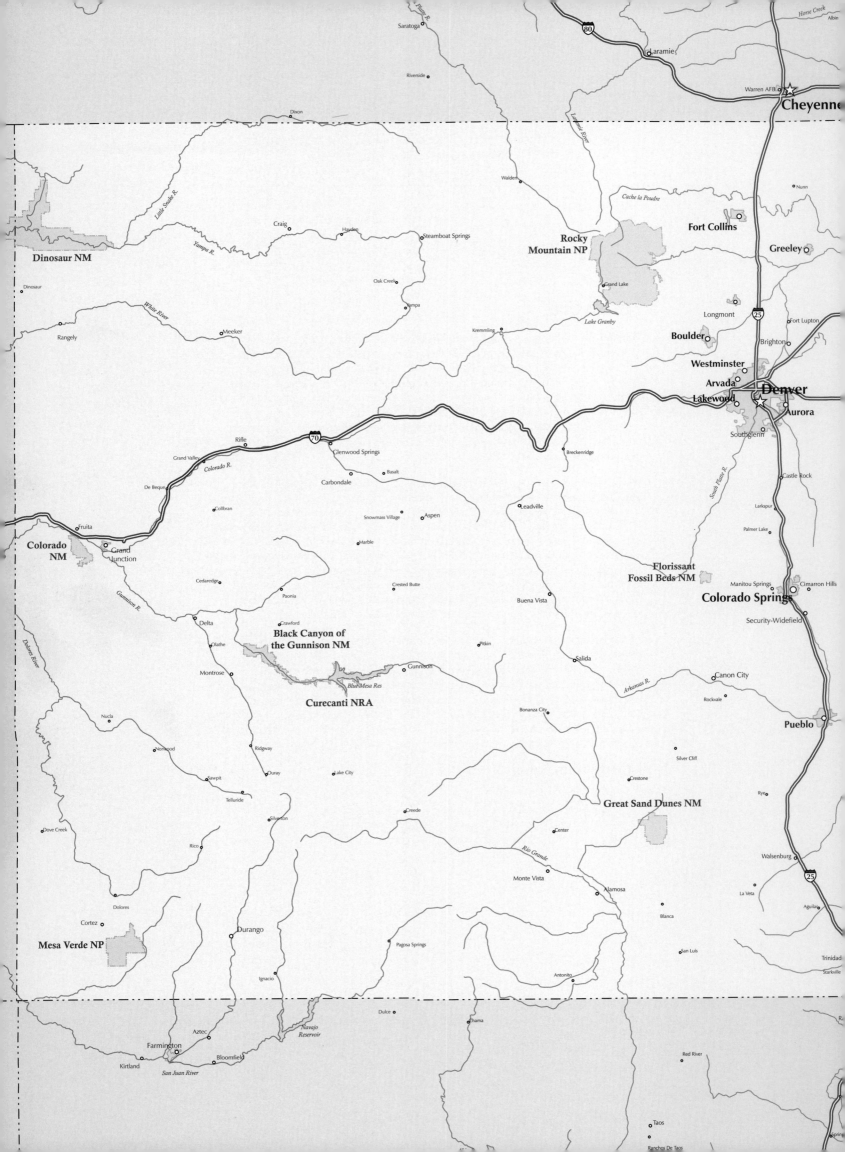

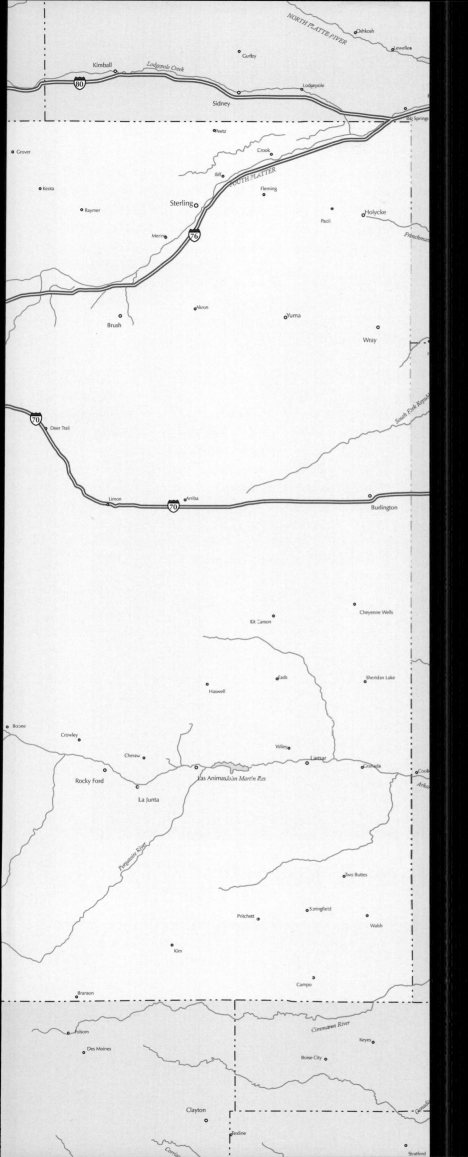

How to use this book

The *Treasures of Colorado* is divided
alphabetically into 14 categories, starting with
Accommodations & Resorts and ending with
Wines, Brews & Spirits. If you want to find a
specific Treasure, just check under the business
name in the Index.

We have provided contact information for each
Treasure in the book, because these are places
and businesses which we encourage you to visit
on your travels through Colorado.

We hope you find this book to be both
beautiful and useful.

Accommodations & Resorts

The Delaware Hotel

The gold that was discovered in present-day Leadville in 1860 was quickly depleted, but then came silver and then came the railroad. By 1886, Leadville was a frenetic boomtown, and the Delaware Hotel was accommodating weary travelers in 50 handsomely furnished guest rooms. The building was fitted throughout with steam heat, hot and cold water and gaslights. It was, in short, the best that money could buy, and indeed the three brothers who financed this so-called Crown Jewel of Leadville spent $60,000 on the project. Today, the Delaware Hotel preserves not only the elegant Victorian architecture of that era but something of its freewheeling spirit. For example, if you stay here and like that brass bed that you slept on, you can buy it. The gift shop provides an emporium-style browsing experience for Native American jewelry, area souvenirs and Victorian clothing. The hotel itself is an ever-changing gallery of antiques put into everyday use in the lobby, halls and 40 guest rooms. Most items are for sale. Adding to the fun, there's tea in the afternoon, parlor games in the evening and an interactive murder mystery a couple of times a year. Enjoy the view to the south of the two tallest mountains in Colorado as you connect with the past at the Delaware Hotel.

700 Harrison Avenue, Leadville CO
(719) 486-1418 or (800) 748-2004
www.delawarehotel.com

Photos by Jim Jensen

Water Valley

Water Valley is northern Colorado's premier resort-style lakefront golf course development. Within easy reach of the Denver metro area, the Rocky Mountains, and Denver International Airport, Water Valley maintains a feeling that is worlds away. Developer Martin Lind, a Windsor native, envisioned a new kind of Colorado, and Water Valley looks as if someone lifted it from a seashore town and set it down on the high arid plains of Colorado. The resort's 1,500 acres include five serene lakes where residents can sail, swim or match wits with wily bass, walleye and crappie. The lakes' white pelicans provide the theme for PelicanFest, the community's annual two-day festival in May. Set against a stunning Rocky Mountain backdrop, the Pelican Lakes Golf & Country Club features a 27 hole layout including the new nine hole Pelican Falls course. The original 18 was designed by Ted Robinson, Sr., one of the top golf course architects in the world. The Pelican Lakes 18 hole course, which winds along the Poudre River corridor and crosses the river four times, boasts more shoreline than any other in the United States. *Golf Digest* gives the 18 holes of the Pelican Lakes course a four-star rating. After golf, visit Austin's Homestead Bar & Grill which specializes in fresh seafood, hand-cut steaks for lunch or dinner and the most incredible sunsets west of the Mississippi River. Water Valley offers an array of maintenance-free housing options, from single-family and patio homes to townhomes, condominiums and luxury lakefront estate homes, there is a residence for almost every kind of buyer. Plans are available from dozens of architects and builders. Coming attractions include the Good Samaritan Senior Living Resort, an independent senior living community slated to open in the spring 2008. Come to a place where people live to play—it's an adult's dream and a kid's paradise. Learn how you can make the Water Valley lifestyle your own.

1625 Pelican Lakes Point, Suite 201, Windsor CO
(970) 686-5828 or (888) 233-5828
www.watervalley.com

Photos by Jim Jensen

Four Peaks Inn

Comfort and convenience would be reasons enough to stay at Four Peaks Inn, but owners JJ and Shannon Bosgraaf treat guests to the kind of extras that add another level of charm to Breckenridge. The 1886 house offers seven bedrooms with European flair, cable television, wireless access and magnificent mountain views. Located in the heart of the historic district, you'll be 300 yards from the Quicksilver ski lift on Peak 9 and just a short walk to the best restaurants and Main Street shopping. If it takes more than that to get you out from under your down comforter in the morning, JJ and Shannon's cooking will do it. Wake up to the aroma of banana streusel French toast with amaretto sauce, eggs Benedict or made-to-order omelettes. In the evening, enjoy a chocolate fondue for two or hand-dipped chocolate covered strawberries. This cheerful Victorian house contains two large common rooms with fireplaces, a kitchenette, outdoor hot tub overlooking the slopes, and steam sauna. JJ and Shannon host intimate weddings and gladly make arrangements with local merchants to make your special day something to remember. Shannon and JJ have put together creative packages for both summer and winter. Enhance your Rocky Mountain escape at Four Peaks Inn.

407 S Ridge Street, Breckenridge CO
(970) 453-3813
www.fourpeaksinn.com

1892 Victoria's Keep Bed & Breakfast

The most romantic bed-and-breakfast in the Colorado Springs area sits at the base of Pike's Peak, within walking distance of mineral springs, shopping and dining in historic Manitou Springs. Occupying an immaculate Victorian home, 1892 Victoria's Keep Bed & Breakfast that has been named three times by *Arrington's Inn Traveler* as the Best Place to Celebrate Honeymoons and Anniversaries. They've also been lauded as having the most comfortable beds of any establishment in the region. Karen Cullen and Jay Rohrer have created one of the best little inns in the West. Victoria's Keep is a creekside piece of heaven with a wraparound porch surrounded by trees. The inn features six unique and elegant guest rooms with private baths, European featherbeds and fluffy down comforters. Many include Jacuzzi tubs for two and a fireplace. The rooms are decorated with period antiques and collectibles, exuding both elegance and comfort. Karen and Jay are passionate cooks who serve the kind of breakfasts that make you want to write songs about them. You'll dine on such delicacies as Grand Marnier stuffed French toast and eggs Benedict over savory waffles. They also offer such special touches as couples' massage right in your room, flower bouquets, and chocolates. If you are looking for an ideal place to hold an intimate wedding, you can't do better than this. The next time you are traveling near Colorado Springs, call Karen and Jay at 1892 Victoria's Keep Bed & Breakfast. You'll leave this cozy retreat feeling pampered and refreshed.

202 Ruxton Avenue, Manitou Springs CO (719) 685-5354 or (800) 905-5337
www.victoriaskeep.com

Ores & Mine
Bed & Breakfast

Ores & Mine Bed & Breakfast was built in the mid-1950s as a family getaway by owner John Cornella's father, Chester "Boots" Cornella, an Italian immigrant and miner. The Cornella Cabin, as it was prominently known, is situated in the shadow of Mt. Elbert, Colorado's highest peak, is 500 feet from the state's largest glacial lake and surrounded by six of the state's 14,000-foot mountains. In 1995, the Cornella Cabin was transformed to Ores & Mine Bed & Breakfast, keeping its original flavor as a rustic mountain getaway. John and Donna offer five separate rustic units reflecting the décor of the early mining era with the amenities of modern day. Each unit has a private bath, gas fireplace and is named after one of the historic gold or silver mines in Lake County. In addition to the comforts of each guest room, a large recreation room is provided for your relaxation. You can enjoy a pool table, ping pong table, juke box, shuffle board, fireplace, board games and an outside hot tub that overlooks the surroundings. A full, distinguished breakfast awaits you each morning in the common room. The menu varies daily to include coffee, tea, juice, fruit, pastries, meat and an entrée. The Twin Lakes area is a playground for many summer and winter activities. Your stay at Ores & Mine can be as relaxing or as adventurous as your mood requires.

6285 County Road #10, Twin Lakes CO
(719) 486-3552
www.oresandmine.com

SummitCove.com

If you are going to rent a condo online for a vacation at Keystone Resort, you will want to know what you are getting. The owners of SummitCove.com, Peter and Cheri Reeburgh, want to know what you are getting, too. They not only take all the photographs for their website, they stay in each condo they represent to make sure it is equipped as described. Summit Cove condos are just minutes away from Keystone Ski Resort's River Run and Mountain House ski lifts and Arapahoe Basin ski resort. Free shuttle service will bring you closer to golf, horseback riding, mountain biking and boating on Keystone Lake. When you return to your condo at day's end, you will find such luxuries as hot tubs and saunas, pools, tennis courts, laundry services and Internet access. The Reeburghs handle 80 assorted properties, from lodges you approach and depart via skis to luxury homes. Many units favor families with young children and include such equipment as cradles, high chairs and toys. Others offer outdoor heaters on the deck. The user-friendly website makes booking your condo and knowing what to expect a breeze. Not only do Peter and Cheri want to satisfy vacationers, they want condo owners to get a fair deal too. They charge a 25 percent commission rate for property management services. Make the most of your Keystone Resort vacation with SummitCove.com.

www.summitcove.com

A Touch of Heaven
Talmar Bed & Breakfast

Welcome to Talmar Bed & Breakfast, an excellent alternative to hotel living. Nestled in the foothills in Golden, this two-acre estate affords Classic Elegance Amidst Cozy, Country Comfort. Designed and built by Kathy Bury in 1976, Talmar expresses all the charm, creativity and commitment to succeed that one woman can possess. The Royal Suite is sheer elegance. Mirrored walls reflect the morning sun, while the sunken bath is accented by a quartz waterfall, five-by-seven-foot Jacuzzi and redwood sauna. With a marble fireplace to warm the ambiance, a white baby grand adds a touch of splendor near the $10,000 dollar English cashmere and cotton king bed. The Starlight Suite opens to a floor to vaulted ceiling stone fireplace, four poster queen bed, merlot jetted tub and private deck overlooking Arabian horses. The Sunshine and Moonlight Suites share a tiled and mirrored bath, yet each have vaulted ceilings and distinctive ambiance. All suites have cable, broadband, music systems, and access to an upstairs snack bar and outdoor spa. Delicious gourmet breakfasts start every day, and cater to your timetable, so whether you are teeing off at dawn, planning a trek up a mountain trail or sleeping till noon, Kathy Bury will tend your needs and treat you to A Touch of Heaven. Rated number one of seven inns in the Golden area by Tripadvisor.com, Talmar is an exceptional choice for honeymoons, anniversaries, birthdays and that special get-a-way. One guest raved of the Royal Suite, "This is by far the most gorgeous and romantic room I have ever seen." Another guest noted, "The breakfasts, including steak and eggs were delicious, while Kathy was a most gracious hostess. For anyone familiar with the area, this is a steal." So, whether you are just married or celebrating your 25th anniversary, Talmar Bed & Breakfast adds romance to any occasion, and is simply A Touch of Heaven.

16720 W 63rd Place, Golden CO (303) 279-4133
www.coloradovacation.com/bed/talmar

Tivoli Lodge

Guests at the Tivoli Lodge enjoy being able to ski from
Golden Peak right to the hotel lift. That's how it's done in
the Alps, where picturesque lodges dot the snowy landscape.
Indeed, with its European-style architecture and ambience,
the Tivoli will put you in the mood to yodel. Oversized chairs
and leather sofas are arranged in front of the floor-to-ceiling
stone fireplace in the lobby. Accept the invitation and stretch
out for a spell. The 62 spacious guest rooms offer a choice of
mountain or village views. Many come with fireplace, and all
are impeccably appointed with fine linens, mini-refrigerators
and large soaking tubs. The Peter Seibert Suite affords stunning
360-degree views of the surrounding mountains. The entire
hotel is wireless and includes such other amenities as a fully-
equipped fitness room, ski storage and two outdoor hot tubs
with mountain views. The staff is ready to accommodate
weddings and group functions of up to 100 people. Built in
the late 1960s as the dream hotel of Bob and Diane Lazier,
the Tivoli is a Vail classic that was recently redone to feel like
new. Car racing fans recognize the Lazier name. Buddy Lazier
won the Indy 500 in 1996, and other members of the family,
including Bob, have raced on the circuit. The penthouse at
the Tivoli serves as the Lazier residence. Relax in fine style at
the Tivoli, a true ski lodge right at the base of Vail's ski hill.

386 Hanson Ranch Road, Vail CO
(970) 476-5615 or (800) 451-4756
www.tivolilodge.com

Paragon Lodging

Paragon Lodging invites you to leave your worries behind and enter the world of breathtaking mountain vistas and the charming atmosphere of Victorian Breckenridge. Several years ago, Johna Rice, Krista Rider and Katie Shocklee dreamed of starting a short-term management company specializing in renting luxury private homes. The tenacious trio realized their wish after preparing myriad business plans, financial forecasts and promotions. Today, your wish is their command. Paragon Lodging adheres to the highest standards as it supplies luxury homes for corporate retreats, family reunions, weddings or much-needed personal vacations. Just pack your suitcase—everything else you need to make your event or vacation perfect awaits you. Year-round relaxation and recreation in Breckenridge entice clients wanting to unwind. Challenging ski slopes, invigorating alpine air and colorful local festivals add to the delight of these beautiful homes. Paragon now represents a number of homes in Hawaii as well. A wedding in Breckenridge followed by a seaside honeymoon could fulfill all of your expectations. Days of downhill skiing followed by wistful nights beside a crackling fire could be your destiny. Whatever your desires, let the dream weavers at Paragon Lodging help you create the time of your life.

325 N Main Street, Breckenridge CO
(970) 547-2122 or (800) 781-4711
www.paragonlodging.com

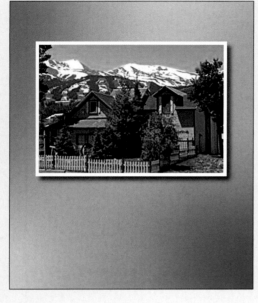

Abbett Placer Inn

It doesn't get much better than bluebird ski days in the Colorado Rockies—unless, of course, you're lucky enough to get a room at Abbett Placer Inn. Owned by Niels Hagen and Emma Walch-Hagen, this homey bed and breakfast is actually a restored 1900 Victorian house. With outside decks overlooking Breckenridge's Main Street, Abbett Placer Inn is close to countless restaurants and shops in downtown Breckenridge. Niels and Emma aim to make every guest feel at home, starting with their legendary mountain breakfasts. The aromas of banana pancakes, coconut French toast, and homemade scones lure the guests down to the family room every morning. Emma does her English heritage proud by infusing traditional recipes and flavors into her menu. The five units at Abbett Placer Inn are equipped with all the basics plus goose down comforters and free wireless Internet. The common areas are comfortably furnished with family crafts and collectibles, making them perfect to relax in after a day of skiing or rafting. For sore muscles, the hot tub is always ready. Nestled in the heart of the Rocky Mountains, Abbett Placer Inn is for those seeking a classic mountain escape with all the comfort of home.

205 S French Street, Breckenridge CO
(970) 453-6489 or (888) 794-7750
www.abbettplacerbnb.com

Boulder Mountain Lodge

The sound of your car's wheels on the unpaved driveway of the Boulder Mountain Lodge welcomes you to this comfortable getaway on Four Mile Creek. Five minutes from downtown, Boulder Mountain Lodge is surrounded by tall trees, wildflowers and majestic rock formations. Wildlife such as deer and high country birds inhabit the relaxing surroundings. The lodge has a community feeling, with picnic tables in common areas and an outdoor pavilion. Each guest has access to the hot tub, seasonal pool and kids' fishing pond. Your pets are welcome with a deposit. The quiet lodge offers 30 units including kitchenettes, full kitchen units, suites, a cabin and several campsites. Suites feature one and two bedrooms with a pull-out sofa sleeper, some with full kitchens, a jetted bathtub for two or an outdoor hot tub on your private deck. You will enjoy fishing in Four Mile Creek or Boulder Creek, rock-climbing in Boulder Canyon and hiking to the breathtaking Boulder Falls. Located in an exceptional setting where the lush green of copious foliage vibrates under the sun, Boulder Mountain Lodge beckons you to enjoy Colorado the best way—naturally.

91 Four Mile Canyon Road, Boulder CO
(303) 444-0882 or (800) 458-0882
www.bouldermountainlodge.com

Mtn Managers

Whether your plans in Summit County involve just you and your soulmate or a whole league of skiers, Mtn Managers can set you up in the perfect accommodations to suit your every need. Owner Eric Gill and his team handle everything from studio-size condominiums to eight-bedroom/eight-bath homes that sleep 28. Do you require a family-size home that is close to the ski areas of Breckenridge, Keystone, Frisco, Silverthorne and Arapahoe Basin? Mtn Managers has lots of them, including many with magnificent mountain views. Some even come with such extras as a tennis court and hot tub. If you need to be close to a boating facility, Mtn Managers can accommodate you nicely. This business has been matching customers with their ideal lodgings since 1981. It has satisfied those who wanted to be able to roll out of bed, step out the door and be on a hiking trail. It also holds the keys to that house on a quiet street for those interested in exploring the shops and restaurants in the area. Come play in the Rocky Mountains, secure in the knowledge that Mtn Managers has found you the perfect place to stay.

1121 Dillon Dam Road, Frisco CO
(970) 668-3174 or (800) 766-1477
www.mtnmanagers.com

Rocky Mountain Resort Management

Whether you're looking to stay in the lap of luxury or just need a place to sleep for the night during your Rocky Mountain adventure, Rocky Mountain Resort Management has just the place for you. The company serves nearly all of Summit and Eagle counties, including Vail, Keystone, Copper Mountain, Breckenridge, Silverthorne, Dillon and Frisco. No matter what you're looking for, Rocky Mountain Resort Management has the accommodations for you, ranging from studios to condominiums to seven-bedroom homes. Many of the facilities have computer and Internet access, as well as a variety of other amenities. The company can even do your grocery shopping for you, so the kitchem will be stocked with your favorite foods when you arrive. It can also provide you with excellent tour packages as well as guidance for activities and dining. Those booking ski excursions and other recreational events through Rocky Mountain Resort Management are eligible for a variety of discounts on items and services, including lift tickets. Order in-person, by phone or on the website. Accommodations are available in both the summer and winter months. Property owners looking to make money with their vacation home can contract with the company for rental services at a competitive rate. Let Rocky Mountain Resort Management satisfy all your lodging and adventure needs on your next Rocky Mountain vacation.

160 U.S Highway 6, #206, Silverthorne CO
(303) 791-3860 or (888) 700-2754
www.rmrminc.net

Colorado Rocky Mountain Resorts

With more than 150 properties in all price ranges, Colorado Rocky Mountain Resorts (CRMR) has just the place for you to rest up after an exciting day on the slopes, trails and rivers of this beautiful region. The company, owned by Diane Wieland and Michael Martin, covers all of Summit County, including Breckenridge, Keystone, Copper Mountain, Frisco, Silverthorne and Dillon. From ski-in, ski-out to secluded cabins and large private homes, most of these properties, recently built, have been thoroughly remodeled and brought up to date in both style and comfort. That dedication to comfort and value is reflected in the fact that between 50 and 60 percent of CRMR's customers are repeats—and most of them recommend the company to friends and family. CRMR partners with some of the finest firms in the travel field, including Orbitz and Expedia to assure you get the best value possible. You'll even get discount cards good for purchases at local restaurants and attractions throughout the county. CRMR can also book activities, including whitewater rafting, snowmobiling tours and sleigh-ride dinners throughout Summit County. Let Colorado Rocky Mountain Resorts put you up in style and comfort on your next Rocky Mountain adventure.

912 N Summit Boulevard, Frisco CO (970) 668-5151 or (800) 662-5368
www.coloradormr.com

Boulder Outlook Hotel & Suites

Opened in 2002, the Boulder Outlook Hotel & Suites reflects the vibrant energy and personality of Boulder, an eco-friendly university town. Start with its comprehensive commitment to using recyclable or compostable material in its 165 guest rooms, restaurant and facilities. The cups might look like plastic, but they are actually made from cornstarch. The pool uses no chlorine and depends upon a liquid solar cover to conserve water. The hotel derives its power partially from wind. The Boulder Outlook has received a Sustainable Business Gold Medal from the Colorado Clean Tech Initiative and was the 2006 Small Business of the Year for Zero Waste. Formerly a Holiday Inn, the 40-year-old hotel building underwent an extensive redesign in 2002, modernizing its appearance with bold color and personality. The in-house restaurant, Skinny Jay's Pizza & Pub, has become a popular blues venue. Alvin Youngblood, Bob Margolin and Philip Walker are among the legendary blues musicians who have played at Skinny Jay's. Get down with the blues while going green at the Boulder Outlook Hotel & Suites.

800 28th Street, Boulder CO (303) 443-3322 or (800) 542-0304
www.boulderoutlook.com

Silver Saddle Motel

The Silver Saddle Motel offers peace and serenity near the heart of Boulder. Thomas and Blanche Taylor built the first row of cabins of the Silver Saddle Motel in 1945 after Thomas came home from World War II. As Thomas was surviving the attack on Pearl Harbor and earning a Bronze Star, Blanche was at home working and saving money. She managed to buy seven parcels of property in the peaceful Rocky Mountains. The couple turned a rockpile, as Blanche refers to it, into a place that thousands of tourists have enjoyed over the years. Today, their daughter and son-in-law, Sue and Dave Remington, run the motel. At the base of Flagstaff Mountain and the mouth of Boulder Creek, which teems with three kinds of trout, the Silver Saddle maintains nostalgic cabins with carports. Surrounded on three sides by mountain parks, the Silver Saddle is an easy walk along Boulder Creek to the open air mall of downtown Boulder. The nine cabins and 28 suites are equipped with air-conditioning, cable television and high-speed Internet. All rooms are smoke-free and provide cooking facilities ranging from a microwave and fridge to kitchenette with cooking utensils. For kids, one of the parks surrounding the motel has a wonderful playground. Enjoy the tradition that the Taylors began more than six decades ago at the Silver Saddle Motel.

90 W Arapahoe Avenue, Boulder CO (303) 442-8022 or (800) 525-9509
www.silversaddlemotel.net

Greeley Guest House

David Clarkson, owner, and Michelle Allen, general manager, love hearing how nice their rooms are at the Greeley Guest House. The compliment means even more to them when guests reveal that someone who lives in Greeley recommended that they stay here. Indeed, many residents know that sending friends and loved ones to this elegant country inn is a great way to show off Greeley. The rooms are comfortable and tastefully done, the setting is quiet, and the mountain views are spectacular. Put it all together, and you have the reason why the Greeley Guest House won the 2005 *Greeley Tribune's* Readers' Choice award for Best Hotel/Motel. The inn offers 19 rooms with fireplaces, mini-refrigerators and microwaves. Three apartment-style suites with a full kitchen lend themselves to longer stays. Two of these suites include a separate living room and a private Jaccuzi bath. Space for corporate meetings and special events is available for groups of up to 75. Complimentary breakfast includes fresh fruit, yogurt and homemade granola in addition to several hot items that are rotated daily. Whether you are staying for business or pleasure, word has it that the Greeley Guest House will make you feel at home while doing Greeley proud.

5401 W 9th Street, Greeley CO (970) 353-9373 or (800) 314-3684 *www.greeleyguesthouse.com*

Animals & Pets

Denizens of the Deep, Inc.

Denizens of the Deep is a store that puts on a one-of-a-kind show. A family owned business for over 20 years, the store offers more than 400 aquariums in the Fort Collins location. Denizens of the Deep is a virtual museum of fresh and saltwater habitats, showcasing colorful tropical fish, corals, invertebrates and plants. It's worth a visit just to behold the dazzling scene of the three, 230-gallon displays featuring replications of the many natural environments. Denizens of the Deep won a national award for aquarium design, which involves not merely an artistic eye but the knowledge to create thriving aquatic ecosystems. Denizens of the Deep is easily one of the largest aquarium suppliers in all of Colorado, but what sets the store apart is its dedication to customer service. Owner Marie Brandt wants to ensure that her customers come away with a thorough understanding of their purchases, how to set up and clean their tanks and how to properly care for their fish. In addition to education, the store offers house calls, installation and maintenance for any size or type of aquarium. Visit Denizens of the Deep for everything you need to put on your own aquatic show in your home or office.

4112 S College Avenue, Suite 112, Fort Collins CO
(970) 229-9361
305 Cole Shopping Center, Cheyenne WY
(307) 635-8311
www.denizensofthedeepinc.com

Bestway Imported Koi

Debbie Weingardt considers herself an advocate for the fish she sells at Bestway Imported Koi. Relying on her knowledge of fish habits, as well as on what the Japanese call a good eye for quality fish, she goes directly to Japan to choose the healthiest and prettiest fish she can find. At the store, she is dedicated to educating her customers about these lovely creatures, which she compares to dolphins. Both are very social and like to be touched, says Debbie. Being named Grand Champion in the Colorado Koi Show three times hasn't made her the least bit arrogant. She bubbles with enthusiasm while sharing her expertise in koi care and pond building with her customers. The health of the fish is her top priority. Noting that koi can live for 70 years, Debbie says that the best thing you can do to promote the longevity of your fish is to give them good filtration. "We will help you," declares Debbie, who, in her 30 years in the business, has guided scores of people through the process of constructing and maintaining a pond full of gorgeous fish. Whether you already have a koi pond or are thinking of starting one, consider making Bestway Imported Koi your source for fish, supplies and expert advice from a passionate advocate.

3951 Creek Drive, Broomfield CO (303) 469-0808 or (866) 469-0808
www.bestwayimportedkoi.com

Tidy Paws

Tidy Paws is a gathering spot for animals and their companions. Locals drop by for grooming, answers to their questions or just to be in the company of other pet-lovers. Owner Colin Towner, along with his wife, a veterinarian, saw a special need for animal services in the Erie area and decided to fill it. Tidy Paws offers a full line of retail pet products such as oatmeal shampoos, grooming brushes and combs, nutritious pet food, and stylish collars and leashes. Toys from squeaky to furry fill the shelves. You'll even find the perfect picture frame for that adorable photo of Fido or Spot. The grooming department offers fancy show dog treatments or a simple bath for the less fussy. Bathing your dog or cat in the self-service area is inexpensive and time-saving. You can do it yourself or the Tidy Paws staff will do it for you, if you prefer. Remember to pick out a delicious treat for your furry friend out of the bakery case or from one of the many other choices. The Towners are strong supporters of organizations such as the Humane Society and events that highlight animal care, for example Bark in the Park, an annual fund-raising celebration. The door to Tidy Paws is always open to dogs, cats and animal lovers. Drop in and pay a visit.

720 Austin Avenue #105, Erie CO (303) 828-4241

Jaws 'N Claws

Home to all manner of critters that creep, crawl, slither and swim, the family-run Jaws 'N Claws specializes in tropical fish and reptiles and their living environments. Within the shop's clear, open space, the colors and quirks of a wide variety of aquatic and land creatures are on full display. Whether you are venturing for the first time into the world of cold-blooded pets, or a veteran fish or reptile owner looking for that rare, hard-to-find critter, Lloyd and Bridget Masters and their daughters are eager to assist. They are very knowledgeable about their animals and will help you to design the ideal living environment with just the right supplies and accessories to make your new pet feel right at home. A long-time dream of Lloyd's, Jaws 'N Claws came to fruition in 2006 when he retired after 20 years of working for the city of Fort Collins. Now immersed in his professional hobby, the outgoing Lloyd is enthusiastic about sharing what he loves. The family at Jaws 'N Claws greets its customers as neighbors and knows many of them and their pets by name. Discover the wonderfully strange world of the small and scaly at Jaws 'N Claws.

1311 N College Avenue, Fort Collins CO (970) 224-5007

Happy Horse
Tack and Saddle Shop

It's not your Grandma's saddle and tack shop. Happy Horse Tack and Saddle Shop provides horse gear and services for the horse fanatic in everyone. Horse lovers flock to this diverse store to find anything from western tack to English riding gear and high-fashion equestrian wear. Happy Horse can custom design boots, chaps, bridles, saddles and more. It also provides saddle and tack repair, washing and consignment. Located in a charming historical home, the shop inspires a down-home feeling and an air of comfort. The welcome sign never comes down, and the friendly, laid-back atmosphere makes horses and riding accessible to a larger audience. It's a great place to network for horse shows and horse-related events. The Happy Horse has been locally owned and operated for 20 years. Owners Jen Wright and Kathy DeWitt have been riding and competing in shows all their lives. They pride themselves on creating an inviting environment where there is no judgment and no pretentious attitude about riding. Above all, they strive to build trusting relationships with all their patrons, maintaining the values of a small-town shop. Find everything you need to outfit your horses and the people they love at Happy Horse Tack and Saddle Shop.

113 Peterson Street, Fort Collins CO
(970) 484-4199
www.happyhorsetack.com

Canines' Canyon

Canines' Canyon offers loving, state-of-the-art boarding, day care and grooming services for dogs. The facility includes spacious indoor play areas and three large outdoor yards. The Cattery can board nine cats. Canines' Canyon provides comfortable indoor kennels each with raised cots. The facility also offers dog training and has a fully functional large outdoor agility course. Owners William and Natividad Bateman made a careful and thorough tour of other Colorado kennels and incorporated the best practices and characteristics of the industry into their fledgling enterprise. Natividad, affectionately known as Natty, is an experienced groomer specializing in large dogs. She is very particular in her craft and insists on a meticulously clean environment. The Canines' Canyon retail store offers excellent prices on all products. The store features the Colorado Kumpi line of dog food, a superior five-meat product which provides more of the protein dogs need. You'll also find a full line of treats dogs and cats. Use Canines' Canyon's gift certificates to introduce friends and family to its products and services. Canines' Canyon pays its employees well and attracts people with the best qualifications. Employees are screened to meet the high standards that follow from the Bateman's philosophy of love and respect for animals. Manager Estela Ortiz ensures that all runs smoothly. For exceptional care and loving service, come to Canines' Canyon.

24060 U.S. Highway 40, Golden CO
(303) 526-9212
www.caninescanyon.com

Blue Springs 'n Katydid Dog Training Center

If your dog is having trouble minding its manners, the folks at Blue Springs 'n Katydid Dog Training Center have the patience and know the techniques to turn it into a well-behaved family member. The center employs 25 compassionate trainers, all of whom have at least six years experience. They are experts at evaluating the personality of dogs, checking their health and then taking the proper steps to correct behavior problems. Classes start at Puppy Kindergarten and progress through Advanced Obedience. The staff is equally adept at training show dogs. In fact, about 40-percent of the dogs that come to the center go on to compete on some level. The center offers classes in dog show conformation, agility, rally and even free-style dancing. Most of the instructors themselves compete successfully in the conformation ring, and some have experience in training canine athletes. Some specialty areas include herding, tracking and sled racing. The center also trains dogs for therapy work in hospitals and rehab centers. The staff is proud to show off its clean, bright facility to anyone who may be considering classes for his or her dog. For a full-service dog training center dedicated to the teaching and betterment of all dogs, try Blue Springs 'n Katydid Dog Training Center.

2980 W Oxford Avenue, Englewood CO
(303) 781-9027
www.bskddogtraining.com

Heavenly Dog

You can wash your own pet or leave your pet for specialized grooming services at Heavenly Dog. Suzy Swett and her dog companions opened the Denver do-it-yourself dog spa in 2002 in the Old South Gaylord neighborhood. The five-block walk from Washington Park makes it easy to stop by for a quick wash or The Works. Suzy provides tubs that meet height requirements for you and your pet along with plush towels, brushes, blow dryers and aprons. You can easily customize the washing, thanks to hypoallergenic shampoo, strong deodorizer and detangling conditioner. The Works includes ear, eye, tooth and breath cleaner plus a paw wax. A cold bowl of water and treat samples help soothe and reward your pet. "We are more than happy to scrub the devil out of your pooch for you, if you don't have time or just don't feel up to the task. Drop them off and pick up a sweet smelling angel," says Suzy. There is a groomer available who is expert at handling all breeds and sizes and specializes in hand-stripping terriers and giving precise trims to poodles and cocker spaniels. Suzy is an expert dog trainer, capable of training the devil out of young and mature pets. Heavenly Dog specializes in all breeds and sells training and grooming aids here. Scrub, Train and Spoil the Devil out of your pet at Heavenly Dog, *5280* magazine's choice for Best Dog Wash.

2224 E Tennessee Avenue, Denver CO   (303) 777-4665   *www.heavenlydog.net*

The Front Range Birding Company

Birding knowledge is just one thing you get when you drop in to the Front Range Birding Company. The store carries supplies such as birdhouses, birdbaths and premium bird food for setting up backyard bird habitats. It also helps both casual birders and professionals with reference books and quality optics, including binoculars and spotting scopes by Swarovski and Vortex. Owners Tom and Diane Bush and their employees are passionate about birds. The couple opened the Littleton shop in 2004 to serve the interests of birds and nature lovers alike. Whenever practical, Tom and Diane stock items made close to home, including nature-based gifts and artistic photos and paintings featuring birds. The couple also sells honey produced from their beekeeping operation. They know that birds reflect what is going on in the environment and act as nature's ambassadors, so they are happy to contribute to bird welfare through participation in the Audubon Christmas Bird Count, International Migratory Bird Day and nature studies for young people. They are avid supporters of many conservation groups. Increase your enjoyment of birds with a visit to the Front Range Birding Company, open seven days a week in the Kohl Shopping Center.

9956 E Remington Place, Suite A-7, Littleton CO
(303) 979-BIRD (2473)
www.frontrangebirding.com

Hounds on the Hill

Who cares enough about your dog to give him a birthday party or throw a party for Halloween so he can dress up in his favorite costume? Give your dog the kind of attention, excercise and fun he'll beg for at Hounds On The Hill doggie daycare. A busy life shouldn't exclude your best furry friend, and it's the perfect place to take him if you've got a long day ahead of you, a lonely dog or a dog who just wants to have fun with his four-legged friends. The "pawprietors" and inspiration of Hounds on the Hill are three lovable dogs named Tucker, Harry and Moose. Each of them suffered from common dog behaviors such as hole-digging, shoe-eating and separation anxiety. Today, each one is happy; they have overcome their problems with obedience training and play-filled days at Hounds On The Hill. Owner and operator Terri Desnica is one of the only doggie daycare providers who is also a professional obedience trainer. Hounds on the Hill offers on-site dog training, behavioral counseling and even private lessons. Westword Magazine designated Hounds as having the Best Obedience Classes in Denver. It also has a natural pet supply store and even offers professional pet photography. Most importantly, Hounds has devoted employees who pamper your pet as if it were their own. Let your dog join Tucker, Harry and Moose for a rambunctious good time at Hounds on the Hill.

960 Lincoln Street, Denver CO
(303) 830-1226
www.houndsonthehillllc.com

The Pet Stuff Place

In 2003, Dick and Sharon Adams left careers in the corporate world to open The Pet Stuff Place in the Castle Pines Marketplace. "We have a passion for companion pets," Sharon says. "They add so much to our lives, and we want to provide products and services that will enhance their well-being." The Pet Stuff Place carries many supplements, natural foods and food samples that can assist those trying to help their pets overcome allergies, skin problems, upset stomach or irritable bowel. The Adams have discovered that sometimes an alternative protein, such as elk, venison or salmon, can make a remarkable difference in pet health. Dick and Sharon's most rewarding experiences come from sitting with clients in the store's living room-like setting to solve food, obesity or behavior problems. If your dog is bedeviled by thunder, Sharon and Dick can help. They care for four dogs of their own and support an area dog and horse rescure. The store carries books about pets, including horses, and arranges support groups for people who have lost a pet. You will find toys, trendy new products and pet-themed gifts for people, including jewelry and socks. Help your pet be happy and healthy with a visit to The Pet Stuff Place, open seven days a week.

562 E Castle Pines Parkway, Unit C-9, Castle Rock CO
(303) 814-6060
www.thepetstuffplace.com

Canine Campus of Castle Rock

Your most memorable teachers were probably the ones who found positive and creative ways to promote learning. The faculty at Canine Campus of Castle Rock, a dog daycare, boarding and obedience training facility, take the same approach to serving the dogs entrusted to their care. These professionals challenge themselves to come up with new, fun-filled activities for the day guests to enjoy. Dogs have a blast and get a chance to practice social skills with costume contests, games of field hockey and specialty parties. Amenities include spacious dorm rooms, wading pools and optional school lunches and bedtime snacks. Owners can even peek in on their pups' day via live web camera. Graduates of the obedience classes go on to become sterling citizens and companions who are gentle with strangers, do not annoy neighbors with excessive barking and refrain from making a mess in the house. A college theme extends throughout this facility, where the lobby resembles a student union, the kitchen a dining hall and the kennels are done up in dorm room fashion with bunk beds for the small and medium-sized dogs. The professors have thoroughly researched canine behavior, animal health and safety issues. In addition, they possess that creative flair that can't be learned from any book. Canine Campus also offers a campus shower so your dog can go home fresh and clean. For a canine facility that meets the Ivy League standard, enroll your dog in Canine Campus of Castle Rock.

780 Kinner Street, Castle Rock CO
(720) 259-2515
www.caninecampus.us

Pet Station

If you enjoy the bonding experience of bathing your dog but can live without mopping up the mess afterwards, Pet Station is the place for you. Pet Station provides three stainless steel tubs for washing your pet, one large enough to handle even a Newfoundland the size of a small bear. Each station is equipped with a hand-held sprayer, scrubber and choice of shampoos and conditioners. After the bath, you can wrap your best friend in the plush towel provided. Each tub and all grooming tools are cleaned and disinfected after each use. Cats are also welcome. Once your pet is clean, you can pick out a new collar from the boutique section at Pet Station. You'll also find premium food and treats for both dogs and cats. Kathryn and Dan Bailey are owners with big hearts who work in conjunction with shelters to get dogs and cats adopted. Once a month, they hold self-pet wash benefits and donate the income to a rescue group. Show your pet some love by taking it for a scrub at Pet Station.

2300 S Colorado Boulevard, Denver CO (303) 757-6800
www.mypetstation.net

B & B for D.O.G.

Of course, you would like to have your canine companion at your side wherever you go, but when circumstances prohibit it, you can feel good about leaving him or her at B & B for D.O.G. This dog daycare and boarding facility was the first of its kind in the entire state of Colorado when it opened in 1995. You can trust the experienced staff to treat your dogs like the playful and social creatures they are. Several times a day, the dogs go outside to play in supervised groups with other dogs of similar size and personality. What dog wouldn't feel like it was at a resort when set free in a 10,000-square-foot playground? The grounds include lush grassy areas, wading pools and plenty of shade. There are even private yards for those who prefer to play alone. Indoors, the solid walls between suites are much better than chain-link fences, allowing dogs to settle down and rest in seclusion. Bowls, toys and bedding for naptime are provided. All you need to bring is your pup's food, along with any medication. Treat your best friend to some T.L.C at B & B for D.O.G., conveniently located on the way to Denver International Airport.

10 S Potomac Street, Aurora CO (303) 361-0061
www.bbfordog.com

Studio Bella

Many times our pets have melted our hearts by turning their faces into expressions of absolute happiness and contentment. Photographer Heather Green, owner of Studio Bella, has been capturing those special looks professionally since 2000, though her love of animals and passion for her art go back even further. Animals can sense the affection she has for them. She has a gift for making dogs and cats comfortable in her presence so that they reveal the essence of their personality to her. "I am an animal lover first and a photographer second," she explains. "It has always been about the animals and the love I have for them." Heather's high-resolution digital portraits reveal her eye for fun, bright and contemporary compositions. She is also known for her fresh twists on black-and-white portraiture. Her accomplishments include providing the cover shot for an issue of Colorado Dog magazine. Studio Bella has been featured in such publications as 5280 and Pet Style News. Heather's expressive imagery graces a line of greeting cards available in gift shops, pet boutiques and other retail outlets. Let Studio Bella produce a portrait that will bring out all that is lovable in your pet.

15797 E Prentice Drive, Centennial CO (303) 514-2422
www.studiobellaonline.com

Four Paws & Co.

Longmont native Carrie Adams has been around animals all her life. She operated a kennel for 20 years and also worked as a veterinary technician and dog trainer. Her consideration for her furry friends motivated Carrie to earn a Bachelor's degree in nutrition, which included animal science and animal nutrition courses. It was what she learned there that inspired her to open Four Paws & Co. in 2003. A dog and cat supply store and more, Four Paws is particularly dedicated to providing high-quality, natural foods. In spite of the many indicators in favor of these foods, most big box grocery stores don't carry them. Four Paws is sensitive to specialty diets, including raw and frozen diets. Carrie also stocks a hand-picked selection of natural supplements for everything from arthritis to anxiety. Her well-schooled and attentive staff keeps customers coming back. Over the years, Carrie has added services to the shop to help make caring for your pet more convenient and affordable. In 2007, she unveiled the 1,700-square-foot do-it-yourself dog wash. The dog wash has six stalls of different sizes to accommodate different-sized dogs, and hand-held showerheads for getting in those hard-to-reach places. You'll find all the bathing and grooming supplies you need at the shop. Carrie has also invited the Longmont Humane Society to host obedience classes at the store. If you're looking for an at-home pet sitter, just ask Carrie when you visit Four Paws & Co. She'll go out of the way to supply the makings of a high quality of life for your pet.

1225 Ken Pratt Boulevard, #108, Longmont CO (303) 485-1565 *www.fourpawsandco.com*

Rover Retreat

Your dog will have every opportunity to blossom into a social butterfly at Rover Retreat, a daycare and boarding operation based on the principle of social interaction. Canine guests play with each other under the careful supervision of employees all day in the large open areas, except when it's time to eat or sleep in the climate-controlled kennels. The staff will introduce your shy dog slowly to the others and ease him into the population. Of course, if your darling already loves mixing with others, she will being having such a good time running after balls and chasing friends that she might not want to leave when you come by to pick her up. Owners Therese Morin and Shaun McMaster, along with manager Mary Houghton, lead a staff whose love of dogs is evident in the energy and patience they bring to work each day. They will quickly learn your dog's name and treat it as their own. Therese sits on the board of the Colorado Association of Dog Daycares, so you know that she is well respected within the industry. This business also offers bath and brush service and is a retail outlet for Kumpi dog food, a local company with an excellent reputation. Encourage your dog to make a bunch of new friends by bringing him to Rover Retreat.

17731 W Colfax Avenue, Golden CO (303) 215-0413
www.roverretreat.com

Lulu Bella

If the expressions and antics of your pet are those of a comedian at heart, you should think about having its portrait done by Julia McClung, owner of Lulu Bella. Julia's paintings, which can be categorized as caricature or pop art, bring out the humorous nature of her subjects. Indeed, although she is classically trained, Julia's art is anything but academic. She goes for bold splashes of color and broad brushstrokes to create images that are offbeat and funny yet always tender. Work begins with a visit to your home to photograph your pet. From these pictures, she will produce the kind of inspired oil painting that earned her the title of Pet Portrait Artist of the Year 2006 from *5280* magazine. Her résumé includes commission work for Kristin Davis of *Sex and the City* and the illustration of a children's book titled *Zooch the Pooch*. Her business is named after her Italian greyhound. Previously, this hip artist performed in a punk rock band and published her own music magazine. Show that you appreciate how much fun pets are by having your dog's or cat's portrait done in Lulu Bella style.

3805 Garrison Street, Wheat Ridge CO (303) 455-6943
www.lulubellaart.com

Sudsy Puppy Pet Grooming

Dogs feel at home at Sudsy Puppy Pet Grooming, where they are free to wander around and check out the scene. Owner Rebecca Cornejo treats each one as if it were her own pet, taking pride in sending them out the door looking all pretty and handsome. Her many regular customers claim that, paws down, she and her staff are the best groomers in town. Grooming from nose to toes is their forte, and their clientele includes not only dogs but cats, ferrets and bunnies, too. Washing and oral hygiene are specialties. Consider bringing your canine diva in for a Pawdicure—a complete package including filing, trimming and painting of the nails. Dogs who like to stand out in a crowd can get a dye job and wild hairdo at Sudsy Puppy, while shedding dogs feel a lot better after a turn with the Furminator. Put the finishing touch on the grooming session by picking out a handmade bow, bandanna or collar charm for your prince or princess. Try Sudsy Puppy Pet Grooming, where dogs are encouraged to make themselves at home.

8971 Harlan Street, #A, Westminster CO (303) 685-7965
6433 W Alameda Avenue, Lakewood CO (303) 233-8406

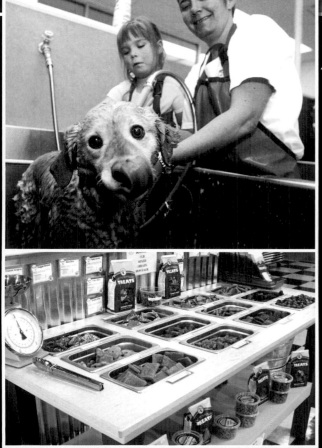

Wag N' Wash Healthy Pet Center

Washing your dog can be drudgery, or it can be something you and your pet anticipate with pleasure. When co-owners Dan Remus and Jef Strauss opened their first Wag N' Wash Healthy Pet Center in 1999, the self-serve dog wash unleashed Colorado Springs' dog lovers. Since then, they've added a second Colorado Springs location and one in Littleton, and they have a Castle Rock operation in the works. Wag N' Wash makes grooming your pet easy with eight well-equipped washing stations that feature waist-high wash basins, temperature-controlled water, grooming aprons, soaps and dryers. Mostly owners bring dogs, but one woman brings a pet goat. The facility is super-clean and doesn't smell like dirty dogs, thanks to an advanced air circulation system. If the task still seems too daunting, consider an appointment for professional grooming services. Wag N' Wash also stocks many natural and wholesome pet foods for your dogs and cats, as well as supplements, collars, toys and beds. Dan's fresh-baked dog biscuits, called Remo's Wag N' Treats after his dog Remo, feature human-grade ingredients and are nicely displayed at the bakery and deli counter. Look also for liver brownies, veggie pizza, quiche and peanut butter pie. If you are celebrating another year of unconditional companionship, you can order a bone-shaped birthday cake to feed as many as four large dogs or eight small ones, not including you. Wash 'em, feed 'em and spoil 'em all in one cool place at Wag N' Wash Healthy Pet Center.

5066 S Wadsworth Boulevard, Littleton CO
(303) 973-WASH (9274)
www.wagnwash.com

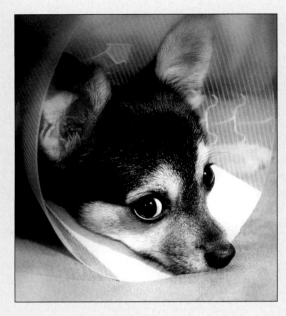

Genesee Veterinary Hospital

Dr. Rebecca Malleck has known since grade school that she wanted to be a veterinarian. In 2001, she fulfilled that dream. Dr. Becky knew she had found home when she purchased Genesee Veterinary Hospital in 2006 after working there for one year. The Kansas State University graduate joins a veterinary team that adores animals and gives them every consideration. You can keep your dog, cat, hamster or bird in tip-top condition with Genesee's thorough checkups and food brands. You can even treat your favorite dog or cat to boutique items, such as stylish collars, leashes, shampoos and treats. Many people have been bringing their pets to Genesee since the hospital opened in 1981. They appreciate Dr. Becky's meticulous care and gentle touch. She shows her love of all animals by working with Golden State Greyhound Adoption and the Clear Creek County Animal Rescue League. Genesee is an easy place to drop off a pet for boarding when you are on your way to the mountains, since it's 20 minutes from downtown Denver at Exit 254 on Interstate 70. Boarded animals have plenty of room to move around as well as the devoted attention of the Genesee staff. Treat your pets to compassionate care at Genesee Veterinary Hospital.

25948 N Genesee Trail Road, Golden CO (303) 526-1655
www.geneseevet.com

Unleashed Ultimate Dog Center

A professional dog trainer for 15 years and the owner of three search-and-rescue German Shepherds, Bernadette Pflug knows a thing or two about a dog's needs. After making the rounds of the dog retailers and washes in Boulder County for about 10 years, she decided she could improve on the concept and created the Unleashed Ultimate Dog Center. The idea of the ultimate dog center is that it provides all your dog services and products under one roof. Bernadette personally heads a schedule of training classes, ranging from puppy socialization to off-leash training. She also offers bathing, grooming and a full retail store. Bernadette has improved on the dog bath by bringing in specialty tubs made just for dogs. Unlike human bathtubs, with their slick, porcelain bottoms and curved shape, these tubs are flat and made of textured fiberglass. They also feature a step, so the bathers don't have to heft wriggling dogs over the edge. She has thought deeply about her retail stock and provided a selection of raw and natural foods, fresh-baked treats and accessories for active dogs, such as backpacks and portable bowls. You'll also find great lightweight, collapsible carry cases and lifelike animal hand puppets. Bring your four-legged friends to Unleashed Ultimate Dog Center, where Bernadette is an expert at unleashing your dog's potential.

1617 Coalton Road, Superior CO (303) 554-9343
www.unleashyourdog.com

Sage Valley Pet Center

Pet owners rejoice. Feel free to leave home and let the experts at Sage Valley Pet Center pamper your precious friends. Dogs delight in the 20-foot clean, covered indoor and outdoor runs with solid dividers offering safety and privacy. Your feline friends reside in lofted indoor runs, and cat families may board together in town-homes. Daily play time allows felines to frolic with individual staff. In addition to providing comfortable, clean lodging for your beloved companions, Sage Valley Pet Center offers gentle and effective grooming to keep pets looking their best. Daycare for dogs and cats relieves pet anxiety for working owners who wonder what Fido is doing from nine to five and includes breakfast, dinner, treats, exercise and playtime. Sage Valley Pet Center is also the home of several pet rescue associations and helps facilitate removing pets from unhealthy situations. The spacious, flower-filled grounds present a beautiful background for your pet's stay. Feel free to book your vacation or business trip and let your pets enjoy a sojourn at Sage Valley Pet Center.

16400 W 54th Avenue, Golden CO
(303) 279-6969
www.sagevalley.com

Doggie Dude Ranch and the O'Cat Corral

A lifelong animal lover, Laurie Mattke wanted to use her property in the country to do something special for her furry friends. She came up with the Doggie Dude Ranch and O'Cat Corral, a revolutionary luxury resort for pets in the Denver area. You have never seen a kennel like this. Laurie is a certified veterinary technician and doggie massage therapist who plies all of her love and skills on her guests. She wards off homesickness with a full schedule of canine activities, including playtime, naptime and afternoon treats. There's an indoor playroom with a rubber floor, an outdoor yard with artificial turf and a swimming pool for dogs. All food is prepared on-site. Drop your pet off for a few hours of daycare or for overnight accommodations. Dogs sleep in temperature-controlled dog-sized hotel rooms on Western-style log beds with blankets. Cats sleep in a separate cat room in private five-level condominiums. Each cat condo has its own air ventilation system, bird window and toys. Guests who stay four days or longer get a complimentary grooming before they go home. Every dog is sent home with a ranch-style bandana and a gift bag with homemade treats and the dog's photo on a magnet. The ranch even offers door-to-door pet delivery service. Laurie has created a home-away-from-home for your pets where you can leave them with a happy heart. Treat your pets to comprehensive loving care at the Doggie Dude Ranch and the O'Cat Corral.

1600 S Quail Run Road, Watkins CO
(303) 366-2498
www.dogcatranch.com

Canine Fitness and Fun Center

Rhonda Siegel took an innovative approach to doggie day care with the opening of Canine Fitness and Fun Center in 2005. Most dogs love to swim, play and socialize with other dogs, which is just what Canine Fitness gives them. Two large indoor swimming pools of varying depths meet the needs of dogs that swim and those that just like a romp in fresh, filtered water. Rhonda and her staff appreciate the fun and exercise value of swimming as well as its benefits for dogs that may be overweight or have joint problems such as hip dysplasia

and arthritis. Indoor and outdoor play areas offer more than 7,000 square feet of tunnels, stairs and running room for the non-swimmers. Your dog will be closely supervised at all times by well-trained staff who are certified as pet care technicians by the American Boarding Kennels Association (ABKA). You can even watch the dogs at play, live from your own computer. In 2006, *5280 Magazine* named Canine Fitness one of eight Super Nannies for your dog. The center came in as a Top 10 Play of the Day on *ESPN SportsCenter* and gets equally high marks from *303Magazine*, *Westword* and the ABKA. To be accepted at the center, dogs must have current vaccines, be neutered or spayed after six months of age and pass a temperament evaluation. Give your dog the gifts of fitness and fun at Canine Fitness and Fun Center.

6336 Leetsdale Drive, Denver CO
(303) 394-DOGS (3647)
www.caninefitnessandfuncenter.com

Pet Outfitters

Where can you find top-notch pet products for the pampered pet in your home? Look no further than Pet Outfitters, an old-fashioned small business pet shop in Greenwood Village. Supplied by several local bakeries, Pet Outfitters provides several different kinds of fresh home baked biscuits for the connoisseur in your pet. Featuring only premium foods for animals, owner Libby Miller can proudly say that none of her foods were on the recall list. If your pet is on a special diet, come into the store for frozen foods and raw-diet foods. In addition to quality food and service, you'll find a variable inventory of leashes, collars and exotic pet supplies. Bring your dog to register for the Furry Scurry retreat, an annual event for dogs and people that brings many breeds of dogs (and dog owners) together. Looking for a breeder or trainer for your special friend? Libby has reputable recommendations on hand for the serious pet owner. Visit one of the annual open houses to take memorable pet photos or network with other pet lovers. Come visit the proud mascot dog, Sabrina Miller at Pet Outfitters and find healthy and unique pet products.

5942 South Holly Street, Greenwood Village CO (303) 290-0430
www.petoutfitters.com

The Little Groomer

When your dog or cat is starting look more like an animated rug than the handsome friend you once knew, bring it to the Little Groomer. Here, Master Groomer Teresa Lask sets up shop with a full bag of tricks for bringing the show star out in your pet. An experienced show-dog groomer who has won grooming awards all over the country. Teresa specializes in hand-stripping hard terrier coats as well as scissoring poodle and bichon coats. If shedding is your problem, shed-less treatments are available. Teresa gives pets the personal time and attention to detail that makes the difference. Even if it just needs a bath and brush, your pet will come out of the Little Groomer hand-fluffed, ears cleaned and toenails clipped. In addition to dogs, Teresa is an expert in cat grooming and recently published an in-depth article on the subject in *Groomer to Groomer* magazine. She is a pet care dermi-tech specialist, meaning that she is an expert on skin and coat care, and offers a variety of treatments for skin and coat problems. A veritable spa for your pet, the Little Groomer even offers coat color treatment and teeth cleaning. Give your pet the royal treatment at the Little Groomer.

1130 Pine Street, #4, Louisville CO (303) 666-0545

Bowhaus Dog Day Care & Boarding

When you go on vacation, treat your dog to one as well. Bowhaus Dog Day Care & Boarding offers a safe and fun haven where your special friend won't get lonely without you. With over 13,000 square feet of outside play area and a caring, dog-friendly staff, Bowhaus is the perfect worry-free place to leave your dog when you can't bring him with you. For cold days, Bowhaus's indoor play area allows dogs to enjoy the same high-energy fun that they would outdoors. Overnight guests are comforted by radiant floor heat or central air conditioning. Webcams provide dog owners a way to see how their dogs are doing. Owners Susan and Dan Nicholson and their dogs have belonged to the Bowhaus family for over six years. They keep the social interaction positive and maintain good doggie habits. In addition to offering one of the biggest daycare and boarding facilities in the area, Bowhaus does not charge extra for holidays, special diets or administering medication. When you're looking for a top-notch retreat for your dog, look no further than Bowhaus Dog Day Care & Boarding.

415 Jones Court, Erie CO (303) 828-4989
www.bowhaus.biz

Beds-N-Biscuits

Boarding doesn't have to be a lonely experience for your dog. A stay at Beds-N-Biscuits, a pet daycare and boarding facility, offers lots of new friends to meet and big, outdoor play areas. Your dog, along with dogs of the same size and temperament, can enjoy exciting games of chase, romp in a wading pool on hot summer days, or just hang out before retiring to a comfy, climate-controlled indoor kennel. Owners Bruce Miller and Andrew MacArthur live on-site and have 30 years of combined experience in the breeding, showing and handling of animals. They lead a staff that is caring, experienced and sensitive to the special feeding and medical needs of guests. Bathing, grooming and spa days are among the services offered. In addition to dogs, Beds-N-Biscuits can accommodate feline boarders in spacious, secure atriums. Local veterinary clinics recommend this facility, which maintains 24-hour access to a veterinary hospital in case of a medical emergency. Treat your dog to a fun, safe and sociable home-away-from-home at Beds-N-Biscuits, a bed-and-breakfast for your best friend.

4219 Xenon Street, Wheat Ridge CO
(303) 940-9188
www.bedsnbiscuits.com

Canine Rehabilitation & Conditioning Group

When Lori Beuerle's young dog, Clark, was suffering with a chronically weak leg, she took him to see Marty Pease. Marty applied her skills as a physical therapist and a certified canine rehabilitation practitioner and Clark was soon completely healthy. This inspired Beuerle to partner with Pease in a new innovative business called Canine Rehabilitation & Conditioning Group (CRCG). The center is a physical therapy and fitness facility for dogs. The specialized therapy treatments include hydrotherapy in an endless pool and underwater treadmill, massage, ultrasound and electrical stimulation. These treatments are used to decrease pain, restore function after surgery and to treat degenerative conditions like arthritis and hip dysplasia. It provides compassionate and experienced advice for conditioning active sport and show dogs, and evaluates and treat dogs with health problems caused by injury, disease, aging or obesity. A large 26-by-18-foot heated indoor pool is open to the public seven days a week for recreational swimming. Life vests are available for dogs that are learning to swim. The clinic's practitioners are certified health care professionals. In addition to physical therapy, the veterinarians on the CRCG team provide acupuncture, herbal remedies, skeletal balancing and nutritional counseling. CRCG was the recipient of the People Helping Pets award. Bring your canine companion for a swim and meet the staff.

3760 S Lipan Street, Englewood CO
(303) 762-SWIM (7946)
www.dog-swim.com

Doggie Styles

Doggie Styles offers professional grooming services for both dogs and cats in a clean and relaxed atmosphere. Customer service is exemplary. This grooming shop uses hand-scissoring techniques to produce the finest cut you'll find. Owners of poodles, Airedales and other terriers know it's often hard to find a groomer who does a good job. The people at Doggie Styles are specialists in grooming and cutting these breeds. This shop delivers a quality cut or grooming every time, with affordable pricing and convenient appointments. This has earned Doggie Styles a loyal local following. TheDoggie Styles staff have a warm and gentle way with animals. Be assured your pet will be comfortable and remarkably at ease in these groomers' capable hands. Doggie Styles can match your schedule. If you need to drop off your pet before the shop opens or cannot pick up your now stylishly-groomed pet until after the shop closes, owner Stefanie Perrine is happy to accommodate you. Stefanie has been a groomer for 21 years. In 1994, she opened Doggie Styles. Stefanie also trains, breeds and shows her own Labradors. Come to Doggie Styles, where pets spread rumors about great groomers.

4990 Kipling Street, Suite 16, Wheat Ridge CO (303) 425-9580

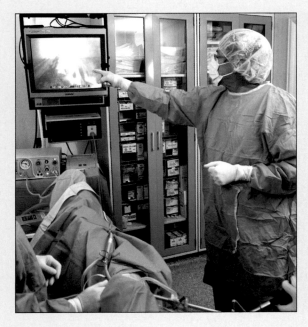

Deer Creek Animal Hospital

Keeping your dogs and cats in good health through a preventative program of check-ups, vaccinations and advanced diagnostics has been an important part of the services at Deer Creek Animal Hospital since it opened in 1984. Deer Creek's 12 veterinarians stay abreast of cutting-edge technology, which means your female dog undergoes less pain from spaying with a laparoscopic procedure, and the reconstruction of a knee ligament could get your best friend out and walking on all fours again. Like other vets in the practice, founding partners Dan Brod and Ray Cox each have their own areas of special interest. Dan's interests involve cardiology, orthopedic surgery and ultrasound, while Raymond is interested in eyes, soft tissue surgery and various new laparoscopic procedures. Still other doctors handle critical care, cancer, dermatology, dentistry and alternative medicine, such as acupuncture. When your dogs stay in Deer Creek's luxury boarding facility, you will be able to watch them online. They all enjoy romping in the outdoor exercise courtyard and swimming pool. Guide your pets toward long, healthy lives with premier care from Deer Creek Animal Hospital, winner of *5280 Magazine*'s Top of the Town awards for Best Vet Clinic and Best Dog Boarding.

10148 W Chatfield Avenue, Littleton CO (303) 973-4200
www.dcah.com

Evergreen Kennel & Grooming

Dogs who know Evergreen Kennel & Grooming can't wait for their owners to go on vacation. Whether the dogs come for day care or overnight boarding, owner Anik Gosch and her staff make friends with their canine charges. In good weather, dogs often stay outdoors for eight or nine hours. In bad weather, Anik's four-legged customers lounge behind the counter with her. The staff finds comfy places for tired dogs to rest and seeks out veterinarian care for sick or injured animals. Anita worked for Peak Kennels before attending dog training school in Arizona and going on to train service dogs in Lakewood. When she heard Peak was closing, she saw her chance to launch a kennel of her own in the Peak location. She's improved security on the property with double gates and split a big yard into three so that small groups of compatible dogs romp together and little dogs exercise separately. The kiddie pool and ball launcher keep dogs busy during the day so they sleep well for their owners at night. Overnight guests receive private, indoor, heated kennels. Anik offers dog training and grooming services. She sells Eagle Pack dog food and such accessories as beds, toys and leashes. Give your dog a second home at Evergreen Kennel & Grooming.

30596 Bryant Drive, Evergreen CO (303) 670-9792

Arts & Crafts

LambShoppe

Long after most yarn shops are closed for the day, LambShoppe is packing people in. When Mary Carol Jehn and Anita Meyer started this business, they vowed to be open hours that would be convenient for their customers. That's why LambShoppe is open seven days a week and open until nine pm four nights a week. People come to LambShoppe for more than just yarn, patterns, needles and other supplies. Often they are looking for a place to sit, knit, crochet and socialize. LambShoppe is the perfect place to get together with folks who love to work on their projects, sip Italian coffee and munch on pastries. The knitting community has its own celebrities and many of them have come by to check out LambShoppe. Vickie Howell, known to knitters through her national television show *Knitty Gritty*, has paid a visit. So have Debbie Stoller of *Stitch 'n Bitch* and world-renowned British designer Debbie Bliss. Those who enjoy knitting and a good mystery love Maggie Sefton, who uses a Colorado yarn shop as the setting in all her stories. Was she getting ideas for her next plot when she came by? It seems that the only person missing at LambShoppe is you, but you can change that by joining the rest of the flock the next time you are in the neighborhood.

3512 E 12th Avenue, Denver CO
(303) 322-2223
www.thelambshoppe.com

Harriet's Treadle Arts

Just as Rocky Mountain National Park is a destination for nature lovers visiting Colorado, Harriet's Treadle Arts is a major draw for quilters passing through the state. Harriet Hargrave welcomes visitors from all over at her shop, many of whom tell her that they have wanted to meet her for years. Harriet's Treadle Arts offers the highest quality supplies for machine quilting, plus unparalleled professional advice. What's more, it offers the chance to chat with Harriet, the author of four books on quilting. Considered to be bibles on their respective topics, they include *Heirloom Machine Quilting*, *Mastering Machine Appliqué* and *From Fiber to Fabric*. The title of her fourth book, *The Art of Classic Quiltmaking*, is also the name of a class she teaches at her shop. All employees are required to take it as part of their training, leaving them ready to answer customer questions. An extensive schedule of classes changes two or three times during the year, offering a wide range of instruction for beginning as well as advanced students. If you are shopping for supplies, be prepared to be impressed. The shop boasts a huge notions inventory, and carries the most complete selection of fabric colors that you are likely to find anywhere. Add Harriet's Treadle Arts to your list of reasons to visit Colorado.

6390 W 44th Avenue, Wheat Ridge CO
(303) 424-2742
www.harriethargrave.com

The Little Wool Shoppe

Connie Huddleson is fond of saying that people come to her Windsor shop to have wooly moments. Naturally the place is called the Little Wool Shoppe, and it's where you will find an enormous selection of wools—tweeds, solids and hand dyed wool—in hundreds of colors. Perfect for your quilting, penny rugs or rug hooking projects, Connie sells the wool by the square inch and would be happy to cut the size you need. When Connie isn't entertaining customers with her wild and wooly personality, she is busy designing patterns for her Starry Pines Pattern Company. At last count, she supplies patterns to about 1,000 quilt shops internationally. Her love of texture and folk art are evident in the Starry Pines designs that adorn the Little Wool Shoppe. She is also a gifted teacher who conducts a full schedule of classes on-site. When we checked the store's calendar, we noticed that most weeks feature two or three classes, making it possible to learn how to make, say, a rag quilt on Tuesday and a wool bag with vintage-looking leather handles on Thursday. Hire Connie for a speaking engagement or workshop, and she will bring not only her great teaching and communication skills but her bubbly sense of humor. Come and spend a few wooly moments with Connie at the Little Wool Shoppe.

505 Main Street, Windsor CO (970) 686-5642 *www.starrypinespatterncompany.com*

Eagles Nest Hobbies

Phil and Sharon Nuckles with a logo of modelers serving modelers. Their shop, Eagles Nest Hobbies, specializes in two things—radio controlled models and friendship. As your friend in modeling, Phil offers his in-store workbench, tools and expertise to help you with your model of choice. Phil has been flying radio control models for over 50 years and has even designed a few models himself. Now located in Longmont, Phil and Sharon moved Eagles Nest Hobbies from Colorado Springs in 2006. The walls of Eagles Nest Hobbies display hundreds of models and loads of hobbyist supplies. Model airplanes from present day suppliers, remote controlled cars by up-to-date manufacturers, wooden ship models, rockets and trains dazzle the child in all of us. Phil instructs beginning modelers and is a member of the local radio control and model railroad clubs. Stop in to Eagles Nest Hobbies and introduce yourself, because to Phil and Sharon there are no strangers, merely friends waiting to meet.

360 Main Street, Longmont CO (720) 494-4144
www.acehobbiesdaytona.com

The Main Street Stitcher's Garden

Not everyone learned the needle arts at an early age like Pat Andriene and Nancy Boggio, but everyone can excel at needlework with guidance and supplies from the Main Street Stitcher's Garden. Pat and Nancy opened the Longmont store in 2005 for fellow stitchers and stitchers-to-be. There you will find everything you need for embroidery, counted cross-stitch, needlepoint, punch needle, Hardanger and Swedish weaving. The store also carries Nancy's designs under the name Sunflower Days Designs. Three permanent teachers plus guest teachers with national reputations offer classes for beginner through advanced students. A visit to the Stitcher's Garden is an opportunity to turn off your cell phone and indulge in a personal therapy session. Pat and Nancy extend stitching camaraderie by hosting spring teas and fall mountain retreats. In July, the Shop Hop takes customers on a tour of needlework shops throughout northern Colorado. The shop supports local charities and the local embroidery guild. It also participates in such events as the stitching exhibition at the County Fair. Come to the Main Street Stitcher's Garden, Where Stitchers Gather for Fun.

331 Main Street, Longmont CO (303) 651-1900 or (866) 739-8425
www.stitchersgarden.biz

Shared Threads Quilt Shop

The Shared Threads Quilt Shop is a quilter's dream come true. This shop has a huge selection of top-quality fabrics emphasizing elegant, traditional patterns. There's always a plentiful supply of fabrics cut into fat quarters to satisfy the urge to add to your quilter's stash. The shop stocks every notion and accessory you might need, along with books, patterns and quilting kits. Bernina and Tin Lizzie are the featured lines of sewing machines. In addition to the Bernina Machine Mastery class series, the shop offers many other classes, ranging from basic quilting techniques to wall hangings and jacket making. Every Saturday morning, the shop hosts a free workshop, a lively social gathering that brings you up to date on the latest in sewing topics, project ideas and what's new at the shop. Owner Judy Lumberg is a prizewinning quilter whose talents have been featured in *Quiltmaker* magazine and the popular book of quilts, *Four Blocks Say More*. She's known for her discerning eye for color and her ability to help you make the most of your color choices. If you love quilting, a visit to the Shared Threads Quilt Shop is a must.

10050 Ralston Road, Suite G, Arvada CO (303) 420-5720
www.sharedthreads.com

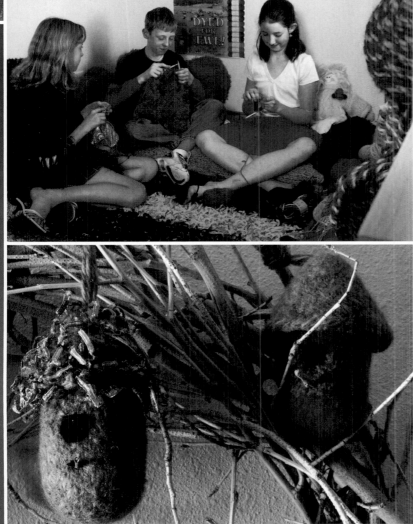

My Sister Knits

For Julie Luckasen, knitting is a form of therapy that helps to relieve the stress of a busy world. At My Sister Knits, Julie and her staff help others discover the joy and release that knitting brings. Julie opened the Fort Collins store in 2004, but her love of yarn goes back much farther. She started knitting at the age of 8, working on projects with her mother and her sister Diana. What started out as a hobby has turned into a career. Today, Julie's store offers what she calls "scrumptious yarns, knitting accessories and encouragement." At My Sister Knits, you'll find a large variety of yarns, most spun from natural fibers. Whether you seek sock yarns, sheep wool or alpaca, you'll find it here. You'll also find a full range of supplies, including felting and darning needles, buttons and stitch holders. My Sister Knits offers books and patterns to help get started. If you need some simple advice or advanced classes, My Sister Knits has plenty of expertise to offer. The store holds knitting and crocheting courses for novices and experts. Julie especially enjoys teaching children the art of knitting. My Sister Knits donates to many schools and community organizations. The atmosphere is homey and quaint. Come to My Sister Knits for all the yarn and material you'll need to keep youself in stitches.

1408 W Mountain Avenue, Fort Collins CO
(970) 407-1461
www.mysisterknits.com

Sew What? Ltd.

With more than 35,000 yards of fabric in stock at any given time, Sew What? is the answer to your fabric needs. You'll find an incredible variety of colors and styles of fabric from all over the world at this shop. Among the most popular are Western and Southwestern fabrics. Whether you're buying by the yard or by the bolt, you'll save money because Sew What? orders fabric direct from the mills. The greatest savings are available to those buying in bulk. If you can't find just the right style of fabric on the shelf, the shop can special-order it for you. You'll also find trim, cushion filler, foam and drapery hardware. Sew What? custom makes draperies, bedding, cushions, pillows and slipcovers. The staff is available to answer any questions you might have, and can help you pick out the perfect fabric for your home. Owners Jack and Lark Ruppert opened the Fort Collins store in 1976. Lark brings a high level of expertise to work every day—she earned a degree in textiles and clothing from Colorado State University. Come in and see why Sew What? is the textiles solution.

1817 E Mulberry Street, Fort Collins CO
(970) 482-7681

Cottonwood Quilts

Amy Rullkoetter and Diane Merritt opened Cottonwood Quilts in 2004, and they have yet to run out of ideas for making their shop a gathering place for creative people. In addition to carrying fabrics, books and everything else quilters need to plan and complete their projects, they host classes and clubs almost every day of the week. You could learn how to make a handbag on one day, explore the use of color the next and return later in the week to work on a project with the hand appliqué club or the paper-piecing club. The doors don't close until nine on many nights to accommodate folks who work during the day. Some Saturday get-togethers even go until midnight. The owners consider themselves a part of the entertainment industry and are forever inventing special events for quilters. Their recent Island Luau, for example, offered a batik sale with free demonstrations and tropical treats. When they aren't busy as social directors, these energetic ladies are creating their own quilting designs, which they sell as kits at the store. Every day is a celebration of creativity at Cottonwood Quilts. Drop by to be inspired, to share camaraderie and to be entertained.

198 2nd Avenue, Suite C, Niwot CO
(303) 652-1711
www.cottonwoodquiltscolorado.com

Studio Bernina

From three-hour workshops to six-month programs, Studio Bernina offers something for everyone who loves the sound of a sewing machine. The school even has classes for children and teens. Traditional tailoring was the focus of the curriculum when Studio Bernina opened in 1985, but the class offerings have grown considerably since then. Currently, the studio's comprehensive curriculum includes fine garment sewing, plus an extensive list of quilting classes, kid's classes and textile arts. Susan Igou, the first woman president of the Custom Tailors and Designers Association of America, owns and manages the studio. Very few institutes teach tailoring as intensively as Studio Bernina, she notes. Going beyond the basics, Susan lets students see clothing as an art form and regard clothing construction as a means of sculpting fabric to fit the body. Studio Bernina is also an authorized dealer of Bernina sewing, quilting and embroidery machines. You can create a portfolio for acceptance into design school at Studio Bernina—or simply enrich your life by learning how to make your own clothing and quilts, or decorate your home.

2460 Canyon Boulevard, Boulder CO
(303) 447-0852
www.studiobernina.com

Tomorrow's Heirlooms

Tomorrow's Heirlooms is a place that will inspire your creativity. Owners Rhonda and Steve Anderson want to share the art of quilting and sewing with others, and have created a wonderful atmosphere to do just that. Their knowledgeable staff will answer all your questions. When you visit, an explosion of color greets you. Beautiful quilts cover the walls and colorful fabrics fill the aisles. Don't miss the wall of thread. Tomorrow's Heirlooms has the largest selection of quilting, embroidery and sewing thread in the area. Customers also love the top-of-the-line fabrics. The shop stocks everything for quilt making and embroidery. It is an authorized dealer for Bernina sewing machines, Gammill quilting machines and Statler Stitcher computerized quilting systems. Come prepared to learn an array of techniques, from traditional to contemporary, artistic to whimsical, quilting to clothing, and embroidery to home décor. Tomorrow's Heirlooms offers classes at every level, including a beginning-quilting course. If you have never quilted before, you will enjoy helpful instruction and the thrill of completing your first quilt. A full set of Bernina classes will build your confidence at every level. Join a Bernina club to learn what your machine can really do. If you have ever wondered what it takes to finish a quilt on a longarm-quilting machine, you will love the longarm introductory classes. The shop invites award-winning quilters from across the country to teach in its incredible classroom. Come in for a demonstration and browse the many fine products. The experience will surely inspire you to create Tomorrow's Heirlooms yourself.

13644 Orchard Parkway, Suite 600, Westminster CO
(303) 457-3888 *www.quiltshop.us*

Promenade's Le Bead Shop

Promenade's Le Bead Shop is the place to go to feed your creativity, a place to revel in embellkishment. From the professional to the beginner, jewelry designers will find that owner Sherri Newson stocks everything they need, including stringing material, instruction books, sterling silver wire and findings (connecting pieces, clamps). The wide range of beads that include glass, Austrian crystal, wood, and both precious and non-precious metals are a delight to the eager artist. You'll also find more unusual beads from around the world that are made of materials such as shell, bone, cinnabar and amber. A selection of rhinestones, sequins, metal studs and appliqués will help adorn any project. Jewelry can be constructed at the make-it-and-take-it table or be left to be completed. The store's bead museum and gallery features exhibits from private collections and fine artists. The staff offers small classes in basic and advanced beading and knotting. Each session includes plenty of personal attention. The shop is open Sunday afternoons as well as weekdays. Whether you want to purchase a finished work of art or stay and create your own, Promenade Le Bead Shop provides a creative environment where customers find enjoyment, pride and fulfillment.

1970 13th Street, Boulder CO
(303) 440-4807

Shuttles, Spindles & Skeins

Have you ever wondered how to weave a rug, knit a shawl or spin your own yarn? A class at Shuttles, Spindles & Skeins will unravel the mystery while unleashing your own creativity. Since 1992, Shuttles has been a gathering place for those interested in weaving, knitting, spinning, felting and basketry. Learning just for the fun of it is the goal at this busy shop, where the staff lends its talents in teaching a full schedule of classes. Being a part of the scene at Shuttles, Spindles & Skeins is a lot like going to crafts college, only you won't have to stress over final exams. Guest instructors come from all over to offer workshops on everything from natural dyeing to the traditions of Estonian folk knitting. The Community Knitters meet once a month to knit for children in need. Located in the Table Mesa Shopping Center, Shuttles, Spindles & Skeins is packed full of colorful yarns, books, patterns and everything else you may need to complete your own projects. Learn, create and shop at Shuttles.

635 S Broadway, Unit E, Boulder CO
(303) 494-1071 or (800) 283-4163
www.shuttlesspindlesandskeins.com

Marci Baker
of Alicia's Attic

Internationally recognized quilting expert Marci Baker completed her first quilt when she was eight years old and has been at it ever since. Her quilting headquarters today is Alicia's Attic, her production offices in Fort Collins. Early on, Marci found that quilting could incorporate her other love, math. Inspired by traditional quilt patterns and looking for ways to make jobs faster and easier, she developed methods that she teaches in her book series *Not Your Grandmother's Quilts*. She also developed several specialty tools that greatly reduce the time and effort of quilting. Her trademarked Know Before You Sew reference cards help troubleshoot the quilting process and provide easy-to-understand solutions to problems. Marci spends much of her time traveling and sharing her enthusiasm and inspiration for quilting through lectures and workshops. She has been featured in *Redbook*, on Home and Garden TV's *Simply Quilts* and on the *Jane Pauley Show*. Marci explains not only how it works, but why it works. At her location, you can peruse the selection of helpful books and tools, which are available to get you off to a great start. Whether you are a beginning or seasoned quilter, Marci Baker's lessons and tools will make your quilting much easier and more fun.

204 Link Lane, #7, Fort Collins CO
(970) 224-1336 or (888) 348-6653
www.aliciasattic.com

Dancing Colours

Dancing Colours is a gift gallery and creative arts studio offering its community an eclectic selection of artist-made gifts as well as ongoing creative classes and supplies. Dancing Colours' fun-loving classes encourage creativity as students learn to use new materials and techniques in a small intimate environment with one-on-one attention. Creative artist-made gifts from both local and national artisans fill the gift gallery along with an artful selection of greeting cards, many of which are small pieces of art themselves. The studio holds a monthly Art Bar, a fun and creative night out in which patrons are served art projects on a platter. As they are creating their projects, waitpersons circulate with hors d'oeuvres and libations. An annual pumpkin-carving contest raises money to benefit the local youth radio program, and Dancing Colours actively supports various other charities and services for youth. Dancing Colours is owned by Cathren and Jeff Britt. Cathren uses her artistic and merchandising background and her creativity to encourage others to open up and create. The studio is inviting and full of whimsy, accompanied by helpful and friendly customer service. Whether you are going to buy, learn, or create, Dancing Colours will stimulate your imagination and give you inspiration.

968 Main Street, Carbondale CO
(970) 963-2965

Recycled Lamb

Customers from all over appreciate the friendly service and top-notch supplies available at the Recycled Lamb. Owner Jeannie Davis provides the very best in yarn, natural fibers, and supplies to her customers. Recycled Lamb is one of Colorado's best and most established yarn stores and has been in business for more years than the Ladies Of The Lamb who work there care to remember. Customers come

from all over the United States, Canada and even parts beyond. Yarn artists and spinners alike will always find exactly what they need at Jeannie's shop. Customer service is the heart of the store and Jeannie or one of the staff members always takes the time to work with you until you find the perfect yarn for your project. The huge stock includes knitting needles and crochet hooks in dozens of sizes (some made exclusively for the store), looms and all manner of weaving equipment. Browse through hundreds of patterns, books, manuals and other sources of inspiration. Dozens and dozens of classes are available in knitting, weaving and special projects. Stop by Recycled Lamb to shop or take a class. Or you can sit and knit or crochet with people who enjoy it as much as you do, in a place that is just like home.

2010 Youngfield Street, Lakewood CO (303) 234-9337
www.recycledlamb.com

What's Needling U

So far, no one has pulled up to What's Needling U in a knitted car, but that doesn't mean that it won't happen some day. Owners Kim Parker and Gail Cummer live by the motto that There's Nothing that Can't Be Knitted. Locals know that they can depend on Kim and Gail for an abundance of yarns, though out-of-towners are always amazed to discover the many natural fibers, including bamboo, soy and corn, as well as the large stock of cotton, buffalo and camel yarns. Indeed, What's Needling U specializes in carrying things that just cannot be found in most stores. The service at the shop is personal and very friendly. Kim especially enjoys applying her keen sense of color to help customers who are starting a project and don't know what colors to use. What's Needling U hosts an open knitting session on Tuesday afternoons, a time for folks to come in and work together and see what each other are doing. A schedule of afternoon and evening classes offers instruction for people who are getting started in knitting, plus workshops demonstrating advanced techniques. Whether your next project is a sweater or a station wagon, get everything you need to complete it triumphantly at What's Needling U.

279 Main Street, Frisco CO (970) 668-0381
www.whatsneedlingu.com

Breckenridge Bead Gallery

If, while taking that vacation you needed in Breckenridge, you decide that you also need a hobby, Kristie Hoffman at the Breckenridge Bead Gallery is the person to see. Since 1996, many people have been drawn into her shop by a longing to try something new and a desire to make something with their hands. Kristie considers her bead selection to be the best in the high country. Remarkable in its variety, it includes delicas, bone and silver, as well as wood, semi-precious stones and glass. The gallery's selection is so wide and the prices are so good that you might set your expectations of other bead shops too high. This beader's paradise carries the books you'll need for instruction and inspiration. Even if you don't plan to stock up on supplies, it's worthwhile just to browse the pre-made jewelry at the shop. Breckenridge stocks fine art supplies such as canvas, paint, brushes and drawing materials. It has a variety of decorative rubber stamps that make it easy to create cards, scrapbook pages and altered books. Let your souvenir of Breckenridge be a new hobby, courtesy of Breckenridge Bead Gallery.

2245 S Main Street, Breckenridge CO (970) 453-1964

Rockywoods Outdoor Fabrics

When her children were members of the Scouts, Audrey Szmyd discovered that quality outdoor fabric can be hard to come by. Audrey reasoned that there must be others searching for the materials that she had such a difficult time locating, so she opened Rockywoods Outdoor Fabrics, a retail shop with a single rack of fabrics. The popularity of the shop proved her right. Today, Rockywoods caters to an international clientele online as well as on location in Loveland. Jared Szmyd is the manager, and the entire operation is staffed by family. Making your own outdoor gear has endless advantages. You can tailor your clothing to fit perfectly and adapt designs to better express your personal style. Rockywoods offers kits to make your own backpacks, gloves and clothing. Materials include Hunting fabrics, waterproof fabrics that breathe, Cordura nylon and fleeces. You'll also find hardware such as zippers, buckles and zipper extensions. Orders are often shipped out on the same day. The Szmyds keep themselves accessible to customers and invite your inquiries and requests. Find affordable, customizable outdoor gear at Rockywoods Outdoor Fabrics.

418 SE 8th Street, A-3, Loveland CO
(970) 663-6163
www.rockywoods.com

Capture

When you visit Capture, you feel like you've entered into a big city paper crafting store. This modern, upscale store offers the latest in high quality scrapbooking and paper crafting supplies in a beautifully organized space. In addition to paper supplies, Capture is equipped with a complete digital center, including Macintosh systems, a high definition scanner, multiple photo printer, a large format printer for 12 x 12 or larger prints, and digital scrapbooking and photo editing software. They are also able to do book binding right in the store. A full selection of classes for adults and kids are provided each month to inspire your creativity. When you see the large, open workroom, you will be excited to take advantage of the tools and die-cutting systems that are available for you to experiment with on your own projects at any time. You can even host your own private cropping parties for your next birthday, shower or just-because party. Capture is a must-see store. Discover the creative possibilities available to help you capture your memories and sentiments at Capture.

838 W Drake Road, Suite 105, Fort Collins CO
(970) 484-0595
www.shopcapture.com

Glenwood Sew

Sandy Boyd always had an interest in sewing, especially the artistic aspect of it, and her husband, Bob, had a knack for repair. Glenwood Sew was a natural progression for them. In the early days of their shop, sewing clothing was the paramount interest of their customers, but over time sewing has evolved into an art form and an activity for enjoyment, most evident in the recent surge of interest in quilting. Glenwood Sew offers Husqvarna and Viking sewing machines, parts, notions and accessories. Contemporary and traditional quilt fabrics, original patterns, supplies and tools are available for you to create your artwork. Customers can sign up for classes or join a club and learn to make full use of the Viking sewing and embroidery machines in a fun social setting. In-house sewing machine repair is always available. A continually evolving quilt show at the shop is worth seeing, even if you don't sew. An offshoot of the business, Glenwood Sewing Press, produces nationally distributed watercolor quilt patterns, stained glass quilt patterns, and many other products. Glenwood Sew participates in the Western Slope Shop Hop where people all over the region visit stores as part of a community treasure hunt. The first Saturday of the month is Saturday Sampler: a drop-in group for piecing quilts. Get ideas and inspiration for your next project with a visit to Glenwood Sew.

822 Grand Avenue, Glenwood Springs CO
(970) 945-5900 or (800) 371-5967
www.glenwoodsew.com

Castle Rock Music

If you dream of making music, Castle Rock Music can help. Owners Jason Bower and Joshua Price bring years of performing and teaching music to their enterprise, offering just the right level of expertise to patrons who hear jazz riffs, Latin percussion or Big Band swing in their heads. Browse through the wide assortment of instruments and decide whether a saxophone or a trombone, an electric guitar or drums is most likely to liberate your inner musician. Castle Rock Music promises competitive prices on instruments and takes pride in providing the right guidance for your musical journey. Offering a full range of lessons featuring many musical instruments and styles, Castle Rock's team of professional musicians can assist beginners and virtuosos alike. Explore music theory or songwriting, or try your hand at jazz trumpet, blues or classical guitar. For a life filled with music, visit Castle Rock Music, because whatever instrument or style calls to you, the folks at Castle Rock Music can help you select your instrument and find your tune, then teach you how to play it.

429 Wilcox Street, Castle Rock CO
(303) 688-0300
www.castlerockmusic.com

Attractions & Recreation

Game Set Match Inc.

Love is more than just a tennis score at Game Set Match Inc. It is also how owner Adam Burbary feels about the game and his stores, which are located in Denver and Littleton. Players find everything they need at Game Set Match Inc. for a great experience on the tennis court. Both locations sell a huge variety of racquets, clothing, shoes and tennis accessories. You'll find major brands, such as Wilson, Prince, Head, Babolat, Volkl, Nike, KSwiss, Asics, Fila and more. Game Set Match Inc. exceeds player expectations by also offering a variety of court equipment and ball machines. Stringing experts are available daily, guaranteeing a 24-hour or less turn around. The stores are an official sponsor of the USTA and the CTA and have provided local league sponsorships for several years. For direct purchase and shipping anywhere in the U.S., contact either store location. Visit Game Set Match Inc. to stay current with all of your tennis clothing and equipment needs.

333 S Colorado Boulevard, Denver CO
(303) 394-1991
8375 S Willow Street, #208, Littleton CO
(303) 790-1991
www.gamesetmatchinc.com

Discount Fishing Tackle

Online or in person, the best supermarket for quality spin and fly fishing supplies is Discount Fishing Tackle. If you equate fishing with breathing, you'll find everything you need to make your next fishing trip one you'll always remember. Knowledgeable staff members give all the anglers great customer service. They pride themselves on finding the hip waders, fly reels, rods and lines to meet your needs. They'll help you hone your craft with a full line of accessories such as fly-tying tools and materials. Personal items such as sunglasses and wading shoes are also in stock. If you're a beginner, you might want to rent equipment before making your final purchase decision. A 24-hour live bait machine is always up and running. Updated fishing and weather reports keep you posted on hot spots such as the Upper Frying Pan, the South Platte River, the Blue River and Spinney Reservoir. The shop organizes guided fly-fishing trips. It also offers hunting adventures on a 6,000 acre ranch outside of Montross, Colorado. You can sign up for a casting clinic, tying class or fly-fishing course. Fishing aficionados of all ages are always welcome. Visit the website and read the kudos from a long list of happy customers. At Discount Fishing Tackle, reel in the quality, selection and service. You won't be disappointed.

1793 S College Avenue, Fort Collins CO
(970) 472-1911 or (866) FOR-FLYS (367-3597)
www.fortackle.com

Fort Fun

Imagine enjoying a sunny day with your loved ones next to the scenic Cache le Poudre River—playing mini-golf and go-karts, relaxing under Colorado blue skies and eating good food. Sound like fun? Then the aptly named Fort Fun is a sure bet for you and your family. Fort Fun is Northern Colorado's premier family entertainment center. It offers playful adventure experiences with both indoor and outdoor activities featuring mini-golf, go-karts, laser tag, paddle boats, mini-bowling, batting cages, an arcade and bumper cars. Relax under the pavilion and watch the gold fish in the pond. Wander through the beautiful gardens. Enjoy the view from the plaza overlooking Blue Herron Lake. The facility is clean and the staff is friendly. Fort Fun successfully embraces the youthful excitement of the new Mountain West while framing itself in a setting filled with nostalgic reminders of the area's historic past. With fun activities, a beautiful setting, great food and more to please the pickiest, Fort Fun can amuse a family of four, a birthday party of 50 or corporate picnic for 400. Fort Fun takes pride in offering playful opportunities for people to connect through laughter and fun. The facility hosts overnight lock-ins for the young and young-at-heart, birthday bashes with pizza and soda, corporate team-building excursions, family reunions and anything else imaginable, as long as it's fun. For a few hours, a day, or even a night filled with wholesome fun and games, make a point to stop at Fort Fun, A Friendly Place to Play.

1513 E Mulberry, Fort Collins CO (970) 472-8000
www.fortfun.biz

Boulder Bikesmith

One of the best ways to enjoy all of the adventures that Boulder has to offer is on a bicycle from Boulder Bikesmith. The company is owned and operated by avid cyclist and head mechanic Jon Stabile. Bikesmith was founded in 1989 as a mobile bike rental service. By the time Jon joined the Bikesmith team as a mechanic in 1998, the shop had been in its current location for six years. He moved up through the ranks until 2001, when he had the opportunity to take over the business. Jon has expanded the scope of the business to include a retail section and custom bike fabrication while maintaining the rental selection and service for which Bikesmith is known. Boulder Bikesmith carries, for rent or sale, a variety of bicycles, including city bikes, cruisers and kids' bikes, along with road, recumbent and mountain bikes. Jon freely admits, however, that his passion lies in the custom bicycle side of the business. Boulder Bikesmith also offers repair and maintenance for everything from a flat fix to a major overhaul. With the emphasis on friendly, knowledgeable service, you are sure to get exactly what you need at Boulder Bikesmith in the Arapahoe Village Shopping Center, located just minutes from the scenic Boulder Creek bike path.

2432 Arapahoe Avenue, Boulder CO (303) 443-1132
www.boulderbikesmith.com

Louisville Cyclery

A road warrior back in his competitive heyday, Scott Adlfinger now shares his enthusiasm for biking with customers at Louisville Cyclery. Scott was a national-caliber racer, but when back problems slowed him down, he turned to the business side of the sport and opened his store in 1980. Louisville Cyclery carries the oldest bike brand in the world, Bianchi, as well as such other top brands as Specialized

and Litespeed. Even though mountain bikes weren't invented when the shop first opened, Scott admires the tenacious attitude of mountain bikers and caters to their needs as well as to those of the road racer and recreational rider. As Scott points out, fit and function are the key with all brands of bikes. Therefore, he is especially proud of his fitting service and of the people who run it. His store is staffed with experts, many of whom have worked here for more than 10 years, so they know how to customize bikes to their riders. You will find a full line of accessories at the store, too, everything from clothing and shoes to lights and mirrors. Louisville Cyclery stays connected to the cycling community by sponsoring teams, events and a club called the Louisville Velo club, which has 120 members. For sales and service from Scott and his staff of biking enthusiasts, race to Louisville Cyclery.

1032 S Boulder Road, Louisville CO (303) 665-6343
www.louisvillecyclery.com

Tortuga Bay

Tortuga Bay, a full-service scuba and snorkel facility, features the deepest heated indoor saltwater pool in the world. Twelve certified instructors teach classes ranging from the intro to instructor level. New divers can complete the necessary academic training on-line, at home or in weekend classes. Then they are ready for confined water training in Tortuga Bay's pool. The open water evaluation, the final stage of training, takes place year-round at the famous Blue Hole in Santa Rosa, New Mexico. At Tortuga Bay, outstanding customer service is paramount. Retail staff members at the dive shop, which stocks major brands of diving equipment, act as equipment counselors, never as high-pressure salespeople. Owner Ron Bland grew up around water, learned to swim at an early age and became a scuba instructor in 1987. He left the corporate world in 1998 to become a scuba bum and to open Tortuga Bay with Jeremy, his son and co-owner of the business. Ron and Jeremy's passion for scuba means that Tortuga Bay exists to make divers, rather than just money. Ron has trained more than 5,000 students. Tortuga Bay arranges multiple travel packages every year to exotic diving destinations. Come discover thrilling underwater adventure at Tortuga Bay, where the staff will prepare you for a lifetime of diving enjoyment.

6200 W 9th Street, Greeley CO (970) 353-DEEP (3337)
www.tortugabay.net

Mountain Whitewater Descents

Brad Modesitt knows that a successful whitewater rafting experience begins with the right guide. At Mountain Whitewater Descents, the guides have medical training and Swiftwater Rescue certifications. They know the Cache la Poudre River and the plants and animals that live here. They also have a sense of fun that just won't quit. Brad opened his company on Colorado's only Wild and Scenic River in 2000. Since then, some 7,000 people make Mountain Whitewater Descents their destination each year from mid-May to the end of August. The company offers thrilling half and full day rafting adventures plus kayak instruction. Early in the season, the minimum age is 13; as water levels change, younger children are welcome. The Poudre starts in Rocky Mountain National Park and tumbles through cliffs and rock spires, offering a continuous adrenaline surge on Class II, III and IV rapids. You can purchase a photo or video of you and your team coursing down the river. The park at Mountain Whitewater Descents invites lingering with frisbee golf, volleyball and a nature trail. You'll also find a hot tub, barbecue and a pond for practicing kayak rolling. Experience the grandeur of the Poudre with the topnotch guides at Mountain Whitewater Descents. Brad, Lindsey and Ella look forward to taking you on your adventure.

1329 N U.S. Highway 287, Fort Collins CO
(970) 419-0917 or (888) 855-8874
www.MountainWhitewaterDescents.com

Rotors of the Rockies

Michael and Regina Fyola know how to get you into the Colorado skies, whether your purpose is to earn a piloting certification or simply to hover over Denver after dark. Michael started Rotors of the Rockies with one helicopter in June 2001. Today it boasts eight helicopters, 12 flight instructors and 100 active students. Helicopter flight training takes place on a Schweizer 300C. The Fyolas also offer fixed wing training on a 2004 Cessna 172SP. The Bell Jet Ranger is their charter helicopter. It can take four people on a half-hour airborne tour of Denver and also stars in a more elaborate evening designed for the romantic. Imagine a limo picking you up at your home and delivering you to the Rotors ramp, where a helicopter will fly you to dinner at The Fort Restaurant. After dinner, you'll enjoy a night tour of Denver before being escorted to the Rocky Mountain Metropolitan Airport, where the limo will whisk you away to a creek-side suite at the Golden Hotel. Rotors also hosts birthday parties, employee appreciation days, trade shows and aviation field trips. It transports wedding couples and gives photographers unusual vantage points. It coordinates search efforts with law enforcement personnel. Rotors also sells helicopters. Michael is a 10-year veteran of sheriff's offices in Denver and Jefferson County. He's also a combat veteran and chief warrant officer for the Army National Guard. Take to the sky with the trusted pilots of Rotors of the Rockies.

11915 Airport Way, Broomfield CO
(303) 635-0496
www.rotorsoftherockies.com

Chipper's Lanes

Remember how much fun you had the last time you bowled? Even if it's been a few years, the folks at Chipper's Lanes say it's all right. Just pick up a ball and let it roll. With 56 lanes at two locations in Fort Collins, Chipper's Lanes provide plenty of opportunities for you to get back into the game. You'll have a lot of fun doing it at the College Center location when you come by for one of the nightly events, such as Moonlight Cosmic Bowl on Saturday or Karaoke Night on Sunday. Early in the evening on Wednesday your first game is just 99 cents, and then a live band kicks in later for Rock N' Bowl. College Night on Thursday features reduced prices on games and draft beer. The Horsetooth Center location is the more traditional league house, hosting senior leagues and high school clubs as well as junior programs that allow kids to earn scholarship money. Co-owner Matt Hoeven is proud to bring safe and fun entertainment to the community in which he grew up. When he took over, he oversaw renovations to update and refresh the lanes, which had been here for decades. He thinks you'll like the bright, modern look. The annual Black Tie Bowling Event, an elegant night of bowling, supports a number of groups and philanthropic organizations. Dozens of other non-profit organizations hold events at the lanes as well. Roll some strikes at Chipper's Lanes.

830 N College Avenue, Fort Collins CO
(970) 484-4777
217 W Horsetooth Road, Fort Collins CO
(970) 226-6327
www.chipperslanes.com

Indian Peaks Golf Course

A well-formed, challenging course, dazzling views of the Rocky Mountains and great customer service rank among the top reasons to play Indian Peaks Golf Course. The land was donated by the Beauprez and Piszek families for the benefit of the community. Championship golfer Hale Irwin designed the course, which was named after the Indian Peaks Wilderness area that is visible from the course. During its construction, 2,500 trees were planted and rye grass fairways cultivated around the six lakes and two creeks on the course. The tournament-friendly course seats up to 150 golfers in the tournament pavilion. Four sets of tee boxes grace every hole. There is also a top-notch driving range, and the practice facility is one of the best in the state. Six professional golfers are available for teaching. They offer excellent adult programs and a junior program that accepts up to 300 junior players. The Peaks Bar & Grill offers an appetizing menu and drink specials for golfers and non-golfers. The staff is happy to arrange catering packages for tournaments and special events. *Golf Digest* gave Indian Peaks a four-star rating. It has also won many local reader's choice awards. Find out why when you play Indian Peaks Golf Course.

2300 Indian Peaks Trail, Lafayette CO (303) 666-4706
www.indianpeaksgolf.com

Mountain Vista RV

Barbara and Tim Albers' dedication to customers and quality service keeps patrons coming back to this established RV service and sales center. Certified to sell three brands of new travel trailers, the Albers also offer a wide variety of used fifth wheels, travel trailers, tent trailers, truck toppers and toy haulers for quads and motorcycles. They promise a relaxed browsing environment where you can survey new and used vehicles without pressure, offering financing once you've made your choice. They also specialize in consignments and are happy to help you sell your vehicle. The well-trained, efficient service technicians stay up-to-date on the latest developments in repairs, and even if you've purchased your vehicle somewhere else, they are happy to give it their time and attention. An emergency service is also available if you need to get back on the highway in a hurry. The well-stocked parts department probably has that battery clip or valve you need, but if they don't carry the exact part, they are happy to order it. If you're driving it, hauling it or need it repaired, Mountain Vista RV can help keep you on the road.

1550 E Highway 34, Loveland CO (970) 667-3175 or (800) 439-3175
www.mountainvistarv.com

BMW Billiards

Shoot with the pros at BMW Billiards in Fort Collins. Owners Judy Mehle, Gary Benson and Warren Woodson were at the national pool competition when they decided that there had to be a better way to run pool and darts leagues in the Fort Collins area. They soon opened a billiards shop complete with retail services, leagues and vending. All the owners take pride in the fact that BMW Billiards need not advertise. With a strong reputation as the best billiard and dart league, word of mouth has kept the shop successful since opening. The most important aspect of BMW Billiards, however, is the league organization. It is the largest operator-owned pool and dart league organization in Colorado and is among the 10 largest nationwide. With over 1,000 combined league participants, BMW can send a large number of skilled players to national competitions. Whether you are looking to become an expert at darts or pool, or you are just looking for a new pool table for your game room, you can find it at BMW Billiards.

6004 S College Avenue, Fort Collins CO (970) 229-1400
www.vnea.com/bmw

Photo by William R. Sallaz

Ski Cooper

With its family-friendly atmosphere and multitude of trails, lifts and services for skiers of all levels, Ski Cooper has come a long way from its origins as an U.S. Army training facility. The skiable area today includes 400 lift-served acres and 2,400 served by Snowcat. Cross-country skiers enjoy 15 miles of trails. Ski Cooper has an all-natural snowfall of 260 inches per year. The Army's 10th Mountain Division trained in this location as World War II raged in Europe and the Pacific, and here it gained the experience and know-how it would need for the liberation of northern Italy. You'll find a monument to the 10th at the entrance of Ski Cooper, and a collection of its uniforms, skis and other memorabilia at the day lodge. After the war, the ski area became a private facility and expanded greatly. Ski Cooper is now home to a variety of races and events, including the Youth Ski League Championship and the annual Snowboard Festival. In addition to the lodge, the base area includes a rental shop, restaurant and bar. Overnight accommodations are available just nine miles away in Leadville. Those looking for a genuine culinary adventure can ski or snowshoe a mile to the Tennessee Pass Cookhouse for elk tenderloin and other favorites. Ski Cooper has recently opened a new Children's Center to house its ever-growing Children's Ski School. Young and old, come ski in the tracks of the famed 10th Mountain Division at Ski Cooper.

U.S. Highway 24 (9 miles north of Leadville), Leadville CO (719) 486-3684 *www.skicooper.com*

Photo by William R. Sallaz

Sol Skateboards

Owner Allan John and his employees at Sol Skateboards don't care whether you have been skateboarding since you could walk or if you are just getting started. They treat everyone with the same personalized service that has put this business at the top of its field. This skater-owned-and-operated establishment has earned Skateshop of the Month honors from *Thrasher* magazine and *Transworld*. The store sells all the major brands, complemented by its own bearings and deck designs. In addition, the shelves and racks are full of shoes and all the gear you'll need to skate and look your best. Since beginning the business in 2003, Allan has aimed for pushing the limits of skateboarding on the local scene. His credentials include teaching for seven summers at Woodward in Pennsylvania, one of the best-known skateboarding camps in North America. He also served as a consultant for the building of Sandstone Ranch, the Longmont skate park considered one of the best in the state. He and his team of skaters/employees compete in contests and promote their own style of skating through the videos they produce. For a skateshop qualified to serve the pro but just as happy to help the novice, go to Sol Skateboards.

627 Main Street, Longmont CO (303) 651-2000
www.solskates.com

Colorado Sports Rent

At Colorado Sports Rent, you can rent top-of-the-line sporting equipment from major companies for a day, a week or a season. In winter, this Arvada business outfits customers for snowboarding, skiing and ice fishing. You can even rent such essential gear as ski jackets and goggles. In summer, Sports Rent prepares many customers for trips to Lake Powell with Sea Doo jet skis and Yamaha WaveRunners. You'll find fishing boats, canoes and kayaks. Watercraft rentals include trailers and permission to take the craft out-of-state. Camping trips come together with ease thanks to the store's tents, stoves and sleeping bags. You can assure camaraderie at your group picnic with equipment for such games as volleyball, softball and horseshoes. Well-maintained dirt bikes and ATVs stand ready to serve you. If you know what you want or like what you try, Sports Rent will sell it to you. The store opened in 1991. Present owner Brad Pester came on as an employee in 1997 and worked for two years before purchasing the company when he turned 21. He's considering expansion, thanks to a customer base that extends to surrounding states. He invites you to rent a piece of the action at Colorado Sports Rent.

8761 Wadsworth Boulevard, Arvada CO (303) 467-0200
www.sportsrent.net

Photo by Iain Cuthbertson

Archery in the Wild

Archery buffs looking for the finest gear and training can't miss at Archery in the Wild. Owner Boyd Wild has been hunting, fishing and enjoying the outdoors his whole life, discovering the joys of archery some 20 years ago. Boyd is hardly alone in his enjoyment of this great sport—archery is one of the fastest growing sports among men, women and children in the United States. As his own father passed his joy of the outdoors down to him, so Boyd has passed his love of archery on to his son, Dusty, who also works full-time at Archery in the Wild. You'll find a full range of gear here, including top-of-the-line bows from BowTech, Mathews and Merlin. Dusty and Boyd make all their own arrows and bowstrings here, using the finest materials available. They can custom-make strings and arrows to your exact specifications, and even have kits to allow you to make your own. Archery in the Wild sponsors archery leagues and lessons for adults and even a Junior Olympic Archery Development program for kids. Enjoy some target practice at the store's indoor range. You'll be right on target with bows, strings and arrows from Archery in the Wild.

1725 Vista View Drive, Unit E, Longmont CO (720) 652-9100
www.archeryinthewild.com

Rollerland Skate Center

Friday nights at the roller rink have been a right of passage and an iconic part of our culture for decades. That tradition continues at Rollerland Skate Center. Now owned and operated by former Olympic speed skater Jondon Trevena and his brother Jathan, it is a thriving center of activity. While times have changed, the fun of skating at the rink has not. Many grownups are rediscovering the fun of the rink while their children are enjoying it for the first time. Many people are interested in skating as exercise—and yet it also provides the opportunity to visit with friends. Rollerland Skate Center offers classes in skating and speed skating for those who want to skate their best. Jam skating classes and private instruction are also available. Rollerland is a great place for birthday parties. You can actually rent the entire rink at a very affordable price. Bring in the family to enjoy fun theme nights such as banana split night, when Rollerland staff build a 50-foot banana split. A favorite with teens is the all-you-can-drink soda night. You'll have a blast at beach party night, which includes beach balls, games and costumes. A skating rink would not be a skating rink without a great concession stand, and Rollerland has one of the best. Of course it offers all of your favorites, including pretzels and slushies. Visit Rollerland Skate Center and join the fun.

324 S Link Lane, Fort Collins CO
(970) 482-0497
www.rollerlandskatecenter.com

Ute City Cycles

In the beginning, one man had a ski tuning shop, and another had a bike service shop. When Bubba Scott and Steven Midlarsky joined forces, they came up with Ute City Cycles. This shop focuses on high end products such as Orbea, and it is the biggest seller of John Parker's Yeti products in the world. Yeti's race teams and tribe members can attest to the bike's outstanding qualifications and leadership in the mountain biking industry. Staff members can fit you to your bike and keep it in optimum condition. Whether you are an experienced rider or just starting out, any one of the staff members can guide you to the bike that is right for you. They ride what they sell and offer knowledgeable, quality service. Bikes are the passion, but clothing and accessories of all kinds are available too. Bubba and Steven have expanded to two locations—with one shop in Aspen and one in Carbondale, it's double the pleasure. Darren Broome is the legendary manager of the Carbondale shop. You'll find experienced customer service, an exceptional selection and the bicycle of your dreams at Ute City Cycles.

555 E Durant Avenue, Suite 2E, Aspen CO (970) 920-3325
580 Highway 133, Carbondale CO (970) 963-2500

Roaring Fork Anglers

Fly fishermen in Glenwood Springs rely on Roaring Fork Anglers and its sister fly shop, Alpine Angling, to keep them provisioned for fishing on area rivers and lakes. The store carries popular gear from such companies as Sage, Scott, Orvis and Ross along with phenomenal numbers of flies. Fly-fishing guru and Manager Drew Reid knows current conditions and what flies are getting results. In winter, you can take fly-tying classes. With five rivers nearby, the store's guided fishing trips are the stuff of dreams. You can take a wade or a float trip on the Roaring Fork, Eagle or Colorado Rivers. The store also offers wade fishing on the Frying Pan and Crystal Rivers and has access to private ranches and spring creeks that yield trophy trout. Each year the shop hosts saltwater fishing trips to Mexico and the Bahamas. Whether you are casting for a finicky eight-inch trout or a 150-pound Billfish, Roaring Fork Anglers has considered your needs. The store got started in 1981 when the first owners started selling flies out of a garage. One of the owners has been the *Post Independent*'s choice for Best Fisherman four years in a row. Before you fly-fish, visit Roaring Fork Anglers.

2205 Grand Avenue, Glenwood Springs CO (970) 945-0180 or (800) 781-8120
www.roaringforkanglers.com

Boulder Mountaineering

Winging it is fine for, say, doing the twist, but when you're climbing a mountain peak, you really need the proper equipment and a plan. That's where Boulder Mountaineering comes in. This guide service run by the father-son team of Bob and Robert Culp has been a Boulder fixture for decades. It offers guided climbs in areas near Boulder such as the Flatirons, Eldorado Canyon and Boulder Canyon. The Culps and their crew frequently climb in the high country of the Colorado Rockies and the Needles of South Dakota. They climb ice in Colorado and Wyoming, and plan trips abroad to such places as the Alps and Dolomites. Rock-climbing instruction is another of Boulder Mountaineering's specialties. Bob, a world-class climber, has proven his passion for the sport while pioneering hundreds of first ascents. His enthusiasm for reaching the clouds has not diminished over the years. In fact, he is always curious to see what technology will bring to the sport next. Boulder Mountaineering uses all of the latest equipment, and enjoys a stellar reputation among the local climbing clubs and schools with which it works. The staff teaches rock and ice climbing at Regis University. Reach the summit with the trusted crew at Boulder Mountaineering.

1335-B Broadway, Boulder CO (303) 444-2470
www.bobculp.com

Boondocks Fun Center

Boondocks Fun Center offers something for everyone. Just a short distance north of Denver in Northglenn, this eight-acre amusement park has been serving up thrills since 2001. A state-of-the-art arcade and redemption area change frequently to accommodate the latest 200 games. Batting cages are a big hit here. Offering slow and fast pitch softball and 40 to 70 mph hardball. Bumper Boats take you on a wild ride, all fully equipped with Master Blaster water guns. You'll find four go-kart tracks for racers of every size while futuristic murals, fog and nine-foot pillars create just the right setting for a laser tag attack. Little ones can jump, swing, climb and slide in the four-story Kiddie Cove soft play area, while would-be daredevils can get turned upside down on the MaxFlight roller coaster simulator. Two beautifully landscaped miniature golf courses offer holes to challenge even the most serious golfer, complete with waterfalls, suspended bridges and a fire-breathing lizard. Boondocks has a delicious restaurant on premises, the Back Porch Grill, which offers pizza, sandwiches and burgers to please the pickiest of eaters. Getting you to smile and return is a goal at Boondocks. You won't regret spending a day at Boondocks Fun Center, open year-round.

11425 Community Center Drive, Northglenn CO
(720) 977-8000
www.boondocksfuncenter.com
or *www.boondocks.info*

Roaring Fork Outfitters

With 45 years of fly-fishing to his credit, it's easy to understand why Dave York's wide selection of flies includes specimens that most fishermen have never seen along with custom-made flies created to attract local fish. Dave operates Roaring Fork Outfitters, the oldest fly shop in the Roaring Fork Valley. He holds permits for the White River National Forest and the Colorado River's Glenwood Canyon, which means his guides can take you out into territory not open to other guide services. Roaring Fork Outfitters also offers wade and float trips on the Roaring Fork, Eagle, Crystal, Frying Pan and Colorado Rivers. Dave introduces newcomers to fly-fishing with a special class and is always glad to offer instruction to his customers. His fully outfitted fly shop, featuring such brands as St. Croix, Wright and McGill, is open year-round. His guided trips include all necessary equipment plus a streamside lunch for full-day trips. For those looking to go farther afield, the shop offers saltwater adventures in the Bahamas. Lodging packages with Cedar Lodge are also available. For some of the best fly-fishing in Colorado, book a trip with Roaring Fork Outfitters.

2022 Grand Avenue, Glenwood Springs CO (970) 945-5800 or (877) 945-5800
www.rfoutfitters.com

Green Mountain Sports

If you ride, Green Mountain Sports in Lakewood is a place you've got to visit. Owned by veteran bicycle racer Corky Grimm, Green Mountain Sports sells top-of-the-line bikes, boards and ski equipment, and serves as an information center for the bike, snowboard and ski industries. Green Mountain is a full service shop, providing sales, rental services and repair work. Kids can try out bikes and even take them home for a trial period before buying. Corky and his staffers are all riders, so they're both comfortable and enthusiastic when talking about the sports they love and the products they sell. Corky himself is a top rider, finishing in Colorado's top 10 in time trials. Green Mountain boasts the number one off-road mountain bike team in the state, and they also won the American Cycling Association title in the age 35 and up open class. Knowledge and customer service are what set this store apart... along with Digger and Tug, the two yellow labs who serve as store mascots and official greeters. In addition to bikes and boards, Green Mountain services mopeds, motorcycles, wheel chairs, baby joggers, electric scooters and more. If you can ride it, chances are good they service it. The next time you're looking for sports equipment, visit Green Mountain Sports. Buying equipment from people who use it makes all the difference.

2950 S Bear Creek Boulevard, Lakewood CO (303) 987-8758
greenmountainsports.com

The Single Track Factory

The folks who work at the Single Track Factory in Denver don't mind being called fanatics. If they didn't need to earn a living, they'd be working out on their road bikes, conquering some rugged terrain on their mountain bikes or carving the slopes on their snowboards. At the Single Track Factory, they get to pass their enthusiasm for their sports and for the latest products to their customers. Their goal is to help customers find the best toy they can. "It can be a stressful world," says owner Brian Isakson, who provides the equipment for stress reduction in the form of Yeti, Rocky Mountain and Maverick bikes as well as Burton snowboards and World Industries Skateboards, to name just a few of the stellar brands found here. According to Brian, these brands are the ones that deliver the most performance and cause the least trouble. He should know. His idea of a fantastic day is one when he gets to ride demo bikes from some of the best makers in the business. He started the Single Track Factory in 1997 with four bare walls and a carpet. The success that he has enjoyed since then allows him to make his business even better. For example, in 2006, he sent all of his employees to a trade show. "It gave them a perspective that helps our customers in all the right ways," says Brian. Get expert service and advice from the fanatics at the Single Track Factory.

1005 S Gaylord Street, Denver CO (303) 733-3334
www.singletrackfactory.com

The Denver Brass

The Denver Brass wows some 75,000 fans a year with the bright, bold sound of trumpets, trombones, tubas and horns. Versatility has been one key to the success of this professional ensemble, which formed in 1981. Its extensive repertoire ranges from elegant classic masterpieces to new works, jazz and the hottest rhythms from around the world. Over the course of its 26-year career, the group has teamed up with everyone from bagpipers and fiddlers to swing bands and steel drums. Visual wit accompanies each high-energy musical performance. The musicians might dress up in Renaissance garb for an early music program or don colorful pirate rags for a musical cruise through the Caribbean. The story of how The Denver Brass began is a tale of two tuba players, Charles Brantigan and Kathy Aylsworth Zeschin, who met, married and turned their obsession with the instrument into a serious commitment to performance. Members of the ensemble are chosen by audition for their technical expertise and their good nature, and once part of the family, they stay on for the long haul. The Denver Brass performs throughout the year at the Newman Center and Bethany Lutheran Church, and is also heard at Red Rocks, the Arvada Center, at schools and hospitals, and on tour throughout the west. Be in the audience for the next exhilarating performance of The Denver Brass.

2253 Downing Street, Denver CO
(303) 832-4676
www.denverbrass.org

Golden Bowl Bowling Center & Chinese Restaurant

Have you scored a perfect 300 in bowling? Join many of the Golden Bowl 300 Club members who have had their pictures placed on the wall for the past 50 years. Golden Bowl Bowling Center was opened in the early 1950s, and is a landmark in the city of Golden. Tom Yang, the new owner, did extensive remodeling in 2006 and refurbished all 24 lanes with automatic scoring, upgraded pin setters and overhead television screens. The center also offers several video arcade games and ping-pong tables. On weekends, you can enjoy a drink or two at the bar, sit back, and sing karaoke. New to the bowling center is a Chinese restaurant managed by Roy, Tom's brother, who has more than 30 years of experience in the restaurant industry. The restaurant serves a generous $1.50 entrée. You can pick from several delicious Chinese favorites such as sesame chicken, beef broccoli and scrumptious cheese wontons. Recently, under Tom's ownership, Golden Bowl has taken an active part in the community, holding many fundraisers for individuals, businesses and non-profit groups. Golden Bowl is most proud to have brought bowling classes back to Golden High School students and sponsored the first Golden High School Bowling League that competed against other high school teams, and to have brought back to the city of Golden an entertainment center for the whole family.

525 24th Street, Golden CO (303) 279-7846
www.goldenbowl300club.com

Lincoln Center for Performing & Visual Arts

Culture is an essential part of life in Ft. Collins, thanks to the Lincoln Center for Performing & Visual Arts, which opened in 1978 on the site of the original Lincoln Junior High School. The facility features a 1,180-seat theater and a smaller theater for 220. Three art galleries exhibit work by local, national and international artists, while conference spaces are available for business meetings and events. The facility also provides concerts and rental space in a beautiful sculpture garden with a covered stage. The performances are as varied as the people of Ft. Collins. The Showstopper Series brings big name entertainers to the stage. The Anything Goes Series offers edgier entertainment, including comedy acts. Music and dance programs abound, including the Classical Series and Dance Series. The Imagination Series provides spellbinding programming for the whole family, while the arm chair travelers enjoy the Adventure Cinema Series. Intermissions are an excellent time to enjoy the center's art galleries, where exhibits change frequently. The annual Fabric of Legacies quilt show, Creative Spaces and bi-annual ArtWear Fashion Week always draw large crowds. The center is also home to many such community arts groups. Conferencing facilities suit everything from large banquets and trade shows to small receptions and training seminars. Experienced event planners will help you with the details for your event. For a joyful celebration of art in all its forms, visit the Lincoln Center.

417 W Magnolia Street, Ft. Collins CO
(970) 221-6735
www.lctix.com

Cycle Analyst

Richard Hodge, owner of Cycle Analyst bicycle shop, doesn't believe in disposable parts. His huge supply of hard-to-find and vintage parts keep bikes on the road long after most bike dealers would tell you that it's time for a new one. When you bring your run-down bike to Cycle Analyst, once of the skilled mechanics on staff will give it a thorough inspection. "If a bike can be fixed, we'll do the job," says Richard. "Perhaps your money would be better spent on a new bike." Any bike that you buy new at Cycle Analyst will be in your life for a very long time. The shop's inventory runs the gamut from cruisers to high-performance racing machines. Cannondale, Electra, Giant, Lightspeed and Merlin are just a few of the featured bicycle brands. Cycle Analyst also carries Brooks saddles, chrome bags, Detours panniers and a host of other parts and accessories. Richard, a racer on the Midwest circuit in his youth, has been in the business since 1967. Located in the Washington Park neighborhood, the shop is a little out of the way, but Richard guarantees a refreshing approach to service and dealership for those who seek him out. Bring your tired and broken bike to Cycle Analyst, or let Richard help you pick out a brand new set of wheels.

722 S Pearl Street, Denver CO (303) 722-3004
www.cycleanalystinc.com

Sundance Stables

A trail ride with Sundance Stables takes you through the wild side of Colorado, filled with scenic vistas and animals such as bear, elk, moose and coyote. The stables, located at Sundance Lodge near Nederland, offer rides of any length to suit your preference and experience. Longer rides include specially prepared campfire breakfasts or lunches. Overnight camping trips into Roosevelt National Forest offer still more opportunity to immerse yourself in the lush meadows and snow-capped peaks along the Continental Divide. Cindy McCollum is your host at Sundance Stables. She understands horses and the importance of keeping guided trips small so that you have plenty of contact with the wrangler leading your ride. She promises "gentle horses for gentle people, spirited horses for spirited people, and for people who don't like to ride, horses that don't like to be rode." Sundance also uses Belgian draft horses for hayrides or to accommodate large riders. You'll be in good hands with Cindy, who owned other outfitting companies before coming to Sundance in 2004. Change your perspective on Colorado with a call to Sundance Stables.

23942 Highway 119, Nederland CO (303) 258-1176
www.sundance-lodge.com

Front Range Anglers

Bill Leuchten and his staff at Front Range Anglers are dedicated to your fly-fishing success. The 25-year-old store, started by A.K. Best and Dick Reeves, offers guided fishing trips to premier fishing spots within an hour and a half of Boulder. It stocks all the gear you need—the top brands in wading gear, rods and reels. Want to craft a black widow midge or an adult dragonfly? The store specializes in supplies for fly tying, because quite a few of its customers pursue this specialized activity. Front Range Anglers offers classes in fly tying, casting and rod building. In winter, the store hosts free fly-tying clinics led by some of the best fly fishermen in the area. Customers receive a free monthly electronic newsletter dedicated to bringing fish and people together. The *Colorado Daily* has voted Front Range Anglers as the Best Fishing Shop in Boulder, and it has received the President's Award from the local Trout Unlimited. The shop is open seven days a week. Whether you are beginning to fly fish or perfecting your skills, come to Front Range Anglers for fine products and instruction that help you catch more fish.

629 S Broadway, Boulder CO (303) 494-1375
www.frontrangeanglers.com

A-1 Scuba & Travel Center

Since 1959, A-1 Scuba & Travel Center has been helping Colorado divers stay ahead of the game. Ernie Busnardo started the shop, and today, his daughter, Lynn Taylor, and her husband, Scott, carry on the family business. A-1 Scuba offers Aquarium Programs & Experiences at the Downtown Aquarium. Sign the kids up for the Swim with the Fish program where they will snorkel with a 250-pound Queensland grouper, moray eels, guitar fish, red drums and 400 other exotic underwater animals. Certified divers can go deep and get up-close-and-personal with that Queensland grouper when they opt for the Dive with the Fish program. For the daredevils, head down to the Sunken Shipwreck exhibit and Swim with the Sharks, including sand tiger sharks, brown sharks, zebra sharks and barracudas. In addition to these underwater adventures, A-1 Scuba offers professional courses and a full-service travel center to book your diving trips. You'll find only the best equipment at reasonable prices, including kid's equipment for ages three and up. There's an extensive underwater photo and video equipment department and development center on-site. A-1 Scuba services all makes of equipment—this is where other dive stores in the state send their equipment for service. The staff are all experienced divers who know what you need in equipment and instruction. You can get your certification here or train as a rescuer or instructor. You'll train in a huge, heated indoor pool with state-of-the-art equipment. When you're ready for a destination dive, you can sign up for one of A-1 Scuba's ongoing group trips or let the travel center create the individual trip of your dreams. You'll find a world of diving at your feet at A-1 Scuba & Travel Center.

1800 W Oxford Avenue, Englewood CO (303) 789-2450 or (800) 783-7282
www.a1scuba.com www.divedowntown.com

Carousel Dinner Theatre

Did you know that Fort Collins has more theaters per capita than any other city in Colorado? Carousel Dinner Theatre distinguishes itself in this theater town by being the only house that operates year round and the only one that focuses primarily on producing Broadway musicals. Folks are still talking about the 2004 staging of Cats, which won a Best Choreography award from the *Denver Post*, though there have been many highly entertaining shows since then and more are yet to come. With all seats within 30 feet of the stage, you'll be able to see the expressions on the actors' faces and to catch every word that they say and sing. Come just for the show, or consider making dinner part of the experience. The menu changes according to the show, though popular demand always seems to put prime rib among the choices. Averaging five shows per year since opening in 1991, Carousel has staged such classics as *Singin' in the Rain, The Music Man* and *Fiddler on the Roof* and has often been the first theater in Colorado to present the latest Broadway smash. Large groups may reserve the theater for an exclusive performance. Enjoy an evening on Broadway without leaving Fort Collins, thanks to the Carousel Dinner Theatre.

3509 S Mason Street, Fort Collins CO (970) 225-2555
www.adinnertheatre.com

Broomfield Bowl & Restaurant

Robert and Kari Warner fell for each other in the lanes of a bowling alley. Today they own and operate Broomfield Bowl and Restaurant, a family place for good, clean fun. The bowling alley hosts tournaments, birthday parties and corporate events in addition to league and non-league play. Open every day of the week, Robert and Kari's main concern is taking care of their customers who are like family to them. The restaurant, which is bustling every day of the week, serves homemade green and red chili, a favorite. You can feed your family for $10 with a 16-inch freshly-made cheese pizza with a topping. Broomfield Bowl and Restaurant also serves other American favorites such as a chili burger or Philly steak sandwich. A pitcher of domestic draught beer is reasonable as well. For those who like to sleep in, breakfast is served until 2:30 pm. Breakfast items include the satisfying huevos rancheros or corned beef hash. Broomfield Bowl and Restaurant has a generous children's menu for little ones. Ready to join a bowling league? Come in and Robert will help get you started. If not, just stop by Broomfield Bowl and Restaurant for a great time and a great meal.

100 Nickel Street, Broomfield CO (303) 446-9700

ATS Helicopter Services

Owner Rich Westra calls ATS Helicopter Services the gold standard of helicopter service. Offering executive transport, tours by air and commercial services such as aerial photography, ATS flies the safest helicopter in the world, the Fly Bell Jet Ranger. ATS pilots have an impeccable safety record and are experts in high altitude flight. From the comfort of an executive leather chair, you can look out the observation window and enjoy the country as you have never seen it before. ATS flies three standard tours of Colorado. The City Night Lights Tour is a memorable evening fit for proposing marriage or rekindling romance as you float together above downtown Denver at night. The Rocky Mountain Experience Tour provides a bird's-eye view of picturesque little towns nestled into the canyons of the mountain landscape. Welcome autumn with the memorable Fall Foliage Tour. You'll be awed by the changing colors, the glorious yellow aspens. Getting married soon? Hire ATS for a dramatic departure from your reception. Choose the gold standard with the comfort and class of ATS Helicopter Services.

7355 S Peoria Street #112, Englewood CO (303) 858-1359 and (303) 825-0815
www.atshelicopters.com

Colorado Railroad Museum

The oldest locomotive in Colorado dates back to 1880, and you can see it at the Colorado Railroad Museum. It's just one of the 90 historic narrow and standard gauge locomotives, cabooses and railcars exhibited outside the museum. The setting, 14 acres at the foot of North Table Mountain, couldn't be prettier. Bring your lunch and enjoy a picnic while enjoying views of the scenery as well as of the trains. The museum building, a replica of an 1880s depot, houses exhibits that tell the story of Colorado's colorful railroad history. Beginning in 1870, after the discovery of gold and silver in the mountains, workers pushed train lines into nearly every canyon and high pass in the Rocky Mountains. The Colorado Railroad Museum is the place where visitors can touch this history through interactive displays and railcars that are open for boarding. See the Cornelius W. Hauck Roundhouse and marvel at the model train displays designed by the Denver HO Model Railroad Club and the Denver Garden Railways Society. The museum operates steam train rides on select dates throughout the year, and hosts Thomas the Tank Engine each fall. Be sure to visit the gift shop to bring home a few souvenirs from the Colorado Railroad Museum, rated by the *Denver Post* as one of Denver's top ten attractions

17155 W 44th Avenue, Golden CO
(303) 279-4591 *www.crrm.org*

Golden Goal Sports Complex

The indoor facilities at Golden Goal Sports Complex assure that the dynamic athlete in the West Denver metro area can play soccer, lacrosse and other sports all year long. Radu and Paula Marcu opened the complex in 2004, offering yearly memberships as well as a fitness room where members and drop-ins stay in shape with weight machines, treadmills and upright bicycles. Two indoor artificial turf fields for soccer and lacrosse host tournament play for adult and youth leagues. Members take advantage of daily hours and a soccer ball machine for practicing your kick. During summer and spring break, Golden Goal offers lacrosse and soccer camps for youngsters. The facility also features a special program that encourages kids and parents to work out together. The complex continues to grow, and plans are in the works for a retail store, saunas, a track, an outdoor synthetic turf field and a hard surface futsal court. Bring your competitive spirit indoors to Golden Goal Sports Complex.

2650 Alkire Street, Golden CO (303) 564-7251
www.goldengoalsc.com

Mountain High Jeep Rentals

All vehicles are not created equal. Mountain High Jeep Rentals solves this problem for the adventuring soul and opens up a world of wildlife, flowers and magnificent mountain views you may never have seen without the aid of a 4x4 Jeep. Mountain High Jeep Rentals is known for prompt and courteous service, but the company offers an arsenal of practical tools with each rental as well. Along with the Jeep, you can get a training session, insurance and a kit comprised of maps, pictures, directions and descriptions from which to set your bearings. You will have an altimeter to help you track your adventure. In winter, ski racks are provided with snow tires, and in summer, bike racks and G.P.S. are available. A high-powered cellular phone comes with every Jeep rental for your security. Mountain High Jeep Rentals is committed to keeping the pristine peaks of central Colorado in their natural state. If you find any litter on your journey and bring it back with you during the summer High Mountain Adventures, the company will discount your next ride by 10 percent. Mountain High Jeep Rentals makes an excellent addition to Breckenridge, a ski resort town with access to a dozen off-road trails. Boldly go where you have never been when you rent a Jeep from Mountain High Jeep Rentals.

620 Village Road, Breckenridge CO (970) 468-6858 or (800) 955-0807
www.mountainhighrentalst.com

Boulder Travel Agency

Do you really want a lawn gnome planning your historical journey to Greece or your wine tour of Tuscany? With today's accessible technology, some may not see the need for outstanding companies like Boulder Travel Agency. We forget the detailed planning and essential knowledge that goes into making a trip successful. The repairmen of Internet vacations, Boulder Travel agents are confident that they can make the planning of your vacation a vacation in itself. President Brian Menk inherited the company from his parents, Don and Helen Menk, who opened Boulder Travel together in 1947. Boulder Travel was one of the few travel agencies savvy enough survive the Internet revolution and has flourished since, says Vice President Lori Loucks. Specializing in corporate as well as leisure travel, the agency maintains a loyal customer base that is ever-growing due to excellent service and knowledgeable staff. An ancient Chinese proverb adorns the agency's website: A journey of a thousand miles begins with a single step. Take a step towards Boulder Travel Agency for the personalized service and expertise essential to a remarkable journey.

1655 Folsom Street, Boulder CO (303) 443-0380
www.bouldertravel.com

Best of Ballroom

Has watching *Dancing with the Stars* got you trying some fancy steps in your living room? If so, then you should take the next step and sign up for classes at Best of Ballroom in Colorado Springs. In fact, this dance studio has its own *Dancing with the Stars* connection in the person of Louis Van Amstel. A professional dancer on the show, he is one of the many world-class instructors that owners Golden Parker and Jaki Brockman bring in from another state to train the staff and students. Best of Ballroom provides instruction in a wide range of styles, from ballroom, Latin and swing to country/western, jazz and hip-hop. Even brides and grooms have enrolled at Best of Ballroom to learn some dance steps for their big day. Some students value the classes here for the social experience and fun aerobic workout. Others come to hone their skills for competition. All ages are welcome, and you don't need a partner to begin. Golden, Jaki and their dynamic staff have won many awards and are all certified with the National Dance Council of America. "The most gratifying thing is to see people improve," say Golden and Jaki, who have been ranked among the top female dance teachers, the top male dance teachers, and the top dance studios in the country by the DanceSport Series. Prepare for the dance floor with a class at Best of Ballroom.

5694 N Academy Boulevard, Colorado Springs CO
(719) 272-9048
www.ballroomdancingcoloradosprings.com

4 Eagle Ranch

Cowboy hats and boots are not mandatory at 4 Eagle Ranch, but they would certainly be in keeping with the spirit of this event center in the Vail Valley. A Rocky Mountain homestead dating back to the 1890s, the ranch was transformed in 1991 into an entertainment venue for corporate parties, weddings and other private group functions. Wide-ranging views stretching all the way to the pristine mountains are part of the attraction. Breathe deeply and fill your lungs with fresh, sage-scented air. Homesteader cabins dot the property and cattle and horses graze in the hay fields. Horseback riding, cattle round-ups in the summer and sleigh ride dinner evenings in the winter are open to the public. Also, don't miss the hoedown on Western Family Night, offered most Wednesdays in July and August. Strolling guitarists and a dance band provide the music while a storyteller spins yarns of mountain men. There are wagon rides, pony rides and a bountiful buffet of steak chili, barbecue and corn on the cob. For private gatherings, let the experienced event staff arrange everything from transportation and bands to food and beverages. Get married wearing your cowboy boots at the 4 Eagle Ranch, or kick your heels at the hoedown.

4098 Highway 131, Wolcott CO
(970) 926-3372
www.4eagleranch.com

The Kangaroo Kingdom

Fun is just a hop, skip and jump away. With its colorful playroom/gym of vinyl-covered foam and variety of programs for parents and children five weeks to five years, The Kangaroo Kingdom is a fun, safe place for families to play. Annadell Burke purchased the gym in 2006 after being a long-time customer. She feels the gym is as much about the development of good parents and encouraging parent-child bonding as it is about the development of the children's large motor and social skills. Annadell and her professional staff offer classes and open-play hours designed to stimulate sensory-motor activity, socialization and curiosity. Along with the core sing and play classes, families can experience music and early immersion language classes, including Spanish, German and French, along with parenting workshops, such as infant massage and Love & Logic Parenting. Open-play hours give children the chance to interact in a non-structured environment. Parents commonly report that their children become more adventurous after exploring the gym. Hop on by to see why The Kangaroo Kingdom was voted Best Toddler Music/Gym Program in Denver Metro by the readers of *Kids Pages* and Best Place to Play with Kids in Boulder County by the readers of *The Yellow Scene*.

1361 Forest Park Circle, #106, Lafayette CO (303) 926-7550
www.thekangarookingdom.com

Mountain Wolf Jeep Adventures

For an intimate, exhilarating experience of Colorado's hidden paradises, see Wolfgang Uberbacher at Mountain Wolf Jeep Adventures. He'll pick you up in his custom-built, seven-passenger, open-air jeep and take you into the heart of the Colorado wilderness. A lifelong naturalist, Wolf boasts an astounding resume of wilderness credentials. He's been a mountain guide on three continents, a wilderness school instructor, an Austrian Army survival trainer and yodeler extraordinaire. His studies in botany and medicinal herbal add a scientific depth to his understanding of the environment. Wolf not only provides you a great photo op, but an insightful introduction to the Rockies. A great storyteller, he'll educate you on the flora, fauna and history of the region, including the native cultures that once thrived here. His two most popular tours are the Horse Mountain Adventure and the West Lake Creek Adventure. The Horse Mountain trip takes you from the desert to the mountain top at 11,000 feet. The West Lake Creek Adventure leads to an old mining site in the White River National Forest. Ask Wolf about his other specialty trips or invent your own with his expertise. Plan on an unforgettable time with Mountain Wolf Jeep Adventures.

Vail CO (970) 926-WOLF (9653)
www.mountainwolfjeepadventures.com

Aerial Dance Over Denver

Whether you're already an accomplished athlete or just looking to improve your fitness and self confidence, Aerial Dance Over Denver is the new sensation you have to try. It's exercise on air, a combination of gymnastics, dancing and flying that's surprisingly easy and undeniably fun. You'll use circus equipment such as hoops, bungee cords, fabric and trapezes to build strength and flexibility. No experience is necessary, and there's no impact at all. Owner Gayle Lynne leads a diverse team of instructors who teach such specialty classes as Aerial Yoga, Lyrical Jazz Dance and Trapeze. Classes are for all ages and include after-school programs, camps and class performances. Cirque de Soliel taught here when they were in town. Swimmers, skiers, rock climbers, choreographers and skaters benefit from increased toning, flexibility, strength and endurance. Gayle was an ice skater for 30 years before experiencing her first aerial dance class. She was so impressed by it that she decided she must bring it to Colorado. "My goal is to offer that inspiration and experience to youths and adults in a way that is affordable, supportive and joyous," she said. Come fly at Aerial Dance Over Denver, the only institution of its kind in the state.

8964 E Hampden Avenue, Denver CO (303) 771-0161
www.aerialdanceoverdenver.com

Bakeries, Coffee, Tea, & Treats

Catalyst Coffee

When two friends got together to start Catalyst Coffee in 2004, their goal was not to get rich but to create a social environment for the neighborhood. These civic-minded saints, Fade Wall and Heather Michalak, use their coffee shop to host meet-the-artist events, storytelling for the kids and crafts sessions. Public school employees get a 10 percent break at Catalyst Coffee, because education is a top priority here. The shop sponsors astronomy nights and catapult building contests. Add free tutoring in math and physics, and you can see why the unofficial slogan of this cheerful place is Your Neighborhood Living Room. The official slogan, by the way, is Brewing Relationships One Cup at a Time, which certainly fits, too. Supporting local artists by displaying their work is important to Fade and Heather. Also, they buy their milk from a nearby dairy and get their coffee locally from Kaladi Brothers, a small organic roaster that uses fair trade coffee. There's so much going on here that you almost forget that the coffee, espresso and specialty drinks always taste superb. "We're always amazed at the wide range of people who come in, from cowboys to hippies," say the owners. See the many faces of Ft. Collins at Catalyst Coffee, a place with a heart as big as the neighborhood.

1003 W Horsetooth Road, Ft. Collins CO
(970) 223-9035
www.catalystcoffee.com

The Chocolate Moose Ice Cream Parlor

Not many ice cream parlors have a wine tasting room, but The Chocolate Moose Ice Cream Parlor in Glenwood Springs does. Featuring Blue Bunny Ice Cream, it is also one of six outlets for the Belvedere Belgian Style Chocolates, and a WI-FI hot spot with a western soundtrack. All of these things set The Chocolate Moose apart. John and Melisa Bellio are hands-on owners involved in every aspect of daily operations. The wines they feature are from Bookcliff Vineyards, a local winery that uses sustainable farming techniques. The chocolates are handmade, Belgian-style, nearly 70 varieties with all-natural ingredients. There are a variety of chocolate gifts and customized chocolates available. Many of the ice cream menu items are named for local attractions such as the Mt. Sopris or Maroon Bells sundaes. The waffle cobbler a' la mode gets a lot of attention, as do the shakes and floats made with Blue Bunny Ice Cream. The waffle cones and bowls are made in-house. The Bellios sell wine by the taste, glass or bottle, and are knowledgeable about each wine they sell, frequently pairing them with the appropriate chocolate treat. They offer an additional selection of sugar-free chocolate and ice cream. Sometimes the good things in life can be bought. Find them at The Chocolate Moose Ice Cream Parlor.

710 Grand Avenue, Glenwood Springs CO
(970) 945-2723

Revolution Donuts

In the doughnut business word of mouth is everything, and the word is out about Revolution Donuts. Owners Ryan Marzec and Michael "Woody" Woodward have taken a new approach to America's beloved treat. Fresh and funky, the store has a bright, warm feel with all glass walls. The selection of doughnuts is wide and all are baked daily in-house using the best ingredients. These delicious handmade treats have substance and character. You can get coffee, milk or other beverages to go with the doughnuts. The store, off the beaten path, is a delightful respite from the hustle and bustle of life. There are plenty of places to sit, so it's a safe late night spot where you can unwind with friends and go on about politics, sports, somebody's awful haircut or whatever. The spacious setup and free wireless Internet access let students set up shop for a while to get those term papers in on time. The hours are convenient, with plenty of opportunity to hang out or satisfy that sweet tooth. For a great selection of handmade doughnuts and a fun atmosphere, visit Revolution Donuts.

1720 W Mulberry Street A-2, Fort Collins CO
(970) 472-1055
www.revolutiondonuts.com

Photo by Shawn Medero

The Jazzy Bean Coffeehouse

Folks gather at the Jazzy Bean Coffeehouse for much more than the espresso, fruit smoothies and food. This business has been keeping the focus on community since 2003 with a full slate of events and activities, including Tuesday morning story time for the kids and Wednesday crafts night. Live music is in the mix on Friday and Saturday nights, when local musicians perform everything from bluegrass and Celtic to blues and, of course, jazz. The coffeehouse offers teens a safe environment in which to hang out on Monday teen night. With so much going on, owners Nancy Wyckoff, Rhonda Trejo and Sandy Tigner work extra hard whipping up specialty drinks and cooking for everyone who drops by. Folks love their homemade ice cream and tell them that their breakfast burritos are among the finest they have had anywhere. The Jazzy Bean gets its espresso from the Devil's Backbone, a small local roaster. Be totally cool and add a hint of frosted mint to your white chocolate latte, made with Ghirardelli white chocolate sauce. Drop by and make yourself comfy in the community living room that is the Jazzy Bean Coffeehouse. The staff is warm and welcoming to everyone who drops by. As their motto says, they turn ordinary into extraordinary.

8110 W County Road 13, Space 2, Firestone CO
(303) 833-3236
www.jazzybean.com

Provin' Grounds Coffee & Bakery

In 2005, the historic community of Leadville got a wake-up call in the form of Provin' Grounds Coffee & Bakery. Partners Chris Albers and Kathy Muller carefully restored one of the community's vintage buildings, constructed circa 1871, and turned it into a popular gathering spot for the town's denizens, who include students, mountain folk, tourists and extreme sports enthusiasts, to name a few. Now, the enticing scents of coffee and freshly baked bread waft though the town each morning. Provin' Grounds Coffee & Bakery serves only Fair Trade Coffee and creates all of its baked goods on-site from scratch using organic flour and other ingredients. The cozy shop serves homemade chai and a wide selection of specialty coffee drinks and tasty treats, such as croissants, muffins, scones and biscuits. The shop is also famous for its monster cinnamon rolls, scrumptious quiches and lunch wraps. In addition to offering great food and an inviting gathering place, the establishment serves as an art gallery by featuring an ever-revolving art exhibit on the walls. A charming retail coffee and tea selection as well as accessories are an added bonus. Savor wholesome cuisine, fabulous coffees and glorious views when you visit the Provin' Grounds Coffee & Bakery.

508 Harrison Avenue #3, Leadville CO
(719) 486-0797

Trompeau Bakery

Pascal Trompeau first came to Colorado from his native France in 1997. He spent more than two years searching for just the right place for the intimate bakery he dreamed of opening. That turned out to be University Park, where the scintillating scents of Trompeau's goods entice shoppers to enter, sit back and savor traditional European delights. Tender quiche, unbeatable croissants and properly brewed coffee drinks are just a few of the temptations that await visitors. Other treats include rosemary garlic bread, classic French baguettes and savory meat and vegetarian croissants made every day from scratch. The bakery provides bread and pastries for several area restaurants. For example, Parisi and Fontano's Chicago Subs both serve Trompeau's bread and use it for sandwiches. Trompeau begins his work each morning at 3 am, baking for patrons who begin arriving at 6 am Monday through Saturday. Enjoy a provincial French breakfast in the heart of Denver with a visit to Trompeau Bakery.

1729 E Evans Avenue, Denver CO
(303) 777-7222

Red Rooster Creamery

Red Rooster Creamery makes dense, super-creamy ice creams by a slow-churning process that minimizes air and maximizes flavor. Since opening in 2004, owners Frank and Tammy Coulter have won four national awards from the National Ice Cream Retailers Association. And these were only for the shop's staple flavors, vanilla, strawberry and chocolate. In fact, Red Rooster offers a dazzling 40 flavors. In addition to such popular flavors as chocolate peanut butter and white chocolate raspberry cheesecake, the Coulters enjoy experimentation, launching such intriguing varieties as Parmesan and Jalapeño. The ice cream is produced on the premises. Many of the most cheerful and intelligent teens in Highlands Ranch find their first job at Red Rooster, where the Coulters apply the same high standards to staff that they do to ice cream. The shop sells smoothies, hand-dipped ice cream bars and all manner of ice cream desserts, including specially themed desserts for parties. For Ice Cream Worth Crowing About, visit Red Rooster Creamery.

4004 Red Cedar Drive, Unit C2, Highlands Ranch CO
(303) 791-9735
www.redroostercreamery.com

Spruce Confections

If you opt for a pastry or cookie when you visit a coffee shop, then chances are you have already tasted something from Spruce Confections, a Boulder coffee shop that supplies baked goods for many other shops between Boulder and Denver. The first Spruce Confections opened in 1992. Today two locations stay packed seven days a week. You can team up your favorite coffee drink with a handmade pastry or a slice of pie. You can also order quiche for breakfast or a gourmet salad, soup or sandwich for lunch. The bakery makes exquisite birthday cakes. Everything is baked fresh daily with all natural ingredients. Spruce Confections sells hundreds of scones a day, including a blueberry, maple and pecan scone that's worth the cost of quitting a diet. Spruce Confections is also the creator of the Old B Cookie, the big, chewy cookie loaded with oats, chocolate chips, pecans, almonds and walnuts that you may have discovered at Whole Foods Markets in Boulder or Denver. Familiarity hasn't dimmed the public demand for the Old B, and you'll still find it at the original Spruce Confections, where owner David Cohen invites you to give in to your own dearest temptation.

767 Pearl Street, Suite B, Boulder CO
(303) 449-6773
4684 Broadway, Boulder CO
(303) 449-5819

Buffalo Moon Coffee & Mercantile

Buffalo Moon Coffee & Mercantile is a favorite local gathering place in the Genesee/ Golden area. Maybe the attraction is the Silver Canyon Coffee from Boulder, or the exclusive drink creations such as the Green Goddess, a green tea steeped with vanilla and steamed soy. The lure could be the four different brews made daily, the Sirius satellite radio, free Wi-Fi, perfectly executed lattes and cappuccinos, and the Moon Secret Sauce served with each sandwich. Perhaps the warm and friendly ambiance is the secret to success. Whatever it is, Buffalo Moon has it. Start your morning with a breakfast burrito filled with scrambled eggs, cheese, baby red potatoes and bell peppers served with sides of salsa, sour cream and then smothered in organic green chile. Then, take a mid-day break for a fruit smoothie with a sandwich built just the way you like it, on a bagel or in a wrap, and top it off with something sweet. One-of-a-kind gifts and greeting cards surround the buzzing coffee chat. The Buffalo Moon is a vibrant place to host your group or join an existing one. Pick up beverages, breakfast or lunch for your office or home gathering. Don't miss Buffalo Moon Coffee & Mercantile.

25948 Genesee Trail Road (I-70 at exit 254), Golden CO
(303) 526-7675
www.buffalomooncoffee.com

Marble Slab Creamery

When you walk in the doors of the Marble Slab Creamery, you're greeted with the aroma of freshly baked waffle cones and the sight of an astonishing array of irresistible ice cream flavors. The Marble Slab Creamery is known for its super-premium ice cream, made-to-order desserts and excellent service. All of the products are freshly made on-site each day. When you've selected your ice cream, staff members scoop it onto a frozen marble slab and combine it with your choice of fresh fruit, candies, nuts and other delectable *mixins*. Choose your desired flavor of waffle cone and you've got a custom-made dessert. Ice cream may be purchased by the cone, cup or even in a five-gallon tub. The shop also offers a tempting menu of ice cream cakes and pies, shakes, malts, floats and fruit smoothies. This is truly dessert heaven. Other treats include made-from-scratch cookies and brownies. The Marble Slab Creamery caters birthday parties and all types of special events. Active in the community, the shop donates both time and delicious product to the yearly Broomfield Bash, as well as supporting the Broomfield Community Foundation. When in Westminster, visit the Marble Slab Creamery, ice cream headquarters for kids of all ages.

10633 Westminster Boulevard, Suite 300, Westminster CO
(303) 460-0988
www.marbleslab.com

Olive Street Bakery

Every Monday through Saturday at 6 am, Olive Street Bakery opens its doors to another day of fine European pastries and the kind of breakfasts and lunches that turn customers into regulars. The coffee is always fresh, the shop always sparkles and the Belgian owners are always happy to see you. Lut and Olivier Campé owned a successful pastry shop in Belgium before they came to the United States in 2002 and bought a Fort Collins bakery with a 60-year history. At first, they reproduced their Belgium bakery, offering such breakfast pastries as croissants, turnovers and scones along with dessert pastries, breads, cookies, Belgian chocolates and special occasion cakes, including wedding cakes. In a few years, they added omelettes and other breakfast fare as well as soups, sandwiches and quiches for lunch. The Campés mix American fare with European specialties in a lineup that showcases Olivier's baking talents and Lut's meticulous organizational skills. You can leave with a tart, a baguette or a dozen cookies. Put some European style into your life with a visit to Olive Street Bakery, winner of Fort Collins Best Bakery awards in 2005 and 2006.

120 W Olive Street, Fort Collins CO
(970) 482-9875

Espresso di Cincotta

Cayenne Kerbs's love affair with coffee began at a coffee shop in Fort Collins that she frequented for more than 13 years. When a friend bought Espresso di Cincotta in 2003, he convinced Cayenne to open a sister shop in Greeley. Cayenne's Espresso di Cincotta offers the same product as the Fort Collins shop, Brazilian coffee beans roasted in Fort Collins and delivered still warm to Greeley. You'll find mochas, cappuccinos and 30 different latte flavors, including Rocky Road, Almond Joy and Tiramisu. On warm days, the frozen frappelattes are in demand. The corner space in Cottonwood Plaza features a patio and a homey gathering of leather chairs around a gas-lit fireplace. You'll find complimentary Wi-Fi and fresh pastries. Employees spend several months mastering the combination of preparation, memory and fast pace that keeps the shop buzzing. Cayenne knows she's found home, a shop like the one she loved in Fort Collins but with more room for lingering. Cozy up to your favorite coffee drink at Espresso di Cincotta.

2308 W 17ᵗʰ Street, Greeley CO
(970) 356-2555

Crown Chocolates

Diane Doderer goes anywhere that her handcrafted chocolates are welcome. You can see her handing out samples of her toffee crunch or aspen bark at grand openings. She sells her hand-dipped truffles and pecan turtles at fairs, craft shows and fundraisers, as well as wine-tasting events and high-country resorts. Weddings and other festive gatherings challenge her to come up with new chocolate specialties coordinating the event to the theme of the occasion. Diane, who founded Crown Chocolates in 2004, markets and distributes these unique chocolates, which are handmade by her mother who watched her own mother make desserts in the kitchen of their 100-year-old dairy farm in Northern Germany. When Diane isn't meeting her customers face to face, she's shipping her fine treats to real estate agents and other professionals who use them as referral and congratulatory gifts for their clients. Crown Chocolates offers several different gift basket ideas, including the three-tiered Executive Tower. For a truly remarkable gesture of thanks or congratulations, send a bottle of Champagne dipped in chocolate. Better yet, give Diane a call and invite her to bring herself and her Crown Chocolates to your next special event.

Westminster CO
(303) 465-0407
www.crownchocolates.com

Caffè Solé

Imagine warming winter-cold fingers around a steamy ceramic mug as creamy chocolate and citrus aromas drift into the sunrise. Make it a reality at Boulder's locally owned Caffè Solé. A laid-back atmosphere invites you to linger and enjoy the aromatic coffees, hand-picked teas and fresh pastries. Owners Ashkan Angha, Noah Westby and Suter Debose pride themselves on providing fresh-roasted coffee in a beautiful setting, with breathtaking views of the Flatirons' jagged peaks. Whether you need a cozy corner to study or an inspiring, airy patio to finally write that novel, Caffè Solé provides it. One of the distinctive features of Caffè Solé is that it has its own accomplished roastmaster, Joel Edwards, who selects and roasts only the highest quality beans. Coffee beans are chosen from different regions of the world depending on the desired final flavor. Guatemalan beans are reminiscent of dark chocolate and nuts while El Salvador's beans brew a cup of buttery caramel richness. Kenya's beans are considered the best in the world. No matter the region, though, Caffè Solé promises you the best cup of coffee you've ever tasted. Caffè Solé invites you to come down and experience the soothing soul of Solé.

637R S Broadway, Boulder CO
(303) 499-2985
www.caffesole.com

Indulge Bakery

Your taste buds will thank you for indulging in a trip to Indulge Bakery. Owners Thomas and Linda Willetto made their sweet dream of owning their own bakery come true in 2006, after 20 years of providing great pastries to restaurants. Indulge Bakery specializes in cakes for weddings, birthdays and other special occasions. Flavor options range from simple chocolate and carrot cake to more exotic offerings, including chocolate raspberry and Lemon Lust cheese cake. You can have your cake specially made in advance or, if your event is last-minute, there is always a variety of ready-to-go cakes at the store. Pie options range from deep-dish apple to pumpkin caramel pecan. You'll also find plenty of pastries and other goodies here, including jumbo cinnamon rolls and chocolate chip cookies made from Linda's grandmother's old-time recipe. Do you have a favorite recipe you'd like to enjoy, but don't have the time to make? Bring it in and Indulge Bakery will make it for you. The homemade gelato is an especially creamy and rich treat. Celebrate today like it's a special occasion with a trip to Indulge Bakery.

1377 Forest Park Circle, Suite 102, Lafayette CO
(303) 926-1676
www.indulgebakery.com

Adagio Baking Company

The Adagio Baking Company offers tempting baked goods that are as good-looking as they are delicious. Virtually everything here is made from scratch. In 2006, *5280 Magazine* named the bakery's scones the best in Denver. The bakery has many other pastries as well to accompany your coffee or espresso. Adiago specializes in magnificent cakes with many choices of flavors, fillings and icings. You can pick up a meal, too—for breakfast, try one of the hefty breakfast sandwiches, including a vegan choice made to order on a challah roll. Choose from several types of quiche, which include the chef's rotating seasonal choice. Adagio offers a mouthwatering lineup of panini sandwiches. The bakery's irresistible cookies range from ginger spice to snickerdoodles. Other treats include snack cakes, bars and tarts, made with seasonal fruits and ranging from bite-size to eight-inch family desserts. You'll find a variety of fruit pies, as well as specialty pies, such as Key lime and lemon meringue. Tiramisu, cannoli, biscotti and zuppa are prepared in the authentic Italian tradition. Office catering services are available. Come to Adagio Baking and see why this popular neighborhood bakery is a beloved gathering spot in Denver's Park Hill district.

4628 E 23rd Avenue, Denver CO
(303) 388-0904
www.adagiobakery.com

Lewis Sweet Shop

If you're looking for sweet treats served up in a 1950s fashion, Lewis Sweet Shop is a cool place to be. The store was started way back in 1949 by Duane Lewis, who, at the age of 94, is the oldest person currently living in Empire. From the beginning, the Lewis family served hot dogs and candy, eventually adding a popcorn machine and ice cream. The business was sold in 1994, and again in 2005. Current owners Peggy and Bernie Hubner have kept the Lewis tradition alive. Lewis Sweet Shop is known for its shakes and malts, taffy and sweets made from the original recipes, including caramel corn, fudge, glass candy, toffee and turtles. Enjoy one of more than 20 shake and malt flavors, or enjoy a scoop of ice cream. Want something to eat before dessert? Try one of the tasty burgers, homemade burritos, or slow-cooked barbecue sandwiches. Sides include such mouth-watering selections as fried pickles, fried sweet potatoes and fried jalapeños. The atmosphere is friendly and retro, with checkerboards painted on each table. Indulge your taste for a shake, sweets and old-fashioned good cooking with old-time service at Lewis Sweet Shop. The shop is open for breakfast, lunch and dinner.

208 E Park Avenue, Empire CO
(303) 569-2379
www.lewissweetshop.com

Fashion & Accessories

Brass Key Menswear and Brass Heart Clothing

Brass Key Menswear and Brass Heart Clothing let Greeley guys and gals add pizzazz to their wardrobes while avoiding the hassle of crowds and carbon-copy mall shops. This delightful pair of stores offers a full selection of fashionable, quality clothing for men and women, along with a choice array of accessories and personal products. Co-owner and area native Debbie Vandanberg founded the popular shopping destination in 2001 after she realized that Greeley lacked a full-service clothing store specializing in contemporary design. Both Debbie and her partner Joann Amlaw, who is in charge of the men's wear shop, work hard to hand-select a diverse inventory of fabulous fashions. They pride themselves on having a little something for everyone. Brass Key Menswear and Brass Heart Clothing feature upscale contemporary clothing, including casual wear, outerwear and shoes, as well as personal care products and a select array of gifts for nearly any occasion. Debbie, Joann and their staff are delighted to offer hands-on service and take pride in going that extra mile to provide complete customer satisfaction. Spruce up your clothing collection or find something special for everyone on your gift list with a visit to Brass Key Menswear and Brass Heart Clothing.

2030 35th Avenue, Suites B & C, Greeley CO
(970) 339-9307 (Brass Key Menswear)
(970) 339-3850 (Brass Heart Clothing)

Sun Logic

Claiming to offer the largest selection of sunglasses in Summit County is bragging only if you don't have the inventory to back it up. Ron McCann needs two stores on Breckenridge's Main Street to hold all of his merchandise. Since 1993, Sun Logic has been known as the place in town to buy shades. According to many aficionados, the huge selection that features Prada, Oakley, Maui Jim and many other top designers might well be the deepest in the entire state. Make a fashion statement on the street, the beach or the slopes with eyewear that offers maximum UV protection while scoring points for fashion. In addition to sunglasses, you'll find such recreation accessories as ski goggles, helmets, caps and mittens. The second store offers a complete line of outerwear in addition to backpacks, watches and many other accessories. If you are looking for an Oakley shirt to go with the shades, this is the place to get it. Check out Sun Logic for sunglasses that deflect the rays and reflect your personality.

**421 S Main Street, Breckenridge CO
(Sunglass Headquarters)
(970) 453-8477
122 S Main Street, Breckenridge CO
(970) 453-0344**

Clotheshorse Boutique

Denver area fashionistas trot on down to the Clotheshorse Boutique to see what's sizzling and sassy. Owned by Sheila Aud and Debbie O'Neil, the boutique caters to women who love clothes and wear them with style. Hand-detailed denim jeans, key to any wardrobe, line the aisles. You'll find the latest selections from Joe's, Christopher Blue and Brazil Roxx. Add a Komarov separate and a fabulous belt and you're good to go. Whether you're a size 0 or 14, professional consultants on-site help you put together a stunning wardrobe. Clotheshorse is for the discriminating buyer who wants designer clothing, but in a price range that's affordable. Jackets, fur coats, lingerie, handmade purses and evening bags demand your attention. Onesole sandals are a best-seller. The sandals have interchangeable, wide neoprene straps that are comfortable and travel well. Aud and O'Neil brought two passions together when opening the boutique—clothes and horses. This unusual shop also carries items for equestrians. It has children's and lady's English riding apparel, Ariat boots and tack, including cinches, bridles and reins for the English rider. Grooming products and horsie gifts for kids are featured. Bring your girlfriends for a private shopping party at the Clotheshorse Boutique. Wine, cheese and appetizers will be waiting.

**10125 W San Juan Way #120, Littleton CO
(303) 933-7777**
www.clotheshorseboutique.com

Hearne's Fine Goods

This family-owned business opened in 1986 in a white brick Victorian house near the University of Northern Colorado in Greeley's historic district. Owner Carolyn raised her children in the business. Today, daughter Maia puts her special touch, depth of knowledge and experience to work in the Old Town Fort Collins shop. The Greeley shop moved to west Greeley in June 2006. Carolyn designed the interior space to showcase the clothing, footwear, jewelry and accessories the shops carry. Solar tubes and full spectrum lighting show true color in the merchandise. A comfortable sofa in each location provides a relaxed atmosphere. Health professionals, teachers and hair stylists are among Hearne's best customers. What do they have in common? All are on their feet all day and appreciate a supportive pair of shoes. Dansko, Birkenstock, El Naturalista, Haflinger, Naot, Earth, Keen and MBT are among the carefully selected brands the shops stock. FLAX, Christopher Blue jeans and jackets, Surrealist and the Jean Ruc clothing lines are accessorized with Zazou scarves, fine native American Indian jewelry and designer jewelry by local artists. Leather briefcases, Ameribags, Baggallini and the hand-painted Anuschka line of leather goods are featured at Hearne's. Special attention is paid to providing small boutique lines and styles not often found in corporate environments. Carolyn, Maia, Tanja, Noelle and Sandee welcome all customers, new and returning, to come play at Hearne's Fine Goods.

1923 59th Avenue, #115, Greeley CO
(970) 352-4653
15 Old Town Square, #133, Fort Collins CO
(970) 224-4653
www.HearnesFineGoods.com

Ron R. Fine Jewelry

A tradition of originality is hard to maintain, but Ron R. Hogsett has kept up such an enviable reputation at Ron R. Fine Jewelry. At the shop, you'll see quality crystal, elegant giftware and custom fine jewelry. Both owner and artist, Ron has designed, created and repaired jewelry for decades. Each custom piece exhibits the innovative style that sets Ron's work apart. He can artfully design and create a custom piece just for you, based on your requirements. Ron is the virtuoso behind the Longs Peak pendant sold worldwide and the sparkling tiaras worn by Boulder County Fair royalty. He also specializes in the fine art of heirloom jewelry restoration. In addition, the shop provides complete service and repair for watches and jewelry. If you have a keepsake ring that does not fit, your ring size has changed or you just want to wear your ring on a different finger, you can have it sized to perfection at Ron R Fine Jewelry. Battery replacement keeps watches going forever, and chains can be repaired to look and function like new. For out-of-the-ordinary excellence, step into Ron R. Fine Jewelry.

452 Main Street, Longmont CO
(303) 651-1125

Over the Moon Kids

Over the Moon Kids sells top-quality, hard-to-find boutique and European brands of children's clothing, as well as a stylish selection of maternity wear for moms, all at affordable prices. The shop caters to little clients from newborns to age six. Over the Moon Kids also carries a hand-picked selection of pristine-condition used children's clothing and maternity wear. *The Yellow Scene* magazine recently named Over the Moon Kids the Best Used Clothing Store. For babies, the shop stocks such brand names as Baby Lulu, Cornelloki and Catimini, as well as the famous Petit Bateau line. Little girls love the beautiful outfits from Baby Nay, Cakewalk and Oilily. The Soup and the Me Too brands are other popular choices. Boy-pleasers include Wes & Willy, Molehill and many others. Owners Dana Keel and Lise McCalpin make yearly buying trips to Europe to bring you the best quality fashions. Their high-end finds are more durable and fade-resistant than comparably priced counterparts you find at the mall. When your kids outgrow their clothes, Over the Moon Kids offers a number of ways to profitably recycle. You choose the method of payment. Get cash up front, store credit or leave current-season clothing on consignment. For kid's clothes beyond your wildest expectations, come to Over the Moon Kids.

2770 Arapahoe Road, Suite 118, Lafayette CO
(720) 890-4928
www.overthemoonkids.com

Snyder Jewelers

Since 1948, Snyder Jewelers has been serving the Boulder
County Community. Through three generations of family
ownership, the business continues to be known and respected
for their honesty, integrity, value, expertise, high quality
craftmanship and unsurpassed standard of excellence. The
inventory is extensive and dynamic. While customer design
is their specialty, Snyder's also offers an exciting selection of
award-winning designer collections. Examples are: Claude
Thibaudeau, Richard Krementz, Mark Schneider, Nouveau
1910 and Hildalgo. The owner, Linda Snyder, says "We offer
unsurpassed customer service, unique and beautiful custom
designs, competitive prices, an extensive selection of finished
jewelry, loose diamonds and gemstones. I want our guests to
have security, peace of mind, and confidence that the purchase
they made was the best possible value and quality in the
marketplace." The expert staff at Snyder Jewelers includes two
master jewelers, gemologists, a Senior Master Appraiser, and a
watch repairman. The members of the sale team are educated,
experienced and committed professionals. Snyder's may be an
older business, but they offer extremely high-tech services. It
was the first store in the world to offer laser-inscribing security
or heritage identification on diamonds in the store, while you
watch. Another laser, (one of only 1000 lasers of its type in all of
North America), is expertly used to make repairs and restoration
on platinum jewelry. Many of these platinum repairs could not be
made using the traditional methods. Linda Snyder and her team
invite you to stop by and see what Snyder Jewelers has to offer.

2201 Ken Pratt Boulevard, Longmont CO
(303) 776-2992
www.snyderjewelers.com

Anspach's Jewelry

Graig Anspach considers it an honor to own Anspach's Jewelry. When he stops to think that three generations of some families have purchased their most prized pieces of jewelry from his store, he sees himself as a part of a larger whole in the small community of Lafayette. His parents started the business in 1955 with pennies to their name. His dad was a watchmaker, a tradition that Anspach's Jewelry continues by offering watch repair, as well as jewelry repair and exquisite custom designs. Whether you are shopping for fine jewelry, diamonds or colored gemstones, you will never feel pressured to buy. Graig and his staff pride themselves on their personalized service, which includes giving folks time to make a decision. They are even happy to do the little things, such as replacing your watch battery for you. With honesty and integrity as the foundation of his business, Graig is proud to have touched the lives of so many people in his community and to have earned their word-of-mouth endorsement. Consider purchasing your next piece of fine jewelry at Anspach's Jewelry.

101-A S Public Road, Lafayette CO
(303) 665-5313
www.anspachsjewelry.com

Classic Gold Jewelers

Whether Ted Willis is repairing jewelry, buying or creating a custom piece to your specifications, he'll spend as much time as it takes to make you a happy customer. Ted opened Classic Gold Jewelers at its present location in 2003 with a focus on excellence. Avoiding excessive mark-ups, he promises fine jewelry at a fair price. His commitment to quality means you can expect to find superior gems along with well-made platinum and gold jewelry that rarely needs repair. Ted carries a large selection of crystal pieces as well as watches by Citizen, Seiko and Skagen. Thirty years ago, he worked part-time for a jewelry store and learned his craft from a German master jeweler. For the past 22 years, he's been in business for himself, earning customer loyalty with a combination of fine taste and superior design and repair skills. He offers watch repair, as well as jewelry, and owns a laser welding machine that makes extremely precise projects possible. To ensure peace of mind and fine workmanship, visit Ted at Classic Gold Jewelers.

383 Main Street, Longmont CO
(303) 774-1322

Becoming Mothers

Becoming Mothers is the place to go for new and expectant mothers who seek the finest maternity fashions, breastfeeding gear and parenting classes. "Our clothes are sassy, fashion forward and comfortable so our customers don't compromise their style while they are pregnant and breastfeeding," says owner Stephanie Moore. Becoming Mothers features maternity brands such as Noppies, Maternal America and Momzee, and is always looking at the collections of new designers. Many of these items are so fashionable that you'll see non-pregnant women shopping here. Accessories include chic diaper bags, baby carriers, strollers, furniture and infant bedding, and a

large selection of nursing bras. Becoming Mothers offers both a mother's registry and an infant's registry that you can customize with special order items. Stephanie is a Board Certified Lactation Consultant and registered nurse with clinical expertise in obstetrics. The store's buyer, Gabrielle Johnson, is a maternity fashion designer in her own right. Gabrielle's clothing line, Bloom Maternity, features the popular Blooming Belly maternity tee which is sold in boutiques nationwide. Becoming Mothers reflects the passions of Stephanie and Gabrielle—fabulous maternity fashions and real-life parenting expertise. If you are an expectant or new mom, come to Becoming Mothers for everything you need to be attractive and knowledgeable during your pregnancy and breastfeeding experience.

2525 Arapahoe Avenue, Suite H12B, Boulder CO
(303) 546-MAMA (6262)
www.becomingmothers.com

Photo by www.peggydyer.com

Photos by Kent Meireis

Kismet

Shana Colbin Dunn believes in Kismet. Not only was actor Rod Colbin, her father, a star in a theatrical version of *Kismet*, but she christened her Denver jewelry and accessories shop with the same name. Kismet means destiny, which is how Dunn presents her unusual store. Enter Dunn's world and you're sure to find the handbag or hat of your dreams. One-of-a-kind jewelry is everywhere. Dunn imports exclusive earrings, bracelets and necklaces from artists worldwide. Items created by local celebrity artist Christy Lea Payne are best sellers. As a wholesale jewelry rep for 12 years, Dunn has access to jewelry that you won't find anywhere else. Useful items such as flip-flops, slippers, shower caps and socks add a unique flair. Wall hangings and artwork provide ideas for filling those empty spaces in your home. Signs reading "Home Sweet Home" or "Coffee, Tea or Me" might be exactly what you're looking for to add some spice to your kitchen or bedroom. If whimsy isn't your preference, select a stunning piece of metal art. At the heart of this eclectic shop is the belief that novelties can be functional. Just venture in and see what Kismet has in store for you.

3640 W. 32ʳᵈ Avenue, Denver CO (303) 477-3378

Lauren Diamonds

"The only difference in jewelry prices is the markup," says Lauren Diamonds owner Gary Casey. With lower expenses than a large diamond chain, family-owned and operated Lauren Diamonds is dedicated to keeping jewelry prices low and service levels high. It's a philosophy that has made the store a fixture in Denver for more than 30 years. Gary and his wife, Sheri, took over the store in 2004. Their staff has a combined 100 years' experience in the jewelry field. Lauren Diamonds is known for going the extra mile to make sure every piece is perfect for the buyer. Your diamond purchase comes with a certificate that guarantees its quality. Gary and has been known to make appearances at weddings to make last-minute adjustments to a jewelry piece when necessary. The store also offers pick-up and delivery for jewelry repairs. Lauren Diamonds specializes in engagement rings, with a beautiful selection in both gold and silver. You'll also find gorgeous pearls, sapphires, rubies and emeralds from around the world. The atmosphere is friendly and informal, the walls covered in autographs. You'll feel even better about your purchase when you find out that 5 percent of each sale goes to your favorite charity. For jewelry that will add sparkle to your loved ones' lives, visit Lauren Diamonds.

410 17th Street, #425, Denver CO
(303) 623-7977
www.laurendiamondsofdenver.com

Princess Kept the View

Deriving its name from Bob Dylan's song, "All Along the Watchtower," Princess Kept the View is a store to keep your eye on. Offering women's fashions, accessories and home furnishings, the Boulder store represents what owner Trinda Weymouth calls "the fashionable Colorado woman." The store specializes in feminine fashion from brands including Max Studio, Jelessy and BCBG. If you're looking for jeans to flatter your form, try Butterfly Dropout. Once you've found the perfect outfit, match it up with just the right shoes, from brands including Bolo and Beverly Feldman. You'll also find plenty of gorgeous jewelry to add sparkle to your ensemble. Princess Kept the View carries antique furnishings to help spruce up your home in Victorian style. Light up your room with a sparkling chandelier, sconce or other beautiful fixture from Princess Kept the View. The friendly staff is always ready to answer your questions and help you find just the right piece. For all the props you'll need to dress your home and person like a princess, visit Princess Kept the View.

1631 Pearl Street, Boulder CO
(303) 442-8439
www.princesskepttheview.com

Fleet Feet Sports Boulder

Fleet Feet Sports offers the best in walking, running and triathlon gear. Owners Kathy Boyd and Jay Johnson make sure that each employee works with a physical therapist on foot biomechanics. As a result, every customer receives a thorough shoe fit through foot measurements and a treadmill gait analysis. Also, staff members constantly wear-test and evaluate running and walking shoes,

giving them the knowledge of how shoes fit and function. The store carries brands that have made a commitment to the running and walking market and support specialty retail shops. You will find top names such as Asics, Nike, Brooks, Mizuno, Saucony and New Balance. Fleet Feet also sells technical running and triathlon apparel, wetsuits, snowshoes and Nordic walking poles. Wearing the right apparel will make your workout more comfortable by keeping you cooler in the summer, warmer in the winter, and always dry. Once you are fit for shoes and find the right apparel, you can join the weekly fun runs, free clinics and physical therapy consultations that the store sponsors to support the community. Visit Fleet Feet Sports Boulder for professional service and the best product for running, walking and triathlon.

2624 Broadway, Boulder CO
(303) 939-8000
www.fleetfeetboulder.com

Snake Vertebrae 18 Karat Gold Necklace

18 Karat Gold Earrings with stars & meteorites

18 Karat Gold Rings featuring ancient coins, seals and fossils

karats

Karats is one of Vail's first jewelry design shops. Dan Telleen is the owner and designer, and his jewelry fuses the natural world with the echoes of the past. Using time as his muse, Dan's creations often inspire insight into a world long gone as he crafts timeless, elegant jewelry from ancient materials into works which touch your spirit. "If there is a theme in the jewelry," Dan says, "it's about time and evolution." You might see an exquisite necklace of black trade beads and a gold-set pendant pairing a Native American arrowhead and an Indian head coin. An aged piece of driftwood holds earrings made from a striking blue tourmaline stone. Be sure to look for Dan's stunning gold collar necklaces. Let his delicately shaped gold rest just above your collarbone while the eye-catching amethyst or natural-occurring geode sets off any outfit. The medallion necklace and earrings pair an ancient silver medallion set in gold with sparkling iridescent beads. While Dan uses only the finest metals and jewels, his media also include relics such as 3,000-year-old Greek coins and 500,000,000-year-old fossils. You'll have a hard time finding any other jewelry store that can make you a necklace with a seal from the Roman Empire. You'll find yourself connected with an ancient history each time you wear one of his pieces. From time to time, other special artists exhibit at Karats as well. Stop into Karats today and let Dan's truly inspired art become a part of you.

122 E Meadow Drive, Vail CO
(970) 476-4760
www.karatsvail.com

True Love Shoes & Accessories

Women looking for fabulous footwear will find true love at True Love Shoes & Accessories. The store has already scored a lot of love from Denver-area publications for its trendy selection and competitive prices. In 2007, Westword honored True Love for offering the Best Cheap Shoes in the city, commenting that owner Sarah Lilly-Ray "has raised the cheap shoe to stiletto-heel heights." The store offers more than 100 styles for less than $50. 5280 magazine also praised the store for its selection, including it in its 2007 Top of the Town issue, saying, "At these prices, you can even buy two or three pairs, if your heart desires." Your heart will desire when you see these shoes, which range from versatile ballet flats to elegant heels for stepping out on the town. Sarah has chosen her stock with love, including love for animals—none were harmed to create these footwear fantasies. You'll also find beautiful bags, sparkling jewelry and sultry sunglasses at the shop. The atmosphere is friendly and full of vibrant colors. Let your feet find true love at True Love Shoes & Accessories.

42 Broadway, Denver CO
(303) 860-8783
www.trueloveshoes.com

Photo by www.pupiloftheeye.com

Colorado Footwear

People who have come from all over the world to ski in Vail often leave town wearing a pair of shoes from Colorado Footwear. This men's and women's fashion shoe store at the base of a Vail ski slope has been serving the public to great acclaim since 1996. The *Vail Daily* has recognized it for Best Retail Experience as well as Best Shoe Store and Best Place to Buy Shoes. Owners Steve and Sally Rosenthal, along with their daughter and buyers, work with shoe factories worldwide to select styles that appeal to their discriminating clientele. Known for its exquisite assortment of styles and its specials, Colorado Footwear even designs a line of its own shoes to complement such famous brands as Frye, Merrell and Via Spiga. Expect to find the latest from Born and Cole Haan as well. The Ice Pick Convertible Boots and Shoes are definitely a must-see. Steve, a veteran of 50 years in the shoe industry, oversees a thriving business that donates hundreds of shoes every year to support worthy causes. After a day on the slopes, treat your feet to a new pair of shoes from Colorado Footwear.

183 E Gore Creek Drive, Vail CO
(970) 476-3130

Well Heeled

Perfect pumps, striking stilettos and beautiful boots. That's what any well-heeled woman will find at Well Heeled. Owners Wendy Lew and Rebecca Hernreich have plenty of what Wendy calls a passion for fashion. Before opening Well Heeled together in 2004, Wendy worked for Bloomingdale's and other fine retailers, while Rebecca made her living as an interior designer. The two friends and partners distinguish their store from the big boxes with their attention to detail and customer service, while still offering competitive prices and shoes you're not likely to find anywhere else. Whether you're looking for something comfy to lounge around in or something glamorous for a night on the town, they have it here. Well Heeled carries fine footwear from renowned designers, including J Renee, Stuart Weitzman and Giuseppe Zanotti, along with the perfect handbags and accessories to match. With its marble floors and tufted settees, the atmosphere at Well Heeled is fashionable and friendly. Put your feet first in fashion with a trip to Well Heeled.

0056 Edwards Village Boulevard, Edwards CO
(970) 766-7463

Niwot Jewelry & Gifts

Perhaps it's no coincidence that the seed for Niwot Jewelry & Gifts was planted in the 1950s, an era that we associate with old-fashioned values such as honesty, integrity and community spirit. During that time, Owen Irby opened a watch repair and jewelry store in Arkansas, where he established a reputation for good work and fair dealing. He became a well-known and trusted member of the Boulder business community after moving to town in the 1960s. His way of regarding everyone who came into his shop as a friend set people at ease and won him scores of repeat customers. Owen has passed that philosophy onto the store's second generation of owners, Vern and Jan Kahl. Irby personally trained Vern in the intricacies of watch repair. Vern will fix your timepiece or help you select a new watch or clock that will last a lifetime. He also does custom work and engraving. Niwot Jewelry & Gifts carries many interesting items that you won't find all over the area. The owners appreciate everyone who drops by and will even help you find things that they don't carry. Go to Niwot Jewelry & Gifts to experience how pleasant doing business must have been in the 1950s.

300 2nd Avenue, Suite 102, Niwot CO
(303) 652-1433

Master Goldsmiths

Jim Miller follows in the footsteps of jewelers dating back 500 B.C., though he is also adept with a laser welder and other state-of-the-art tools. With everything from modest sterling silver to extravagant engagement jewelry, Master Goldsmiths embraces the new and the old while appealing to people of various tastes and budgets. It has been a part of Boulder since 1977, and many customers seem like family. Helping people commemorate special moments in their lives is what his business is all about, Jim says. Perhaps something in his display cases will catch your eye and warm your heart. If not, he is ready to turn your ideas for custom pieces into beautiful rings, necklaces and bracelets. Repairing and reworking jewelry are also specialties, and the shop has from time to time rescued pieces damaged by less competent shops. Jim is assisted by his son, Colin Miller, and a full-time jeweler who, according to the owner, is one of the best stone setters in the world. Jim acknowledges that the Internet has changed the way that people shop for jewelry, but it cannot, he notes, replace the experience of visiting his shop. Jim and his friendly and helpful staff are experts on the entire process of jewelry making, from the mining of the stones to the subtlest detail of the crafting. Drop by Master Goldsmiths and see for yourself what personal, knowledgeable service means.

951 Pearl Street, Boulder CO
(303) 444-4653
www.mastergoldsmiths.com

Prima Bodywear

Prima Bodywear meets the specific clothing needs of dancers as well as those who practice yoga, Pilates and gymnastics. The Ft. Collins shop employs teachers, dancers and performers who draw from personal experience to point you to the right brands. You'll find leotards, tights, jazz pants, yoga and active-wear in sizes up to women's XL. The yoga wear comes from independent labels not available chain stores. Children and Adults will find dance shoes suitable for ballroom, tap, jazz and ballet. Prima is the only full-service dancewear retailer in Ft. Collins and attracts customers from throughout the region, including neighboring states. Owner Mary Pat McCurdie has been an amateur dancer all of her life. She worked briefly at the store while in graduate school at Colorado State University, and purchased the store in 2002 after leaving a career in the high-tech industry. Prima Bodywear understands the needs of active adults and children for apparel and accessories and opens seven days a week to meet those needs. For clothing that moves with your moves, visit Prima Bodywear.

123 N College Avenue, Suite 112, Ft. Collins CO (970) 484-2623
www.primabodywear.com

Little Mountain

When your child climbs Everest some day, you'll be glad that you started your adventurer off right by buying his or her first pair of hiking boots at Little Mountain. This Boulder retailer specializes in high-quality and high-value outdoor gear for kids. "It's easy to get kids involved in family outings, but they need the right stuff," say owners Dan and Lori Nichols. To address the need for comfortable, durable and dependable gear for the junior trekker, Little Mountain offers children's clothing, sleeping bags and backpacks from some of the finest names in the outdoor industry. Patagonia, North Face and Columbia are just a few of the featured lines. Clothing ranges from sleek jackets to sun-protective swimwear. Has your future John or Jane Muir not begun to walk yet? Then the snow shoes can wait. For now, you will want to check out the nice selection of carriers and strollers. What fun you will have shopping for your active young ones all the way through middle school. For gear that will make your child want to blaze trails, visit Little Mountain

1136 Spruce Street, Boulder CO (303) 443-1757
www.outdoorgearforkids.com

Trail Kids

Outdoor adventures can be expensive when you have kids, who outgrow their outerwear so fast. Scott and Sue Reardon formed Trail Kids to solve this problem with new and used kid-sized outerwear and equipment. The Reardons opened the shop in 2004, quickly earning a reputation for their expertise and the quality of their products. They know first-hand how challenging it can be to outfit children from trying to keep their own three kids in gear. A name-brand fleece jacket may have a life of 10 years, but a child will likely outgrow it in one season. Through Trail Kids, another youngster can benefit from the jacket. Trail Kids offers specialized clothing for infants through teens, along with such items as sleeping bags, Alpine and Nordic skis, bicycles and climbing harnesses. You will find jogging strollers and child carriers, too. You can trade in equipment as your child grows. The shop also offers telemark ski rentals. Beyond gear, the Reardons offer advice on how to start hiking with your children and where to take them. They can give you the skinny on camp spots, ski areas and trails and analyze the pros and cons of their products for your family. Prepare your kids for outdoor pursuits at Trail Kids.

2750 Glenwood Drive, #3, Boulder CO (720) 564-1300
www.trail-kids.com

Galleries & Fine Art

Shooting Star Glass Studio

Deborah Carlson is one of the few glass artists who works in several glass techniques, combining the disciplines of hot, warm and cold glass for highly original art glass. Deborah has worked out of Shooting Star Glass Studio in Greenwood Village for about 25 years. She creates award-winning pieces for galleries and shows as well as architectural pieces for public and private installations. Deborah's work extends from leaded glass windows, mosaics and carvings—known as cold-worked glass—to such warm-glass techniques as kiln casting and fusing, as well as hot-glass blowing and torch work. Much of Deborah's work is interactive, including the observer in the creative process. She produces wall pieces and one-of-a-kind sculpture, such as a pod series with glass leaf capsules separate from the glass seed clusters. You are bound to break out in a smile when you see her miniature collectible hats that are held aloft on glass pedestals. Customers appreciate inventive goblets and a series of organic blown and carved inspirations are available in varied color combinations. Also included in the organic series are the blown pears, which invite the owner to pick them up and turn them in the light. "Each piece starts with a simple human thought and then develops into its own personal poetry," Deborah says. Deborah teaches at her studio, or stop by for a short demonstration. Call for an appointment. Some work can be viewed locally at Pismo Art Glass, Cherry Creek in Denver.

5600 E Powers Avenue, Greenwood Village CO
(303) 689-9072
www.deborahcarlson.com

Michael Stano

Michael Stano is a sculptor of timeless magic. His pieces, created through a very personal process with a high degree of physical and intellectual involvement, transcend mere form. Their unmistakable ethereal quality weaves together primordial echoes of ancient stories with an emotionally charged connection to the natural world. Stano's wooden and life-sized cast bronze sculptures are heavily influenced by Eastern European mythology tales that speak of worldly survival and enchantment through the exploits of spectral animals. His early pieces were combined with rich, evocative narratives. As he continued his process, the visual art eclipsed the need for stories as they became their own narratives and began engaging viewers in their own dialogue. Stano begins with a drawing, then translates this into cardboard templates and follows with a wood skeleton. The animals take shape in a naturalistic way, with texture and color the last to come. Stano's works are widely exhibited in galleries, including the Gallatin River Gallery in Big Sky, Montana, the J. Cotter Gallery in Vail and the James Ratliff Gallery in Sedona, Arizona. They are found in the homes of celebrities and people from all walks of life. Take the opportunity to visit the art works of Michael Stano and participate in a mystical communion of your own.

1800 Hoyt Street, Lakewood CO
(303) 638-3895
www.michaelstano.com

Show of Hands

While there have been plenty of great days during the 24 years that Show of Hands has been in business, none has been better than August 10, 2006. That's the day when the owners of this Cherry Creek North gallery announced that their establishment had been recognized as one of the top 25 craft retailers in the nation. A place where creativity thrives, Show of Hands promises visitors an uplifting and inspiring experience from the moment that they pass through the delightful garden entry. This showcase of fine American craft represents some 200 artists working in clay, fiber, wood, metal and mixed media, their styles ranging from elegant and chic to whimsical and funky. Furniture, garden art and ceramics are just a few of the specialties, along with wearable art such as scarves, jewelry and handbags. The only craft retailer in the state of Colorado to win the prestigious top retailer award presented by *NICHE Magazine*, Show of Hands enjoys a reputation for superb customer service and giving back to the community. The gallery participates in the Cherry Creek Arts Festival in July, donating a portion of its sales of animal-related art to Golden Retriever Rescue of the Rockies. This is a good time to shop for everything from metal dog sculptures to colorful limited-edition prints of happy canines while supporting a worthy cause. Visit Show of Hands and see for yourself what makes it special.

210 Clayton Street, Denver CO
(303) 399-0201
www.showofhandsdenver.com

Vail Fine Art Gallery

Owner James G. Tylich of Vail Fine Art Gallery has spent a lifetime selecting masterpieces from all over the world to adorn his family of galleries. Jim has traveled to virtually every fine art museum in the world, which serves him well in visiting artist studios and homes, looking for the touch of the master. For Jim, art has always been an emotional thing, and he makes it a point to involve his heart when making an art purchase. In addition to showcasing master painters like Dali and Picasso, Jim has an uncanny ability to discover the new masters of our time, some of whom have had little exposure to the world. For example, Vail Fine Art is one of the few galleries in the nation with such a large collection of fine Russian art. Russian art is hard to come by and little-known in the United States because of its inaccessibility. Russia's artists are revered as celebrities, and even an experienced art dealer needs connections to meet the artists, let alone acquire their pieces. Jim has managed to find an "in" to the Russian art world, and you'll find the results at Vail Fine Art Gallery and at his other galleries, located throughout Colorado and in Santa Fe, New Mexico. For exceptional art that is sure to impress novice and expert alike, contact Jim Tylich of Vail Fine Art Gallery.

Vail Fine Art
227 Bridge Street, Vail CO
(970) 476-2900

Beaver Creek Fine Art
210 Offerson Road, Suite 162, Beaver Creek CO
(970) 845-8500

Breckenridge Fine Art
421 S Main Street, Breckenridge CO
(970) 453-9500

Aspen Fine Art
400 E Hyman Avenue, Aspen CO
((970) 920-0044

Wall Street Fine Art
232 Wall Street, Vail CO
(970) 476-7192

Santa Fe Fine Art
221 W San Francisco Street, Santa Fe NM
(505) 820-0045

www.vailfineart.com

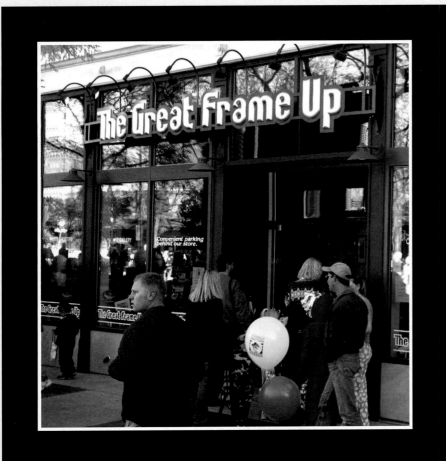

Metropolitan Frame Company
Formerly Animal Crackers Framing & Art Services

"The frame is the reward for the artist." That quote, courtesy of Edward Degas, provides the philosophy of the Metropolitan Frame Company—formerly known as Animal Crackers Framing & Art Services. Owner Andrew Stemple came up with the store's original name while in college. As he was writing a plan for a then-fictitious business, a care package arrived from home with a package of animal crackers. That college project has since grown into a business that *Décor Magazine* has called one of the Top 100 Frame Shops in America. Established in 1990, the company has escalated into working with the regions top collectors on million-dollar works to entire exhibits for institutions, such as the International Museum of Photography in New York City. Consumers are the real winners benefiting from Metropolitan's professional relationships with collectors, museums, interior designers, galleries and art consultants. Products range from inexpensive simple mouldings for family snapshots to gold leaf on hand-crafted period frames. The level of craftsmanship here is unmatched. Let Metropolitan Frame Company bring out the best in your art.

Downtown Denver: 2845 Walnut Street, Denver CO
(303) 446-2265
Denver Country Club: 387 Corona Street, Denver CO
(303) 350-4766
(800) 204-5709
www.metropolitanframe.com

The Great Frame Up

Since 1995, The Great Frame Up has been known for its impeccable picture framing services; satisfying customers with with its huge selection of frames, knowledgeable staff and beautiful results. As successful as the early years were, they were only a warm-up for The Great Frame Up of today. In 2004, owners Dave and Pam Inannazzo expanded the frame shop into a rotating gallery by moving into a 6,000-square-foot historic building in downtown Longmont. With its move to this central location, the Great Frame Up became the place to be in the local arts community. The gallery today showcases 12 to 14 artists each month, most are regional artists, but some national as well. The owners are excited to be part of Longmont's Art Walk three times a year and the Gallery Hop on the second Friday of every month. "Being at this beautiful location allows us to do more for the community," Dave points out, "such as hosting art events, raising money for local nonprofits and showcasing local talent." Whether you need something framed or are looking for original artwork from local artists, consider the Great Frame Up, named the Longmont Small Business of the Year in 2006.

430 Main Street, Longmont CO
(303) 772-7293
www.Longmont.TheGreatFrameUp.com

Painting by John K. Harrell

Painting by Anita Mosher

Painting by Kit Hevron Mahoney

Brushstrokes Studio Gallery

Creativity is in the air at Brushstrokes Studio Gallery in Denver. As you enter, gorgeous paintings line the walls, while one of the gallery's three owners and resident artists intently creates his or her next masterwork. Guests are invited to watch as renowned artists John K. Harrell, Kit Hevron Mahoney and Anita Mosher work, and even ask questions of them. The three artists work in a variety of styles. John, who got his start courtesy of his artist grandmother's encouragement, creates vibrant, impressionistic florals and cityscapes. Kit draws on 20 years of experience in fine arts and graphic design to create texturized canvasses covered with colorful florals, landscapes and contemporary abstract. Anita's still lifes, figures and landscapes combine Russian-style training with a predilection for American Impressionism. The three artists can answer your questions about any of the art in the gallery. The atmosphere is friendly and inviting. Brushstrokes Studio Gallery presents shows of all three artists at various points throughout the year. The artists invite you to come watch their creative process in action and bring home its beautiful fruits.

1059 S Gaylord Street, Denver CO
(303) 871-0800
www.brushstrokesstudio.com

The Little Cottage Gallery

The Little Cottage Gallery, the longest standing art gallery in Lake County, showcases the work of the artistic Mullings family. You'll find work by Ted Mullings and his wife, Audie, here. Their daughter and Ted's brothers also show artwork here along with many other artists. Born and raised on a ranch, Ted painted as a hobby while growing up and later became a rancher and a regular on the amateur rodeo circuit. Although he had an art degree from Adams State College, Ted worked as a day laborer for the Climax Molybdenum

Mine until his bosses discovered his artistic talents. During his 30 years with the company, Ted created more than 7,000 detailed, isometric drawings of the complex, block-cave mining system, so supervisors could explain the mine set-up to new hires. He also created company calendars and drew cartoons for the company's safety pamphlets. He continues to illustrate for mining organizations all over the country. In 1979, Audie opened the Little Cottage Gallery with another artist, Thea Richardson, to sell their watercolors and as an outlet for her family's artwork. When Ted retired in 1983, he started working at the gallery, too. Ted's representational art continues to reflect his lifelong interest in ranching, mining, Western landscapes and horses. Come visit Little Cottage Gallery and discover Western paintings, sculptures and crafts created by the Mullings family and other talented artists.

108 W 8th Street, Leadville CO
(719) 486-2411

Adrian Davis Photography

Adrian Davis is deeply familiar with the landscapes of northern Colorado and captures them with medium and large format film cameras. You can view his work at local shops and galleries, including the Collective Fine Art Gallery and Alpine Arts Gallery in Fort Collins and Mountain Crafts Gallery in Red Feather Lakes. The galleries carry both poster-size prints of his landscapes and copies of his books. ReMax, the national real estate firm, has used Adrian's photographs on several occasions for stock views of northern Colorado. Adrian is also an independent publisher of pictorial books and posters. He produces 24-inch by 32-inch limited edition fine art prints, complete with mats and frames. Adrian performs all parts of printmaking himself, from the photo, which is shot with slide film, to high resolution digital scanning and giclee printmaking. Artists often come to him for this high quality reproduction work. His website carries original photos, art prints and stock photos from his work in 23 states. If you need fine art printmaking, let a well-known photographer put his skills to work for you at Adrian Davis Photography.

1524 Freedom Lane, Fort Collins CO
(303) 906-7700
www.cachelaphoto.com

Myriad Art & Framery

Personal service, a keen eye for art and expert framing skills have built a loyal clientele for Myriad Art & Framery. Co-founder Doris Hime took time off from her duties as assistant professor in the Department of Textiles and Clothing at Colorado State University to help her son, Gary get the business on its feet. She never went back. Gary passed away in 1992, but in his stead, Doris has built Myriad Art into one of the most respected frame and art print stores in Fort Collins. Her experience in color, design and pattern-making makes her a natural framer as well as buyer. All of Myriad's thousands of frames and print samples are offered at excellent prices. Doris believes that all students should be exposed to art, so they receive a 10 percent discount on every purchase. Support a worthy local retailer and get much more in return when you shop at Myriad Art & Framery.

3500 S College, #11, Fort Collins CO
(970) 224-4616

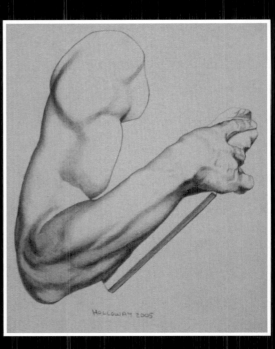

Colorado Academy of Art

Established just five years ago, the Colorado Academy of Art
(CAA) is a private fine arts academy that offers programs in
classical drawing, painting and sculpture. The faculty includes
experienced, classically trained artists, art historians and scholars.
Last year, the Art Renewal Center named the CAA as one of only
40 internationally approved classical training academies. The one-
to-four year foundation program allows candidates to experience
art training in the most classic sense. In addition to practical and
theoretical classes, students meet regular studio requirements. CAA
is a working studio that encourages advanced students to participate
in professional commissions. CAA artists have worked on projects
ranging from sculpture for municipalities, murals for community
projects, logos for businesses and private portraitures. The CAA
also offers the public 30 community classes per week in painting,
drawing and sculpture. Budding artists, ages 10 to 17, can enroll in
CAA's Young Artists Program. The CAA's new facility encompasses
6,000 square feet of classrooms and private studios plus an on-site
art gallery. Whether you seek art education or simply wish to view
an impressive gallery, the Colorado Academy of Art is worth a visit.

2897 Mapleton Avenue, Boulder CO
(303) 442-0669
www.coloradoacademyofart.com

Felicia

Felicia creates powerful Southwest-themed sculptures at her Denver studio and gallery, open since 2002. The gallery is home to limited edition sculptures in varying sizes, made in quantities no larger than 36. Capturing the heart and soul of the Native American women of the Southwest is Felicia's specialty. She works with live models, renders a strong likeness and simple lines. Her signature touches include stones, high polish lines and painted beads. "My sculpture represents a well-designed image full of graceful movement, soft curves and massive presence," says Felicia. Felicia began her artistic career as a painter at the Art Students League in New York City. She began sculpting full time when she moved to Denver in 1980, creating contemporary Southwest vessels and figures in bronze. She has been invited to many juried shows, has won many awards and displays her sculpture in galleries throughout the country. In 1995, Felicia was inducted into the National Association of Women artists in New York City. In June 2002, she completed a life-size bronze fountain of a family of Cahuilla Indians for the city of La Quinta, California. Come under the spell of sculpture by Felicia.

300 W 11th Avenue #C, Denver CO
(303) 570-5534
www.feliciasculpture.com

Image of Africa Gallery

Roland McEldowney was working as a geologist exploring for gold in Ghana when he was charged by an elephant. During his recovery, he re-discovered an old love: capturing images of animals and people in their natural environment. Drawing on his deep rapport with indigenous people of Africa, Roland spent the next ten years capturing unforgettable images of their culture and homeland. His dynamic photographs include a limited series of the seldom-seen Wodaabi tribe conducting their annual autumn ceremonies. He has since traveled to exotic landscapes and communities all over the world, from Mayan Mexico to Alaska. Roland's award-winning work has shown in galleries all over the United States and at the major art festivals of Colorado and Arizona. Highly sought by contemporary interior designers, it hangs in permanent corporate and university collections. He is currently on commission to provide landscape photographs of all of the national parks to decorate Grand Luxe railroad cars. Roland's Image of Africa Gallery is open by appointment. Open your eyes to the vibrant world of remote cultures caught by Roland McEldowney's lens.

29434 Greenwood Lane, Evergreen CO
(303) 674-7585

Fox Ridge Fine Art Glass

To experience an entirely new genre of art, visit Fox Ridge Fine Art Glass. Featuring glass art by renowned artists from around the nation, the 2000-square-foot gallery and store radiate inspiration. Ranging from inconspicuous and delicate vases to vivid, breathtaking centerpiece bowls, each piece is an original work of art. If you're looking for a piece to accent your home or business, Fox Ridge is sure to have it. The artists can also create custom pieces based on what you see or duplicate a piece for a whole set. Artists featured at Fox Ridge have also been exhibited at prominent galleries such as the Smithsonian and the Corning Museum of Glass. Owners Johanne and Jared Picken describe stepping into Fox Ridge as "stepping into a kaleidoscope." Visit Fox Ridge Fine Art Glass to satiate your appetite for original glass art.

411 South Main Street, Breckenridge CO
(970) 547-8192
www.foxridgegallery.com

The Art Source

When architects, art consultants, interior designers and collectors go on a shopping spree for art, they often head to The Art Source. Amy Wilhelm began building her reputation as an art resource with masterful client services 25 years ago. She opened her Denver wholesale fine art showroom in 1994 and moved to the Osage Lofts in 2002. The Art Source schedules appointments to show off a collection that represents 500 regional, national and international artists. You'll find original art, limited edition prints, works in metal, pottery and some fine art glass in the showroom, which strongly appeals to those decorating corporate offices, healthcare facilities, hotels and residences. Amy and her associate, Kate Aragon, select the artwork directly from the artists and the New York Art Expos. They pride themselves on all styles of classic framing design. The Art Source carries pieces suitable for environments as different as a Tuscan villa and a contemporary urban condominium. It can be surprisingly affordable to decorate with original art, according to Amy and Kate, who serve about 60 percent commercial customers and 40 percent residential ones. They offer many price points and insight into trends and styles that suit particular establishments. Find artwork from celebrated and emerging artists at The Art Source.

1111 Osage Street, Suite 10, Denver CO
(303) 685-4750
http://artsourceofdenver.com

Mount-N-Frame

A certified professional picture framer since 1993, Linda Osterberg has certainly framed her share of artwork, not to mention everything from sports memorabilia and military uniforms to awards and diplomas. In fact, about the only things that she and her staff at Mount-N-Frame haven't figured out how to frame are their smiles. Not that they would want to. Those smiles work best when they appear spontaneously to greet customers and to assure them that their framing project is in good hands. Voted Best Service with a Smile by the *Vail Daily* in 2003, this frame shop—the oldest in Eagle County—has earned scores of repeat customers from Vail and beyond by showing that service is just as important as product. Linda offers customers many frame styles that simply cannot be found anywhere else in the world. Mount-N-Frame is also a gallery, specializing in Vail images. Are you looking for an artistic souvenir of your time spent enjoying this beautiful town? If so, Mount-N-Frame features skiing posters, vintage posters and photographs of Vail Village and Vail Mountain. These images, suitable for framing, also make a lasting gift for the hiker, skier, snowboarder or mountain lover back home. Linda has personally trained her staff so that any of the three is capable of handling your framing needs. For a business that has mastered the art of framing as well as the art of customer service, stop at Mount-N-Frame.

953 S Frontage Road W, Suite 110, Vail CO
(866) 476-4172
www.mountnframe.com

Showcase Art Center

Showcase Art Center has fulfilled art needs and solved art problems for clients since 1986. From metalwork and murals to framing and commissioned work, owner and artist Colette Pitcher creates memorable art in virtually any media. Showcase Art Center also displays the work of other local artists and provides classrooms for art lessons for all age groups and in all media. A piano studio and art supply shop support creativity in the community. A full-time artist for more than 20 years, Colette specializes in painting and sculpture. She communicates particular feelings and evokes moods through dramatic use of light and shadow, vibrant color and expressive brushwork. For the past five years she has exhibited bronzes at the prestigious Loveland Sculpture Invitational Show, the world's largest outdoor sculpture show. Colette also counts graphic design, illustration and fabric designs among her talents, plus writing for magazines, calligraphy and consulting. Showcase Art Center, her mini-mall, combines a variety of businesses under one roof, including a hair salon, sewing alterations and dress shop. Come experience the joy that infuses Showcase Art Center, where you can watch artists create or take the first steps toward creating your own masterpieces.

1335 8ᵗʰ Avenue, Greeley CO
(970) 356-8593
www.colettepitcher.com

Rose Weaving Gallery & Studio

No matter how many times she does it, Harriet Rose still finds something magical in taking strands of thread and turning them into gorgeous weavings. She opened her shop, Rose Weaving Gallery & Studio, to promote weaving as an art form. You'll find beauty in every square foot of the gallery, where Harriet sells new and vintage fabric art from all over the world. On display are wall hangings and other decorative pieces as well as beautiful jackets, vests and scarves. The shop also carries yarns, looms and other weaving supplies. Local artisans play a key role in the business, contributing work to the gallery and teaching classes. Harriet notes that at least half the people who take one of the introductory weaving classes at the studio stick with it. She moved to the loom back in the 1990s after starting as a knitter and now describes her passion for weaving as something of an addiction. As you browse her beautiful shop, you'll be forced to disagree and call it a blessing. Discover treasures from the loom at Rose Weaving Gallery & Studio.

7508 Grandview Avenue, Arvada CO
(303) 424-ROSE (7673)
www.roseweaving.com

The Madison & Main Gallery

The Madison & Main Gallery showcases the talents of Northern Colorado artists working in a variety of media. In 1987, a group of artists joined together to support each other in their work, starting a co-operative gallery where their pieces could be displayed and sold for the benefit of everyone involved. Two decades later, the co-op has grown to include 20 member artists with nearly 50 artists represented on consignment. Tucked between a bookstore and a coffee house, the gallery holds a treasure trove of handcrafted items, including vibrant stained glass, pottery, wood crafts and paintings. You can find a unique sculpture for your home or a delicate necklace for a friend. The show changes every two months, with a new guest artist each time, so you can always discover something different. Show themes take their cues from the seasons, colors and other inspirations. Stop by Monday through Saturday and get a chance to speak directly with the artists about their latest works. Come to the Madison & Main Gallery to immerse yourself in the works of some of Colorado's most talented artists.

927 16ᵗʰ Street, Greeley CO
(970) 351-6201
www.madisonandmaingallery.com

Meko's Gallery & Framing

Flair and functionality intersect in the classy setting of Meko's Gallery & Framing. With nearly 20 years in business, Meko's has evolved from a tiny picture framing shop to the upscale frame store and gallery it is today. Offering over 2,500 frames and hundreds of mat colors, Meko's specialty is originality and quality of design. Whether you want your art to whisper along an inconspicuous hallway or shout vibrantly from across the room, Meko's design team can help you do it. They'll help you find the perfect frames for a wide array of media including fine art, needlepoint and fabric arts. Redesigning an entire room or business space? Innovative and experienced staff can aid in interior design. One of Meko's main focuses is furnishing commercial spaces such as banks, restaurants and medical offices with exquisite pieces to enhance the décor. The staff has over 30 years combined experience in custom framing and design. In addition, Meko's offers something for the art observer as well as the collector. The gallery at Meko's features the works of local artists in several genres including oil, pastel, watercolor, photography, sculpture and pottery. Come in to Meko's Gallery & Framing to find the art aficionado in you.

133 Remington Street, Fort Collins CO
(970) 221-4208
www.mekosgalleryandframing.com

The Metal Forest

First, Mike and Nina Stanton used their finely cut metalwork in the lighting and décor of their hand-built mountain cabin. Then they used their artistry to launch the Metal Forest. This Fort Collins business specializes in metal wall art and lighting fixtures. A sconce of an aspen forest hiding a bull elk is a Metal Forest favorite. Mike cuts the intricate, nature-inspired shapes from metal, stone and glass using a waterjet. Nina creates the graphic designs, focusing on a mountain theme along with other topics such as horse herds, tractors and fly-fishing. Both partners apply the hand-painted finishes, which include unusual rust and copper-green patinas. The Stantons' specialty is creating mix-and-match pieces that allow customers to design their own unique wall art and to fill odd spaces. They also have a collection of kitchen and bath accessories, clocks, switch plate covers and coat racks. The couple started out in summer artisan festivals and then branched out into the local mall for the Christmas season. In 2006, they opened their gallery. For metal art that captures the strength and beauty of nature with striking silhouettes, visit the Metal Forest.

#1 Old Town Square, Suite 107, Fort Collins CO
(970) 407-1677
www.metalforest.com

Roadside Gallery

The side of the road is a big part of the experience on road trips. The Roadside Gallery of Americana gives a glimpse into road trips of the past, and celebrates a time when the view was not so homogenized. A vast selection of nostalgic photos of Route 66, classic cars, motorcycles and old architecture energize the gallery space. Vibrant portraits of mom and pop motels, diners and gas stations hearken to a pre-digital past. You'll see pictures of wall murals used to sell brands of soda, beer and blue jeans that are no longer made. Recall a time when the main forms of advertising were the neon sign, artwork on a wall, or the distinctive body shape, grill or hood ornament of a particular car that could be recognized from a mile away. These things were a colorful, integral part of the landscape. The photographer and owner of Roadside Gallery is Marty Garfinkel. He has been working on his craft for 20 years with the purpose of preserving and archiving the past. His high quality, giclée or canvas prints can be customized to size. Roadside Gallery also offers a photo restoration service, making new, undamaged prints from old photographs. Collect some pieces of the past for your home or office at Roadside Gallery.

320 Main Street, Carbondale CO
(970) 963-9333 or (866) 963-9332
www.roadsidegallery.com

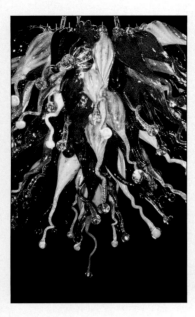

Agnes of Glass Studio and Gallery

Since 1999, Agnes Sanchez has been sharing her love of glass art at Agnes of Glass Studio and Gallery in Denver. Agnes has studied art locally and taken advanced training in Italy. She says she is "a one-of-a-kind person" and demonstrates this in her art. She loves the combination of wind, fire, earth and water that go into every handblown glass creation. Agnes believes the glass truly has a life of its own. "The piece selects me, not the other way around," she says. "My work expresses who I am and how I view my world. Glass is my passion." Some of her most impressive pieces are actually made from recyclables. Much of the gallery's blown glass selection is architectural glass art, which includes unusual lighting fixtures, doorknobs and glass blocks. Agnes' Medusa chandeliers, made up of hundreds of individually blown pieces, are capable of casting their very own spell over a room. You'll find sculpture, accent pieces and jewelry here. Agnes offers custom services, too. She also offers glass blowing classes through Front Range Community College and Colorado Free University. She is happy to arrange for private lessons or to rent studio time to those who already know the basics. Agnes' work appears in galleries throughout the state and has been displayed in London. Let Agnes of Glass Studio and Gallery be your first stop when it comes to beautifying your home or office with glass art.

2717 E 40ᵗʰ Avenue, Denver CO
(303) 399-4066
www.glassartists.org

Cove Gallery

Jon R. Tamm's oil paintings start in the open air, where he can glory in the Colorado landscape he loves so much. At Cove Gallery in Boulder, Jon brings the beauty of his native state to the world. For more than 15 years, Jon has hiked mountains and stood in

river marshes painting the changing light and stunning landscapes of Rocky Mountain National Park. One stroll through the Cove Gallery puts the visitor in direct contact with the rich life and rugged vistas of the Rocky Mountains. John attributes his creativity to "the excitement of experiencing the place and the ever-changing light." He also attributes his interest in artwork that teems with life and vibrant color harmonies to his exposure as a young child to the work of his step-grandfather Walter Fardon. Jon paints still lifes and portraits, but the bulk of his work is focused on landscapes. His work has been featured in such magazines as *American Artist*. Jon is a regular participant in Boulder's Open Studios, where each fall Boulder artists open their studios to the public. He is happy to discuss artwork by commission. The Cove Gallery, located in Jon's home, is open by appointment only. Experience the people and places of Colorado through the eyes of Jon Tamm with a visit to the Cove Gallery.

7534 Brockway Drive, Boulder CO
(303) 499-1695
www.jontamm.com

Halsman-einstein: "Albert Einstein, 1949"
©*Philippe Halsman*

The Camera Obscura Gallery

Hal Gould's fascination with artistic expression through photography is the basis for the Camera Obscura Gallery in Denver. Gould worked as a commercial photographer for many years before turning to fine art photography. In the 1960s, fine art photography was not a recognized art form, and establishments like the Denver Art Museum would not display photographs, so Gould set out with others to create a venue for displaying fine art photography, and that venue grew to become Camera Obscura in 1979. "Art is in the artist, not in the medium," says Gould, who displays both vintage work and the work of emerging artists here. Back in the Sixties, his gallery exhibited the work of Matthew Brady, whose Civil War photographs represent the first photo documentation of war. Camera Obscura gave fine art photographer Sebastião Salgado his first show in America and showcased the nature photography of James Balog. Gould displays his black and white work here, which includes Western themes. The Camera Obscura is one of the oldest, if not the oldest, gallery in the country devoted exclusively to fine art photography. The gallery offers archival framing with an eye to special matting and composition. It also features the largest selection of photographic books in Colorado. Come see photography in a whole new light with a visit to the Camera Obscura Gallery.

1309 Bannock Street, Denver CO
(303) 623-4059
www.cameraobscuragallery.com

Health & Beauty

Salon Hether's

While cutting and styling hair since 1984, Hether Champlain felt like she needed more, so she opened a salon in Olde Towne Arvada in 1999. Her positive energy can be felt as soon as you walk in the door. Lila Neigh of the Arvada Economic Development Association certainly feels it. "Hether's is a fine example of what an upscale shop can be," she says. "Customers come from throughout the metro Denver area, the state of Colorado and some even fly from other states to visit Hether's. Historic Olde Towne Arvada is proud to have such an innovative and distinctive enterprise, which draws a sophisticated and polished clientele to our area." The salon is such a great place to work that the majority of Hether's employees have been with her for at least four years or longer. They include nail technicians and hair stylists. All are committed to continuing their education so that the service they provide is second to none. Salon Hether's carries Goldwell hair color and hair care products, which is from Germany. It also carries Bumble and bumble hair products, which are available exclusively from New York, and only the top one percent of the salon's in the world are permitted to carry. The salon is located inside a beautifully restored building in the historic district. Call and book an appointment at Salon Hether's. You'll look great as you help build the community.

7423 Grandview Avenue, Arvada CO
(303) 421-8500
www.hethers.com

Photo by Carl Scofield/www.CarlScofield.com

Bodyworks Spa & Massage

Once in a while, existence should be effortless, with everything taken care of for you. For those times, Bodyworks Spa & Massage offers a fulfilling escape from the ordinary with traditional health and beauty treatments from around the world. Owner Jayne Marino opened the spa in 1990, making it the oldest spa in Summit County. Your hosts will treat you as an honored guest, attending to your comfort with natural beauty products and environmental purifiers such as ozone and ultraviolet light. Body scrubs, wraps and facials at the spa incorporate such natural healing ingredients as wildflower honey, yogurt, oats, essential oils and exotic spices. Enjoy the comfort of steaming hot towels with the Japanese facial and foot massage or exfoliate with a Swedish Dry Brush Scrub. You can nourish the tissue around your eyes with a collagen eye treatment or loose inches and reduce the appearance of cellulite with a detoxifying herbal body wrap. Get ready for summer with a Brazilian Bikini wax. Talented massage therapists use hot stones, aromatherapy, acupressure and energy work as well as Swedish, deep tissue and pregnancy massages. Everyone loves a spa gift certificate. Bodyworks' certificates never expire and come wrapped in pretty paper with ribbons and wildflowers. Take mind, body and soul on a nourishing spa journey with the highly trained staff at Bodyworks Spa & Massage.

101 Forest Drive, Unit L, Frisco CO
(970) 668-5859
www.friscobodyworks.com

Amara
Massage Therapy Center

The goal at Amara Massage Therapy Center is to make life better in a natural way. Owner and therapist Mike Mazza has a personal approach to massage therapy. To make sure every client receives the best possible care, each one is interviewed and matched with the most appropriate expert therapist. All staff members have at least 1,000 hours of training and a strong dedication to health and wellness. One of the main benefits of massage is to increase blood circulation and lymph flow, bringing fresh oxygen to the tissues. Studies show that massage significantly increases the number of white blood cells, enhancing your immunity as well as lowering stress, anxiety and tension. The deep tissue massage is designed to relieve pain; the results are often wonderful. Sports and medical massages help muscles become more pliable and can aid in recovery from injury. Hot stone treatments work through tired and sore muscles. Amara's spa treatments include the sea nutrients hydrator. For some great add-on treats, try the honey sugar foot scrub, a sweet way to enliven the senses. Or bring complete relaxation to your massage through aroma therapy—you can choose any of ten aroma blends. In a world of deadlines and schedules, be sure to take some time and enjoy a massage at Amara Massage Therapy Center.

100 W Olive Street, Fort Collins CO
(970) 484-2629
www.amaramassage.com

Cohayla Salon & Spa

Who is the most important person in your life? Your compassion is admirable if someone other than yourself comes to mind. Maybe it indicates that you haven't been nice enough to yourself lately. The dedicated and caring professionals at Cohayla Salon & Spa would like to change that by putting you first. They offer a full menu of salon and spa services designed to pamper your body and spirit. Relax in the jetta tub, indulge in a facial or enjoy a therapeutic massage or body wrap. You can even come out of Cohayla Salon & Spa sporting a sexy tan after spending time in the tanning booth. Owner Kymm Barton's seasonal pedicures—namely, the peppermint scrub in winter and the margarita scrub in summer—are extremely popular. A nail tech for 15 years, she decided about eight years ago to go back to school to add new areas of expertise to her repertoire. She now handles all aspects of hair, including cutting, coloring and perms. Sensitive to the mood of each customer, the staff wants you to relax and feel at home whether you come in to enjoy a quiet day or to socialize and chat. Remember, the emphasis is on you at Cohayla Salon & Spa, so shed your responsibilities and let yourself be pampered.

1515 Main Street, #A, Longmont CO   (303) 651-0499
www.cohayla.com

Narcissus Hair Salon

The historic building on Grand Avenue in Glenwood Springs has been a barber shop since 1907, and in 1997 tradition met innovation with the opening of Narcissus Hair Salon. Owner Sharon Wright was a hairdresser for 17 years before realizing the dream of her own salon. At Narcissus, she leads one of the best-trained hairdressing teams in the state and has been voted Best Local Hairdresser in the *Post Independent* Locals Choice awards. Narcissus is an Aveda concept salon, and Aveda is a hair-styling institution known for its environmentally-conscious products and business ethics. Sharon believes in continuous training, and Aveda offers some of the most advanced training in the industry. Stylists Sara, Natalie, Nicole and Jenifer know all about the latest hair cutting techniques and are expert colorists. Aveda hair color is naturally derived from plants and minerals, free of ammonia and less harmful to your hair and health than alternative products. Aveda shampoos, conditioners and other goods offer simple, natural solutions to common hair problems. Aveda sources its ingredients from sustainable farms and traditional communities all over the world. Like Aveda, Sharon runs a thoughtful business at Narcissus, where you'll never be just a number. Come to Narcissus Hair Salon for cutting-edge hair solutions that will make you feel great about your hair and the your impact on the earth.

726 Grand Avenue, Glenwood Springs CO   (970) 945-4247
www.narcissushairsalon.com

Colorado's Pro Gym

Colorado's Pro Gym has brought fitness and good shape to the Wheatridge community since 1995. You'll find fitness programs here to suit every member of the family. Whether it's weight-lifting programs or sports training, Colorado's Pro Gym is up to the task. If you're simply out of shape and want to get buffed up a bit, this neighborhood gym can help. Weight-lifters will find all the equipment they need. The serious body builder can make good use of all of the gym's popular aerobic and weight-training machines. All of the staff are involved in the pursuit of fitness themselves and are qualified to help you meet your goals. Owner Harry George is committed to your good health and a fit body. He knows that the personal relationship between you and your trainer works best when your goals are matched with your trainer's expertise, forming a bond of trust that brings the results you desire. The gym is currently expanding its women's programs, especially in aerobics. Unlike high-priced clubs, Colorado's Pro Gym offers reasonably priced programs and packages that will benefit your wallet as well as your physique. Join Harry and his team at Colorado's Pro Gym and get the shape you desire.

4240 Kipling, Unit B, Wheatridge CO   (303) 456-0076
www.coloradoprogym.com

City Drug

Oh, what a fun store. City Drug looks like a set for a 1960s sitcom, and in many ways, a trip to City Drug is a trip to a bygone era. In fact, the history of the business goes back further than that. City Drug is the oldest surviving business in Fort Collins and traces its origins to 1873. Housed in an old time building with older fixtures, "it isn't retro, it just is," says Berni Wilkins, pharmacist and co-owner. Charles and Silvia Wilkins, daughter Barbara and son Berni all work at the store. The pharmacy is the heart of the business. City Drug pharmacists have degrees in both pharmacy and chemistry, they do compound prescriptions and they give their customers a quick turnaround time. City Drug also offers a full range of durable medical equipment such as rollabouts, wheelchairs, hospital beds and lift chairs for both sale and rent. All four of the Wilkins are certified orthotic fitters, and a large fitting room provides both comfort and privacy. The shop stocks the largest selection of compression stockings in Northern Colorado. Other wares include gifts, foods, household goods and toys from Europe and other countries. City Drug also carries a collection of Colorado, Fort Collins and Colorado State University souvenirs. If you can't find it anywhere else, try City Drug. The store's in-house museum exhibits period medicine bottles and many other historically intriguing items. Come to City Drug, where you'll receive personal care and concern that remind you of visiting an old friend.

101 S College Avenue, Fort Collins CO
(970) 482-1234

Figaro's Salon

Keeping abreast of the latest European hair designs has been the concern of Figaro's Salon since 1973. Customizing these designs to capture the spirit, style and attitude of each client is the challenge that the team of stylists accepts with pride daily. "I believe no two lives are the same and such should be said for a hair color and cut," says owner Sung Park. He oversees a salon that breeds loyalty both in his staff and his customers. Indeed, many clients have been getting their hair done by the same stylist at this establishment for more than 10 years. Among the corps of regulars are even a few who have called Figaro's their salon for the 30 years it's been in business. Ask the owner what sets his place apart from the competition, and he will quickly say that it's the experience and dedication of his professional team. These stylists routinely turn skeptics into believers, as clients come to them doubting that the latest style is for them, only to leave praising their new look. Professional skin care and nails to perfection are other specialties. Try Figaro's Salon for the hair cutting and coloring ideas that are sweeping Denver.

5494 E Evans Avenue, Denver CO
(303) 691-9110
www.figarossalon.com

A Colour of Harmony

On some days, you might be able to restore harmony to your life with hair color and a perky new cut. On other days, you are going to need the works—a pedicure, manicure, facial and massage. This long-standing salon began in 1988 under a different name, and since the beginning the lucky folks in Dillon have turned to these professionals to fine-tune body and soul. A Colour of Harmony often fits in last-minute tourists, too. The family-owned and -operated business offers generous hours, including convenient evening hours. Husband and wife owners James and Lisa Rode are the professional hair stylists and colorists. They form strong relationships with individual clients and offer counseling on many aspects of health and beauty, including diet and skin care. Guests can also choose from a range of massage treatments to condition tired muscles or provide deep relaxation. Body wraps, such as the detox treatment, improve the look and function of your body. Much of the clientele at A Colour of Harmony comes through referrals, which means loyal customers are walking around with some spare change, because the Rodes discount services by $25 to $40 each time you bring in a new customer. When life takes away your tranquility, get it back with a visit to A Colour of Harmony.

325 Lake Dillon Drive, Suite 104, Dillon CO
(970) 485-1136
www.acolourofharmony.com

Cha Do Day Spa

Cha Do Day Spa has been located inside the historic Antlers Hilton in downtown Colorado Springs for 20 years. Their longevity stems from the expertise of their staff and the quality of the treatments. At Cha Do, you will find a wide range of packages and treatments, from a Quickie Retreat, where you'll get a manicure, pedicure, mini-facial and hair style, to full-day treatments where every aspect of your wellness will be considered. Owned by Kerry Earle, Cha Do employs the services of world renowned massage therapist Ruby Singh and 13 highly trained technicians. People come into Cha Do for the tranquility, and they keep coming back because of the quality. At Cha Do, your long-term well-being is the main concern. Signature services include a cellulite body wrap, Synergy Anti-Aging Treatments, a grape peel pedicure, and their popular couple's night, where you and the one you love will be pampered, caressed, and massaged with a series of treatments guaranteed to transform your body, mind and spirit. The next time you visit Colorado Springs, take time to visit one of the most remarkable spas in Colorado.

60 S Cascade Avenue, Colorado Springs CO (719) 577-4441
www.chadospa.com

Femme Fitale

Owner Christine Neff calls the workout gear at Femme Fitale functional equipment, because it requires your body to do the stabilizing. Balance boards, medicine balls and free weights are some of the circuit training tools used at the all-female Boulder gym, opened in 2006. Christine specializes in pre-designed workouts that target individual goals. You can train specifically for skiing, triathlons, rock climbing,

weight loss or a healthy pregnancy at the 24-hour gym. Christine spent 14 years as a personal trainer before opening her gym. She wants women to operate with pride, self-confidence and a positive body image. Being crunched for time interferes with many fitness goals, so Christine seeks ways to help you fit a workout into your busy day. Her ConSHEerge service works together with local businesses to get some of your chores done while you work out. Order groceries online from Aspen Grove Market to pick up when your workout is over, or get your oil changed next door at Jiffy Lube. You can also have a healthy meal delivered to your door or someone run your errands for you. Christine knows that when you take care of your body, you can handle the demands of your life. Are you ready to tackle your fitness goals? Then visit Femme Fitale.

1810 30th Street, Suite F, Boulder CO (303) 489-1505
www.femmefitale.com

On Broadway Hair Studio & The Boulder Spa

Whether you come in for a cut, color or perm or try a spa treatment or facial, you can be sure the products used at On Broadway Hair Studio & The Boulder Spa are plant-based and easy on you and the environment. On Broadway's founder, David Martinez, and co-owner Joy Lanzano use the Aveda brand, because they like Aveda's natural products, its proactive stance on the environment and the Fair Trade partnerships it makes with indigenous people. You can choose aromatherapy with a therapeutic massage and melt away stress with such lavish body treatments as the calming Caribbean Therapy and the invigorating Eucalyptus Mud Wrap. Still other treatments use salt and fragrant herbs for relaxation and deep cleansing. A Vichy shower is part of every spa treatment. Bridal parties come for updos and makeup applications. On Broadway is serious about our planet's health and does its part by recycling and operating a wind-powered facility. It also supports local charities. It was named an Aveda Earth Month Hero in 2005 and 2006. Be good to yourself with a visit to On Broadway.

380 Arapahoe Avenue, Boulder CO (303) 444-0330
www.boulderspa.com

Breckenridge Hair Company

Breckenridge Hair Company, the longest running salon in Breckenridge, buzzes with energy as a dynamic crew of seven stylists, three manicurists and an esthetician ply their trade while keeping things merry. They've been known to break into song at the mention of a phrase that sparks a musical memory. Working at this salon is a dream job for these folks, many of whom can claim longevity of 10

years or more. Hair design and hair color are specialties, as well as perms and highlighting, and scores of loyal customers drive nearly an hour and a half from Denver to get theirs. The staff especially looks forward to those days when an entire wedding party is scheduled to come in for hair services, facials and manicures. Melanie Gallegos began doing hair at the salon in 1993 and soon became one of those happy professionals who couldn't imagine working anywhere else. Located on a corner off Main Street, this business has been part of the community since 1979. When it went up for sale in 2004, Melanie jumped at the chance to own it. She and her staff contribute to charitable projects galore, often donating their earnings to help fight breast cancer. Get acquainted with the upbeat personalities who make Breckenridge Hair Company such a joyful place to visit.

100 W Ski Hill Road, Breckenridge CO (970) 453-0800

Ambrosia Day Spa & Salon

The staff at Ambrosia hasn't taken an official survey, but it has noticed that people don't seem to require a special reason to treat themselves these days. Sure, ladies preparing for their weddings and proms are among those scheduling appointments for a hair styling, facial or relaxing massage. But a simple case of the winter blues or long-overdue Girls Day Out is just as good an excuse to visit Ambrosia, whose name evokes delicious aromas and a place of refuge and renewal. Ambrosia had been open just four months when it received the *Greeley Tribune* Readers' Choice Award for Favorite Day Spa. "I was humbled and very appreciative of the honor," said owner Julie Mackenzie, who leads a highly trained staff at the spa, including her daughter Nicole. You'll find specialists in such exotic services as Belavi Facelift Massage, eyelash extensions and high-style hair cutting using clipper, razor and dry cutting techniques. Or come to Ambrosia for routine waxing and nail treatments in a relaxing atmosphere. No matter what your reason for visiting, close your eyes and let the staff at Ambrosia take care of you.

1919 65th Avenue, Suite 4, Greeley CO
(970) 330-6811
www.ambrosia-dss.com

Photos by Brad Edwards Photography

Salon Mariani

Jennifer Mariani, owner of Salon Mariani, is a professional
dedicated to providing the best in products and services.
All of her staff are highly qualified experts with years of
experience. Salon Mariani has been newly remodeled
and is fresh, contemporary, comfortable and conveniently
located. A full-service facility, Salon Mariani offers cuts
and styles for men, women, teens and children. You can
have your hair colored or add highlights with confidence,
knowing your stylist hears what you want and can deliver.
Whether you add curls or have them relaxed, you will look
stunning. The salon specializes in hair extensions. It also
has products to promote hair growth and deep conditioning
treatments that give your hair that strong and healthy look.
Be sure to try the lavender steam-towel conditioning for
an extra-special treat. For a designer brow, try the salon's
skillful waxing services. Salon Mariani offers complete nail
services, including manicure, pedicure, fiber or silk tips and
acrylics. Talented make-up artists are on staff as well. All
products used in the salon are diversion free, that is, you can
only find them in professional salons. This helps ensure that
the highest standards are maintained. Visit Salon Mariani
for friendly, accommodating and professional service.

9956 W Remington Place, Littleton CO
(303) 979-5300

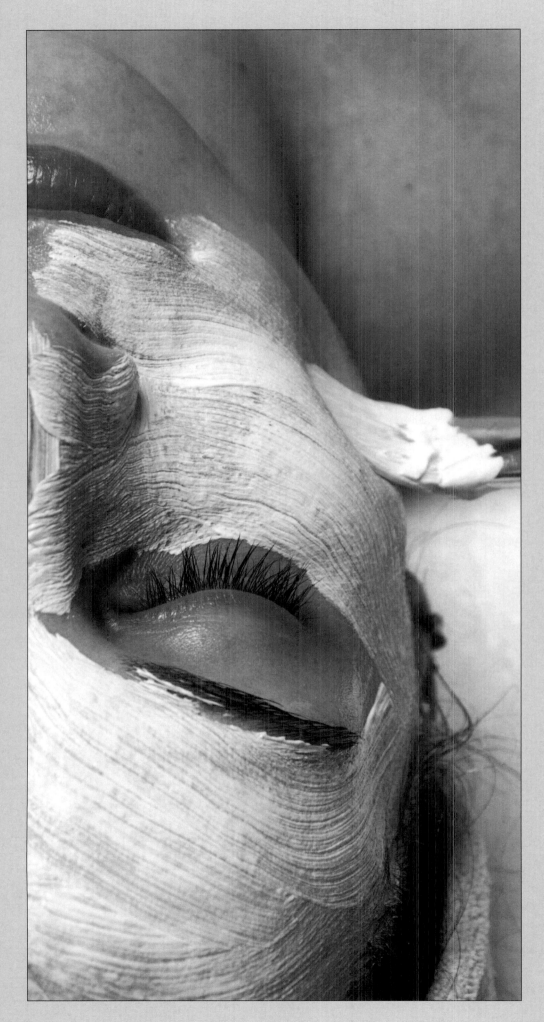

Mystic Garden Spa and Salon

A beautiful mural, rustic garden furniture and a bubbly fountain state the garden theme as soon as you walk into Mystic Garden Spa and Salon. When Shirley Kasperbauer opened her spa, her goal was to create the most relaxing place possible for her clients. For inspiration, she looked to the garden in her own yard. "It's my serenity and my refuge," says Shirley, "a place where I can go when I'm feeling stressed." The menu of packages and a la carte services at the spa builds on the theme. The Gardener's Integrative Massage is a blissful whole-body treatment designed to treat sore muscles after a day of digging and planting or other labors. Spa packages featuring facials, peels and mud treatments bear such creative names as the Garden of Eden and Tilling the Soil. For aromatherapy, you can choose from as many scents as ride the breeze in a botanical garden. Shirley had 30 years of experience as a hair stylist when she started her own business, so understandably hair services are a specialty. You can also get your tan in the rays of the Mystic Garden. Shirley and her team cater to wedding and birthday parties and to friends and family seeking to spend a day of relaxation together. Find a fine assortment of beauty, spa and bath goods at Shirley's place. Book an appointment at Mystic Garden Spa and Salon, a restorative sanctuary for body, mind and spirit.

600 Airport Road, Building C, Suite D, Longmont CO
(303) 774-2541
www.mysticgardenspaandsalon.com

Wind Water Vibe Center

Cleansing your body of toxins from the inside out is as easy as stepping inside the Wind Water Vibe Center. This metaphysical store provides the tools to energize and invigorate your body and soul. Visitors are immediately drawn to the trademarked VIBE (Vibrational Integrational Bio-photonic Energy) machine. This energy device uses an electromagnetic field to bring the vibrational level of your body back to its natural state of being. The first VIBE session is always free. The EB cellular ionic bath is for relaxing and restoring your feet using positive charges through your body and out your feet into the soothing water bath. Wind Water Vibe Center also offers massage therapy and acupuncture. Healing stones, crystals, incense, aromatherapy candles and essential oils are available for purchase, as well as a myriad of books. The co-owners are Suzanne Engrav and Cynthia Morger. Take time to explore a new world of calm, peace and good health waiting for you at the Wind Water Vibe Center.

931 12th Street, Greeley CO (866) 915-6224
www.windwatervibecenter.com

Hair Atelier

It's like going to a friend's house to get your hair done. That's how customers describe the experience at Hair Atelier. The fact that the salon is located inside an old house certainly contributes to the feeling. Rooms are separated, resulting in a semi-private atmosphere in which guests can relax and get comfortable. It goes without saying that all members of the dynamic hairdressing team are skilled at what they do, whether it be cutting, coloring or threading. What deserves special note is that owner Ann Marie Craven only hires hairdressers who are gifted, upbeat and a lot of fun. The divas with attitude are welcome to work elsewhere. Hair Atelier has been around since 1975. Ann Marie, a native Coloradan, became a big fan of the place when she moved to Fort Collins after high school. Jumping at the opportunity to buy the salon when it came up for sale, she now feels like she is living out her dream, and she strives every day to communicate her joy in running such a great business. Walk-ins are welcome at Hair Atelier, located in the heart of Old Town. Consider making this salon with the friendly attitude your choice for hair care.

330 E Mulberry Street, Fort Collins CO (970) 482-0461
www.hairatelier.com

Cabana Salon & Spa

Many customers have experienced every service that Leslie Thomas and her staff provide at the Cabana Salon & Spa. Their willingness to try everything is a credit to the affordable prices. "Plus," says Leslie, "we have everything that anyone could need," including hair, waxing and massage services in addition to nail care, facials and sunless tanning. The homey atmosphere also has a lot to do with the repeat visits. Leslie runs her business with the heart of a social director who genuinely enjoys being around people and getting to know her customers. She says that she has been to posh salons and that she is trying for something different in her business. If you are looking for a salon and spa where you can relax and be the tender-hearted, wise-cracking or even lovably grouchy person that you are, then Leslie and her staff would love to see you at the Cabana. Booking a Cabana Package is a great way to get acquainted. For two hours of pure luxury that will get you ready to face anything, try the facial and full-body massage package. Cabana is also the place to shop for salon products and, curiously enough, sunglasses. "Because the sun is always shining at Cabana," explains Leslie, who hopes to see you many times.

1119 W Drake Road, Fort Collins CO (970) 472-1111

Donna Bella, Sensual Dance & Fitness for the Everyday Woman

At Donna Bella, Sensual Dance & Fitness, women are discovering their sexy side, which they never knew or forgot they had. They are also finding that pole dancing, sensual dance, hula hoop and belly dancing are a lot more fun than the typical drudgery of using weights or a treadmill to burn calories. The Donna Bella approach to fitness encompasses working out the entire mind, body & soul, providing women with increased self esteem, confidence and empowerment as each student begins to realize just how beautiful they really are. All classes combine yoga and pilates with sensual movement which combines fitness with a sexy twist. Donna Bella is run by women for women in a safe, non judgmental environment where they feel cherished and begin to love themselves. Edwards says that all women are beautiful, regardless of the age, shape or size. Real woman do not come airbrushed as they do on TV or in magazines and they are tired of society's definition of beautiful. The average client, who ranges between 25 and 65, arrives unsure of what she is getting into. Many have taken classes out of curiosity, as a part of a team building activity, or booked a private party lesson for a special occasion. They find the experience so exhilarating, they want to take all of the classes offered. Women are so excited about this new concept that they have driven over 2 hours to attend the classes. One client said that she was a very shy woman before taking the classes, but she now understands the meaning of walking with confidence. Every woman needs to experience this. Dancing and working out at Donna Bella has changed lives. This is what being a sensual, confidence & fit woman is all about.

6811 W 120th Avenue, Broomfield CO
(303) 466-1387
www.donnabelladance.com

Tonic Oxygen Bar

The Colorado mountain air is fresh and invigorating, but customers are breathing something even more remarkable at the Tonic Oxygen Bar. They come in to sit back on couches and inhale a stream of aroma-infused, 85 to 90 percent pure oxygen. Sessions last anywhere

from 10 to 40 minutes and customers report an increase in energy, clearer thinking and relief from stress after regular visits. The oxygen comes in a variety of flavors and aromas. Try a blend of rosemary, juniper and nutmeg for energy, or the eucalyptus, peppermint and spruce blend for respiration. The lavender is said to be calming, while sandalwood supposedly helps eradicate negativity. Medical experts agree that breathing deeply is important for good health, yet most people typically fail to do so, either out of habit or as a reaction to stress. The owners of Tonic Oxygen Bar aim to change that by offering a tranquil setting for health-conscious people to practice deep, relaxed breathing. An oxymassage combines an oxygen session with a chair massage. The bar also serves healthful teas, fruit juices mixed with Chinese herbs and other elixirs. Fill your lungs with the pure prana at Tonic Oxygen Bar.

2011 10th Street, Boulder CO (303) 544-0202

Photo by Tim D' Antonio/D' Antonio Photography

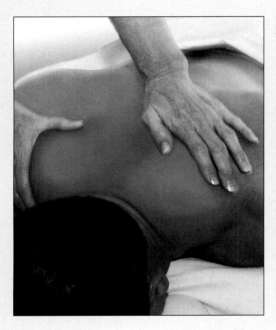

Able Body Massage Therapy

Marietta "Marita" Kerby started Able Body Massage Therapy in 1985, graduating from the Boulder College of Massage Therapy, and is dedicated to improved health through bodywork. Marita's skills relieve pain and discomfort, increase circulation, and improve muscle function and flexibility. Massages are by appointment and Marita keeps flexible hours to accommodate clients' needs. "Regular massage teaches you to listen to your body," says Marita. "You learn to recognize your body's warning signs of stress and tension and are able to do preventive care, keeping yourself healthy." Stress causes muscle tension and reduces optimal body functioning even as injuries from accidents and sports do. Athletes use Marita to recover from workouts and improve performance. Supple muscles cannot pinch nerves or contribute to chronic pain. Increased circulation improves all tissue by accelerating toxin removal. Marita is a Reiki Master and expert in deep tissue, trigger point, orthopedic, sports, PUSH and myofascial release. She helps clients recover from injuries, surgeries, TMJ, chronic pain, stress and more. Add more detoxifying with ionic foot baths. Maintain your well being with regular visits to Able Body Massage Therapy.

1244 S Wadsworth Boulevard, Lakewood CO
(303) 936-6646
www.ablebodymassagetherapy.com

Frizz

Does getting your hair done make you feel like a million bucks? Does getting a massage put you at peace with the universe? They will at Frizz, where you can get both, plus many other services designed to bring out your beauty and nourish your spirit. From facials and body care to waxing, nail care and tints, owner Colleen Herman and her staff do it all. The list of massage options alone is extensive. The buzz that this full-service salon and spa created upon opening in the Cherry Creek area in 2006 has yet to die down. Frizz has been nominated for the A–list, a recognition of the best local businesses sponsored by a Denver television station. Being very picky in hiring stylists is paying off for Colleen. Her clients appreciate service by the most experienced and knowledgeable professionals in the field. The professional tone is set by the tasteful and squeaky clean look of the salon itself. The staff approaches its work with dedication and seriousness, yet is friendly and approachable. Clients love to linger and shoot the breeze. Treat yourself to a feel-good day by going to Frizz.

235 Fillmore Street #280, Denver CO (303) 377-4100
www.frizzsalon.com

Home & Garden

Indochine

It didn't take Hugo Brooks long to discover that Boulder and Asian imports were a perfect match. Locals and visitors alike flocked to his store, Indochine, right from the start. In 1995, just two years after opening, he added a 10,000-square-foot warehouse for all the furniture, home accents and antiques that wouldn't fit in the showroom. By 2003, the store had doubled its original size. Indochine features many hand-crafted pieces made from rare woods, metals and stones. Tables, chairs and architectural design pieces are among the best-sellers. The inventory moves in and out fast, so you had better snatch that lovely tea set or captivating garden statue if you really want it. Owning the store keeps Hugo connected to the cultures he experienced when he was younger. After graduating from college, he lived in various places in Asia for six years, developing an affinity for the styles and traditions in this part of the world. He continues to travel to Asia and the Pacific Rim countries, meeting traders and craftsmen and purchasing items for Indochine directly from them. Eliminating the middleman allows them to keep prices low. Add Asian flair to your home by shopping at Indochine.

Store: 2525 Arapahoe Avenue, Boulder CO
(303) 444-7734
Warehouse: 1779 Valtec Lane, Boulder CO
(720) 565-8262
www.homeimport.com

Fossil Creek Nursery

Ft. Collins gardeners find the plants, the inspiration and the expertise they need at Fossil Creek Nursery, which sits on 15 park-like acres overlooking Benson Reservoir. Many gardeners appreciate the nursery's bare-root trees and shrubs, available in early spring. The staff here can give advice on how to plant these affordable and reliable specimens. As the season progresses, the nursery teems with annuals, perennials and container-grown trees. Getting started can be the most daunting part of any garden project. Fossil Creek offers a jump start with personal gardeners who will visit your site, make design suggestions and provide professional drawings. Although there is a fee for the service, customers receive coupons from the nursery that allow them to apply the cost of the service towards plant selections. Each year, the nursery offers seminars on such topics as water gardening, pruning, irrigation and container gardening. When pests threaten your plants, simply bring a sample of the pest or the problem and let the staff suggest a solution. Local families look forward to special events held on the nursery grounds, such as an annual Easter egg hunt. You can also celebrate Apple Fest here with apple tasting, carriage rides and pumpkin bowling. The staff invite you to take a stroll through Fossil Creek Nursery.

7029 S College Avenue, Ft. Collins CO
(970) 226-4924
www.fossilcreeknursery.com

Raven Architectural Artifacts & Antiques

Owners David and Lori Bredemeier combine their passion and flair for collecting and salvaging items from the past to bring you the eclectic shop called Raven Architectural Artifacts & Antiques. Raven's ever-changing inventory provides early American antiques and other architectural design elements that can create a stunning focal point in your home or office. Specializing in primitive and unusual pieces, the Bredemeiers offer a wide variety of choices for beginning and seasoned collectors. Highlight your table settings with decorative glass and dishware. Vintage birdhouses, dazzling fountains and eye-pleasing ironworks create an aura of whimsy in your garden. Raven buys and sells in all categories including architectural, vintage bath and garden, farmhouse and country, cabin and rustic items. Truly, there is something for everyone. If you are restoring an older home, you'll uncover hard-to-find pieces to personalize your dream house. Raven is a full-service dealer that offers estate and auction services, on-site appraisals and free local pick-up and delivery. Patrons come from miles around to buy antiques and soak up the atmosphere. If you've got a story to tell, you can always find an audience here. Stop by Raven Architectural Artifacts & Antiques to browse, buy or just enjoy a delightful stroll into the past.

600 N 2nd Street, La Salle CO
(970) 284-0921

Earth, Wood and Fire

From wood stoves to warm the winter night to hot tubs that enhance a summer eve, Earth, Wood and Fire has all your seasons covered. Owner Scott Hudgin began installing wood stoves in 1983. In the early 1990s, he brought Mike Cash on board as well as their spouses, Fran and Terri. Together, the foursome plotted to extend their offerings to fireplaces and hot tubs. Suppliers include the finest vendors available. Beachcomber hot tubs bring elegance and comfort to your backyard. Vermont Castings BBQ grills add flair to your summer meals. Heat & Glo, Lopi, Avalon and Fireplace Extraordinair fireplaces and stoves supply efficient heat to any room in your house. Choose between gas, wood or pellet models, antique or cast iron. A full line of accessories such as wood, gas, and pellets are also available. The co-owners offer complete installation, servicing and repair on everything they sell. In the early planning stages, the co-owners enjoyed a glass of wine and the mellow tunes of the band Earth, Wind and Fire, hence the business name. Whether you're adding some warmth your home, upgrading your vacation cabin or adding some highlights to your place of business, call on the experts at Earth, Wood and Fire.

3313 35th Avenue #A, Evans CO
(970) 506-WOOD (9663)
www.earthwoodandfire.net

Castle Cleaning & Oriental Rug Company

Phil and Virginia Auserehl, owners of Castle Cleaning & Oriental Rug Company, offer high quality handmade rugs and a proprietary system of cleaning your rugs and other textiles that is thorough yet gentle. Their Berthoud showroom resembles an art gallery or museum more than a retail store, showcasing handmade artifacts from around the world and scores of one-of-a-kind rugs that they've collected over more than 30 years. Phil's motto is Real Rugs at Real Savings, and their upfront pricing, minus the haggling, lets customers enjoy the experience. Phil and Ginny want to be your rug consultants, not salespeople. They offer free decorating advice and show you the difference in a $5,000 rug and a $10,000 rug so you can invest your money wisely. "We don't sell you a rug," says Phil. "You can buy one from us, but without the knowledge and education, one cannot make a smart decision." The flip side of their business, Castle Cleaning, offers the Auserehlian Cleaning System, a world-renowned rug cleaning process that Phil developed. By utilizing compressed air and a submersion bath, rugs and other textiles are cleaned thoroughly yet safely. Cleaners come from all over the world to become specialists in this authentic hand-washing technique. Castle Cleaners also does expert repairs, reweaving and appraisals of fine rugs. Stop by, browse and enjoy a unique shopping experience at Castle Cleaning & Oriental Rug Company.

565 Third Street, Berthoud CO
(970) 532-2187
www.orientalrugcleaning.com

Groundcovers Greenhouse and Nursery

Owner Keri Luster knows that when it comes to planting a successful garden, quality starter plants make a difference. At Groundcovers Greenhouse and Nursery, Keri backs her starters with a five-year warranty on shrubs and trees and a three-year warranty on perennials. Keri is the second-generation owner of the Denver-based Groundcovers, started by her parents, Gary and Alison Luster, in 1980. Standing out among a myriad of garden shops can be challenging, but Keri manages it, winning a Best Neighborhood Nursery award from *Westword* magazine in 2000. The shop carries a large selection of decorative pieces, including concrete birdbaths and fountains for every taste. Your vines can climb in style on ornate cast-iron trellises and arches. Everybody smiles when they see a resin fox, toad or bunny peaking out of the greenery. You'll also find appealing hanging baskets, including sphagnum baskets that create big balls of bloom, and staff to help you make the right plant choices. Keri attracts customers year-round, adding pumpkins in the fall and Christmas trees and poinsettias during the holidays. She enjoys bringing the neighborhood together and holds an annual Ladies Nite, an opportunity to show off your handmade arts and crafts. For gardens that get noticed, come to Groundcovers Greenhouse and Nursery.

4301 E Iliff Avenue, Denver CO
(303) 758-8957

Backyards Plus

Everyone needs a vacation, but with the rising cost of fuel and increased airport security travel seems more complicated than it once did. What if you could create a vacation paradise in your own backyard? Whether your fantasy is lounging in a hot tub surrounded by forest, musing on a bench in a quiet garden courtyard or gathering with the family around a fire pit in the twilight with the sound of a waterfall in the background, Backyards Plus can put it within steps of your door, year-round. To explore the possibilities for your backyard, visit the impressive showroom on I-25 or visit the website for hundreds of outdoor living photo ideas.

5010 Acoma Street, Denver CO
(303) 635-0085
www.backyardsplus.com

O'Toole's Garden Center

Since 1979, O'Toole's Garden Center has supplied the community with top-notch plants, garden supplies and service. The nursery has an appealing neighborhood feel even as it stocks an inventory that rivals the large chain stores. Friendly and knowledgeable staff members can answer all of your gardening questions and direct you to choices that suit your needs. Low prices and an unbeatable selection have earned the nursery a loyal and dedicated following. Each week, a new or unusual variety is the featured plant, giving you a chance to learn about a new idea for your landscape or home. Along with perennials, bedding plants, roses and bulbs, O'Toole's Garden Center carries an wide choice of grasses to suit any situation. Colorado's Choice Water Saver Lawn food is the center's recommended fertilizer for area lawns. For landscaping needs, choose from an array of trees and shrubs. Patio pots and hanging basket arrangements can fill your porch, patio and balcony with glorious color. Tomato lovers love the huge variety in stock. The nursery is also known for its excellent selection of Christmas trees. Founder Jim O'Toole was known as a man of great integrity, and today's owner Adele O'Toole carries on his tradition. O'Toole's Garden Center believes in giving back to the community and is a generous donor to local schools, Scout troops and other charity organizations. If you're a gardening enthusiast, you won't want to miss O'Toole's Garden Center at any of three metro Denver locations. (See the website for the center nearest you.)

1404 Quail Street, Lakewood CO
(303) 232-6868
www.otoolesgardencenters.com

Donath Lake Greenhouses

There's nothing as tasty as fresh garden fruits and vegetables. Donath Lake Greenhouses is home to the largest selection of transplant vegetables in Northern Colorado. Sitting on 54 acres of farmland, the greenhouses offer a wide array of plants, flowers and vegetables. Ranch owners and horse lovers from miles around come to Donath Lake for the quality hay. It's no wonder that the business maintains such a large and loyal customer base with its one-stop-shopping for fresh, natural foods and beautiful perennials. Father and son Ken and Jeff Goldsberry pride themselves on running this H2O-friendly farm. Donath Lake uses a natural pond to water all plants, vegetables and flowers. Because of their commitment to water conservation, Ken and Jeff's greenhouses have flourished through many droughts. In addition to being your feed, seed and weed store, Donath Lake Greenhouses features solariums, skylights and conservatories for sale. Make your home a horticultural haven with these plant-friendly products. Whether you're looking to plant sweet strawberries or create a sanctuary full of wholesome vegetables, Donath Lake Greenhouses can make it happen.

8420 S County Road 13, Fort Collins CO
(970) 663-6636

Picadilly Nursery

Picadilly Nursery started small with just two employees, but today the family-owned and operated business employs 20, thanks to customer loyalty. Attentive customer service is standard, so you'll meet at least one of the staff as soon as you come in. Someone will even walk you through the store if desired to help you select the right bedding plants, shade trees and shrubs for your yard. Dave Rock started growing plants on the family dairy farm in 1984, selling them cheap from that original location in the boonies just to give people a reason to make the drive. The same emphasis on pricing continues as the second generation starts, with Dave's son Davey assisting in managing the nursery. It's not at the expense of quality—Picadilly Nursery grows its stock on 140 acres in Kansas, where horticulturists can watch its progress and nurture it to its full splendor. The retail store in Brighton sits on 10 acres and features a huge selection of plants that are native to Colorado. Take your pick of beautiful trees, flowering plants and bushes at Picadilly Nursery.

21750 E 152nd Avenue, Brighton CO
(303) 659-2382
www.picadillynursery.com

The Koi Lagoon

When you live in the high, dry Rocky Mountains, there's something irresistible about a cool, clear, botanical lagoon. Kathy and Ray Smith have been catering to this thirst since 1997 with the Koi Lagoon, their full-service pond-supply shop. The Smiths always had aquarium fish and an interest in aquatic plants. This grew into a growing and viable business, which funneled into the Koi Lagoon where they run all operations personally, from customer service to design and installation. They can take one look at your property and know instantly what will and won't work on the landscape and how to mechanically achieve your vision. Walking into their shop, you'll enter a cool, blue-green paradise full of exotic plants, Koi and turtles. A magnificent show-pond in the front of the store demonstrates the range of possibilities, including fountains, waterfalls and under-water lights. As you browse the extensive selection, you may meet Fred the giant desert tortoise, who wanders the floor freely. Return customers will find a well-stocked mechanical division for keeping their pond in top shape and looking great. Visit a Koi pond paradise and dream up your own at the Koi Lagoon.

2000 E Lincoln Avenue, Fort Collins CO
(970) 484-9162
www.koilagoon.com

Stickley Fine Furniture

No matter how much you stuff into a Stickley drawer, it will glide smoothly without scraping or sagging. This kind of workmanship, along with appealing styles, has been a trademark of the Stickley brand since Leopold Stickley and his brother John George first began their manufacturing operation in 1900. Today, Stickley has more than 1500 employees, a nationwide dealer network and 13 company showrooms including Westminster and Centennial in Colorado. Unlike most modern furniture, Stickley furniture appreciates as it ages. It is built to exacting standards, marrying time-honored methods of joinery with state-of-the-art machinery. Whether you live in an urban condo, a turn-of-the-century home or a mountain lodge, you'll find Stickley pieces to match your lifestyle, thanks to the ongoing work of the company's in-house design team. Craftspeople carefully sort such fine lumber as the quartersawn white oak, cherry, black walnut and curly maple, using discarded pieces to heat the Manlius, New York factory and employees' homes. Finishes are hand rubbed; hardware is solid brass or copper. Alfred Audi grew up learning to respect the integrity of the Stickley furniture sold in his father's New York furniture store. In 1974, Alfred and Aminy Audi purchased Stickley, assuring the continuity of the Stickley values and the loyalty of the company's exemplary employees. For American furniture you will pass on to your grandchildren, visit Stickley Fine Furniture.

9180 Wadsworth Boulevard, Westminster CO
(303) 467-2777
8130 University Boulevard, Centennial CO
(720) 493-5677
www.stickley.com
www.stickleyaudi.com

Encore! Home Styles

Mother and daughter duo Judi Supplee and Dena Blackburn have great taste. As home stylists, Judi and Dena were urged by their friends and clients to use their talents to open a shop that carried their kind of hip, whimsical and classic home décor. Thus, Encore! Home Styles was born in historical downtown Longmont in 2006. Encore has everything you need to create a customized style for your home, including art, furniture and dishes. You will surely find an item you can't live without at Encore! If you are not sure how to best display your item after taking it home, Dena and Judi will come to you for a consultation, or act as stylists and arrange it for you themselves. Encore! also carries the wildly popular line of cocktail glasses by Lolita. Customers come in daily seeking the distinctive stemware to give as gifts or for their own collections. The inventory at Encore! Home Styles is constantly changing, and the shop owners are committed to providing you with fun shopping. Come in for one visit, and the Encore! Home Styles experience will entice you back for many return visits.

347 Main Street, Longmont CO
(303) 485-7446

Nesch Foundry

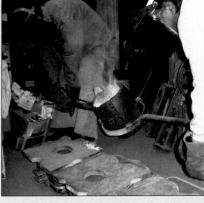

Sand casting is a dying art, says Jim Nesch, but he is too busy doing it to mourn its imminent demise. Specializing in brass, bronze and aluminum castings, Nesch Foundry is one of the few remaining sand casting foundries in the country. It produces, among other things, subdivision signs, memorial plaques and golf putters. Antique car owners hire Jim to make various car parts just like the original. Those restoring old houses see him for specialty door knobs, drawer pulls and lamp parts. The Old Court House in Boulder features Jim's reproductions of door hardware. He's also done work for such historic local hotels as the Armstrong and the Northern. Jim learned his craft from his father, who apprenticed at the Weiner Foundry in Kansas City. Nesch Foundry uses a particularly fine sand called stove plate that comes from the Kansas City region of the Mississippi River. Since Jim assumed sole ownership of the business in 1986, word of mouth has been his biggest advertiser, a testament to the work that he produces. Whether you need one reproduction or several thousand castings, consider bringing your project to Nesch Foundry.

201 N Link Lane, Fort Collins CO
(970) 221-0787
www.neschfoundry.com

Wadoo Furniture Co.

When Amy Satterfield started looking for eclectic art furniture for her home, she had a hard time finding what she wanted in the stores around Ft. Collins. In 2006, she started her own outlet, Wadoo Furniture Company, a shop filled with wall-to-wall color and artistry. The one-of-a-kind furniture pieces here represent the work of more than 40 acclaimed artists and designers from across the United States. Much of the work is award winning, and occasionally Amy will bring together many pieces by a single artist for a special showing. You'll find jewelry, pottery, textiles and many accent pieces here, too. Amy puts it this way: "Here you'll find the one-of-a-kind armoire that gives focus to the room, the necklace everybody notices, the mosaic mirror you hang as fine art, the stop-sign table that starts conversations, the hat that transforms bad hair days into photo ops, lamps that shed light on your character, purposely mismatched socks, and gifts you've never seen before." Because she has an intimate knowledge of each artisan's style, she knows where to turn for custom pieces when you need something that's not on display. The bright and friendly store invites browsing and tends to build excitement as visitors gather ideas from the creative assortment. Amy is always happy to offer insight or advice. When Ordinary Just Won't Do, it's time to visit Wadoo Furniture Company.

314 E Mountain Avenue, Ft. Collins CO (970) 223-4012
www.wadoofurniture.com

Elliott Gardens

You can see the expertly grown annuals, perennials, edibles and bedding plants of Elliott Gardens in garden centers all over the Denver region. For the wholesale price and the complete selection, though, you'll want to visit the gardens themselves. Open April through October, the gardens are owned and operated by William and Donna Elliott with the help of their children, Brett, Bill and Marie. Annuals and perennials are the best-sellers, but there is also a strong crop of vegetables and fresh herbs. During the 1980s, a local chef came to William and Donna and asked them to grow fresh herbs for him. The food industry quickly caught on, and today Elliott Gardens supplies fresh herbs to select grocery stores in the region. William Elliott was a truck farmer when he had the idea to build a greenhouse to help the farming community start plants early. He had so much fun starting plants that he decided to go into the business full-time, bringing his family with him. Today, Elliott Gardens continues the tradition of starting everything from seeds. Find plants brought up right at Elliott Gardens.

6321 Lowell Boulevard, Denver CO
(303) 428-4043
www.elliottgardens.com

Glenwood Gardens

A long history lies behind Glenwood Gardens' greenhouse facility. One of the greenhouses was first built by Colorado Fuel and Iron Corporation founder John Cleveland Osgood to supply flowers for his estate. The greenhouse was moved to West Glenwood Springs after his death. Over the years, it passed hands a few times until the current owners, Hugh and Molly MacPherson, moved to the area specifically to purchase the business in 1992. Glenwood Gardens consists of eight greenhouses on four acres of land, including the famous dome greenhouse built between 1896 and 1906. Glenwood Gardens built its reputation on an excellent selection of annuals, perennials and foliage grown on-site. Laura and Erik MacPherson specialize in custom planters that offer attractive assortments of plants in their prime. These have become a strong asset to the business and very popular with the local community. An eclectic mix of gifts discovered at gift shows throughout the year, along with gardening and plant supplies, are also available for purchase. Allow time to linger when you visit Glenwood Gardens, because you will want to take your time exploring everything there is to see.

51993 Highway 6, Glenwood Springs CO
(970) 945-6747

Splash Home Furnishings and Design

Splash Home Furnishings and Design believes homes are for relaxing. As an exclusive dealer of Sundance Spas, Splash carries beautiful indoor and outdoor hot tubs that are recognized for advanced technology and superior design. Spa shoppers also find a complete line of patio accessories, including seating, umbrellas and fire pits. A second showroom adjacent to the original Splash site in Glenwood Springs focuses on making the bedroom the most relaxing and comfortable room in the home. You'll find a fabulous selection of beds and bedding, including mattresses by Serta and designer Vera Wang. From cozy furnishings to soft lighting and hot tubs, you'll find everything you need to turn your master bedroom into a stress-free sanctuary. "With our superior design staff, we can get a project done quickly," notes Splash owner Alice Pendleton, adding that her designers can accommodate any style, from contemporary, casual and classic to rustic, mountain modern and relaxed Western. Furnish your home for maximum relaxation at Splash Home Furnishings and Design.

2316 Glen Avenue, Glenwood Springs CO
(970) 928-0029
0105 Edwards Village Boulevard, Edwards CO
(970) 926-8185
www.splashhome.net

Garden Thyme

Tonya Dunn and Ivan Andrade, the owners of
Garden Thyme, have been offering horticultural
services for the discerning homeowner for 14
years, which is exactly how long some customers
have been with them. Since day one, the team
at Garden Thyme has been winning clients
over with its high level of professionalism.
Embellishing homes with perennials, annuals
and seasonal falderal is their specialty. The
beautiful results are there for everyone in the
neighborhood to admire. That's why the owners
rarely advertise. Once someone on the block hires
Garden Thyme, the word spreads like wildfire
that this is the company to contact for a beautiful
job done with a professional attitude. Garden
Thyme focuses on upkeep, so customers usually
call them after landscaping has taken place.
Landscape architects and designers love Tonya
and Ivan's work, because it not only maintains
the original look but enhances the beauty of the
garden or yard over time. Garden Thyme works
throughout the year, doing planting, fertilizing
and pruning as well as decorating at Christmas.
Its clients include the owners of many homes
featured on garden tours in and around Ft.
Collins. Find out what Garden Thyme can do
for your home, and you'll be pleased to pass the
word on to the next discerning homeowner.

2660 Bainbridge Street, Ft. Collins CO
(970) 416-9000
http://GardenThyme.net

The West End Gardener

You'll discover something new every time you shop for gardening supplies and accents at the West End Gardener. *Garden Design* has named this nine-year-old store one of the top garden shops in America. Fragrances welcome you and beauty surrounds you as you step into this store. Kim Dunning, a talented gardener, says that her shop was inspired by nature. It is designed, in turn, to inspire those who share her passion for creating beautiful spaces around plants and flowers. The West End Gardener is filled with a mix of vintage and new, including iron benches, granite fountains and birdbaths. It is also the place to find torches, lanterns and unusual pots. For Kim, the shop reflects who she is. "It's a personal creative endeavor," she says. "I am living out who I am every day." Kim started out as a garden designer, creating indoor and outdoor spaces that add charm and coziness to the home and garden. If you have felt the calming effects and curative powers of gardens, Kim speaks your language. You'll get the professional help you deserve when you visit her at the West End Gardener.

777 Pearl Street, Boulder CO
(303) 938-0607
www.westendgardener.com

Birdsall & Co.

A visit to Birdsall will provide you with the inspiration you need to turn your backyard into a beautiful haven. For starters, outdoor furniture, perfect for the patio, is featured at this home and garden shop. Birdsall is an authorized dealer of Barlow Tyrie Teakwood Furniture, regarded as some of the finest outdoor furniture made. Are you thinking of adding a fountain to your garden? Birdsall stocks an astounding variety. To help you weigh the choices, the staff at Birdsall has composed a fact sheet that covers the advantages and disadvantages of each type. Fine garden tools and implements were the original focus of this store, which started with a mere 500 square feet of showroom space in 1988. Gradually trellises, arbors, pots and sculpture added to the mix. With enough merchandise to fill 4,000 square feet of interior space and an additional 7,000 square feet of exterior exhibits, Birdsall is worthy of the attention it has received in several national magazines. Find a home and garden collection to inspire your backyard dreams at Birdsall.

1540 S Broadway, Denver CO
(303) 722-2535
www.birdsallgarden.com

3240 Design and North Larimer Antiques

Just as no two people are alike, no two living spaces should look the same. The eclectic selection of vintage pieces, architectural items, contemporary art and accessories at 3240 Design allows shoppers to achieve a completely customized look, reflecting their individuality. Owner Laura Phelps Rogers opened the shop, gallery, warehouse and design service in Denver's up-and-coming NoBo (North of Broadway) shopping district after many years of collecting art and antiques. Inside the shop, you may find an antique hutch for your dining room or a pair of mid-century turquoise lamps for the bedroom. Neon business signs and 20th century advertising stand in juxtaposition to the quiet elegance of an Asian designed piece or Federal Period mirror. The result is a fun, funky and ever changing place of style and design to shop and gather inspiration. The store even offers guidance, design consultation, supplies for urban gardening as well as western, Native American and tribal items. The gallery participates in First Fridays, staying open late on the first Friday of every month to introduce patrons to local artists. Give your home a splash of personality with a little help from 3240 Design and North Larimer Antiques.

3240 Larimer Street, Denver CO
(303) 292-0076
www.3240design.com

The Rock Garden

From the great pyramids to the Great Wall of China, some of the world's most awe-inspiring landmarks have been made of stone. The Rock Garden has what you need to create your own natural stone masterpiece. A leading supplier of stone to architects, masonry contractors and landscape designers, this company also makes its product available to homeowners for such projects as retaining walls, fireplaces and patios. The retail outlet is itself made of stone and serves as a showcase. Look closely and notice that no two pieces are exactly alike, though each is striking in its color and texture. Owner Jim Striggow says that finding new sources and methods of presenting stone is a passion that goes beyond just doing business. Professionals value the Rock Garden's stone for many reasons, including its contemporary earth tones, obvious beauty and durability. Because the company mines its stones directly from its own quarries in northern Colorado, customers enjoy ready availability, the absence of stone brokers and a high level of quality control. The team of experts at the Rock Garden shares its knowledge of the products with genuine enthusiasm and politeness. They are ready to provide rock solid inspiration for your project, so drop by and let them help you get rocking.

167 Spaulding Lane, Fort Collins CO
(970) 472-1115
www.therockgardensite.com

Walnut Street Woodworks

Tom Deiss and Chris Connors, owners of Walnut Street Woodworks, never know what they will be called upon to make next. It could be a coffee table, an armoire or an entire dining room ensemble. An interior designer might provide them with a detailed draft of a piece of furniture, or they might have nothing more than a homeowner's rough sketch on a napkin to guide them. No two jobs that they undertake are alike, and every chair, desk or cabinet that they create is one of a kind. Tom, Chris and the top-notch craftspeople they employ have been collaborating with clients since 1993 to produce works of functional art that can be passed down through generations. Their specialty of working with veneers allows for elaborate designs with inlays. A Denver couple imported a piece of the world's oldest wood, Kauri, from New Zealand, and had Walnut Street Woodworks make a table from it—a project that was featured on the style pages of the *Denver Post*. Another noteworthy commission was the crafting of about 75 pieces of furniture for the high-end suites at the Hyatt Regency Denver at Colorado Convention Center. Experience the pleasure of being involved in the design process by bringing your ideas for furniture to Walnut Street Woodworks.

3440 Walnut Street, Denver CO
(303) 297-9515
www.woodworkstudio.com

City Floral

Founded in 1911, City Floral is the oldest garden center in the Denver area. Its selection, quality and knowledgeable staff make it one of Denver's favorite garden centers. The 1.5 acre greenhouse has a large selection of annuals, perennials, trees, shrubs, tropicals, roses, aquatic plants, gardening supplies, pottery and fountains in the middle of the city. It also has a large gift shop to treat yourself, a child or a friend to a special find at any time of year. Whether your passion is growing herbs and vegetables or beautiful gardens, City Floral is prepared to get your attention. From aisles filled with hanging baskets and blooming plants in spring to fall mums, bulbs and pumpkins, and Christmas displays of trees, poinsettias and holly, City Floral has the goods gardeners desire all year long at this store. Supplied primarily by local producers, City Floral manages a stellar selection and fair pricing. If you are perplexed over a problem with a plant or a lawn, or just need some new color for your home, bring your concerns to City Floral, where a staff of avid gardeners will diagnose your problem and offer the perfect solution. Turn your garden into the paradise you've dreamed about with a visit to City Floral.

1440 Kearney Street, Denver CO
(303) 399-1177
www.cityfloralgreenhouse.com

The Linen Kist at Vail/Beaver Creek

Nancy Rehder, owner of the Linen Kist at Vail/Beaver Creek, believes that your bedroom should take your breath away when you walk into it at the end of a long day. The bed linens should evoke tranquility, comfort and belonging in their colors, and they should hold the promise of feeling silky and smooth against your skin. Your towels should beckon you into the bath or shower and fill you with the anticipation of being wrapped in plush Egyptian cotton. Offering bed and bath linens since 1989, the Linen Kist is the place to go for an wide range of luxurious fabrics, colors, textures and styles. Brands in stock include Sferra, Anichini, Yves Delorme and Abyss. The shop has a workroom on the premises, so customers have the option of designing their own bedding and bathroom accessories. Nancy, who has lived in the Vail Valley since 1978, handles the custom work along with two other designers. Maggie Brown, a Vail resident since 1972, earns kudos from Nancy for her calm way of dealing with customers' linen emergencies. As for Thanh Nguyen, a native of Vietnam, Nancy says, "Her creative touches are what make her pieces so unique and enjoyable." Drop by the Linen Kist at Vail/Beaver Creek to browse the fine selection, or to put the design team to work for you.

142 Beaver Creek Place, Avon CO
(970) 949-7166
www.thelinenkist.com

Bonzai Kid, Inc.

At Bonzai Kid, owners Shan Liu and Dan Sensho understand the importance of design in all aspects of life. Shan Liu offers web and graphic design while co-owner Dan Sensho, a feng shui consultant and bonsai master, teaches people to reduce stress by communicating with plants. By applying the principles of feng shui, which seeks to balance the five elements of metal, fire, water, earth and wood in one environment, customers can create positive energy in their personal spaces. Bonzai Kid offers bonsai plants, furniture and home décor items as well as custom designed gardens for homes and offices based on feng shui guidelines. Dan's family has worked with bonsai for 12 generations and has cultivated at least one bonsai tree for more than 400 years. He maintains that plants have feelings, can achieve an unlimited life and enjoy all types of music, just as humans do. Dan believes that happy plants create positive energy. By designing gardens for hospitals in the community, Master Sensho reduces patients' stress levels by transforming the negative energy of pain and suffering to a positive atmosphere of peace, balance and harmony. Dan also invites everyone to enjoy the peace and positive energy in his store, where he teaches his students and customers the way of bonsai. All are encouraged to walk around freely and enjoy the beauty and soothing sounds of waterfalls in Dan's gardens. Come learn how you can bring this beauty and tranquility into your own life at Bonzai Kid.

6590 W 120th Avenue, Unit B-1, Broomfield CO
(720) 566-4949
www.bonzaikid.com

Mountain Woods Furniture

What makes Mountain Woods Furniture so Colorado? Well, like most folks in the Rocky Mountain state, owners Chris and Jamie Brown cherish the outdoors and prefer a rustic style that makes a connection with nature. The finely crafted aspen and pine log furniture that they offer in their store fits right into this lifestyle. Chris and Jamie carry over 200 furniture designs for every room of your home, cabin or ski lodge, including full kitchen sets and bedroom suites. All pieces are created using Rocky Mountain woods and are handcrafted, from the peeling and sanding to the finishing. If you truly appreciate log furniture, you'll see for yourself that the craftsmanship of Chris and Jamie's pieces is first-rate. If you don't see exactly what you want, Mountain Woods Furniture can build and upholster pieces to your specifications. The Browns and their staff are proponents of a more laidback approach to retailing. Maybe it's the fresh air and clear skies that relaxes people in Colorado. Whatever the cause, the mood at Mountain Woods Furniture is casual and friendly. You're never pushed into buying anything. When Chris and Jamie decided to go into business in their adopted home of Colorado, they wanted it to reflect everything they love about this beautiful state. Mountain Woods Furniture fulfilled their desire. For furniture that captures the essence of Colorado, visit Mountain Woods Furniture today.

11 Old Town Square, Suite 121, Fort Collins CO
(970) 416-0701 or (877) 686-9663
www.mwlogfurniturecolorado.com

P Design Gallery

Paul and Pifuka Hardt are too busy shaking up the Denver style scene to reflect on how to categorize their business, P Design Gallery. They spend their day greeting customers, making contact with young designers and planning exhibitions that challenge modernist notions of art and craft, design and decoration, function and content. Still, the question sometimes nags them: Are they running a furniture store? An art gallery? The area's most bizarre gift shop? Perhaps the closest one can get to defining this enterprise is to call it a showcase for ultra contemporary furnishings and decorations that can be called art. Displayed items may include bed frames and tables as well as vases, plates and jewelry. After highlighting quilts and other textiles, Paul and Pifuka may mount a show that shifts the focus to tableware, lighting and other contemporary home design pieces. Expect anything from classic designs to pieces that will make your jaw drop. Perhaps because it is so outside the mainstream, this business earned two Best of Denver 2006 awards from *Westword*: Best Design Store and Best Design Exhibition. Satisfy your ultra modern taste for irony and unpredictability at P Design Gallery.

2590 Walnut Street, Denver CO
(770) 259-2516
www.pdesigngallery.com

The Windsor Gardener

The Windsor Gardener, a seasonal nursery and garden center, specializes in colorful, robust plants selected for their ability to grow well locally. Owners Pat and Amanda Weakland love sharing their secrets for successful Colorado gardening and have deep roots in the industry. Growing up on a farm gave Amanda a solid agricultural background, while Pat, a third generation nurseryman, worked in his father's greenhouse in Longmont as a kid and has four brothers in the nursery business. Pat and Amanda opened Plant-Scape in 1991 with a small mobile greenhouse they set up and took down each year. In 2001, they expanded their operation to 11,000 square feet of greenhouse space on 10 acres and changed the name to the Windsor Gardener to more accurately reflect what they offer. Choosing to forego trees and shrubs allows them to concentrate on seasonal nursery stock, which includes annuals, perennials, vegetables and colorful hanging baskets that they put together themselves. They grow more than half of their own plants and offer many plant varieties suitable for growing in containers. Decorative items for both home and garden include an expansive selection of pottery and many gifts. The nursery is open from March to July. Pat and Amanda support area schools and enjoy passing on their experience to students by giving them their first jobs. At the Windsor Gardener, the selections are always changing, so stop in and see what's new.

6461 Highway 392, Windsor CO
(970) 686-9771
www.thewindsorgardener.com

Denver Art Glass

The art of stained glass is "not a cookie-cutter business," says Mike Delva of Denver Art Glass. That's why Mike offers free estimates and consultations, where you can leaf through a portfolio of styles, ranging from classic to contemporary. Whether he's designing glass for the governor's mansion or for your private home, he'll tailor the design to the location and the needs of his client. Denver Art Glass has been in business since 1980 and in its current location in Greenwood Village since 1985. In addition to traditional stained glass, the company also offers etched and beveled glass options, including chamiso, a contemporary carved glass that resembles molten lava. You can call Denver Art Glass for stained glass repair and restoration work too. The craftsmanship and attention to detail you'll find at Denver Art Glass is second to none, resulting in a look that complements the building's design. If you're considering adding the beauty of stained glass to your home or office, make a difference, visit Denver Art Glass.

6801 S Emporia #106, Greenwood Village CO
(303) 792-9012
www.denverartglass.com

Markets & Delis

Choice City Butcher & Deli

In three years, Choice City & Deli has become an unbreakable habit for many folks in Fort Collins. Owners Rus Robinson and Derek Kennedy offer the highest quality meats, from beef through lamb to kangaroo and ostrich. The butchers on staff know their meat and are ready to answer your questions. There's always something new in the butcher's case. The cheese selection is wide, as well. While at the deli, check out the star of the menu, the fabulous buffalo-meat Colorado Rueben. Locally, Choice City is actually as famous for its beer as for its meat. The collection of brews is both unusual and unusually good. You can also sample any of 40 sodas and a variety of specially selected wines. Breakfast is available Wednesday through Sunday, sandwiches from the deli are up anytime the doors are open, and dinner is Thursday through Sunday. Check Choice City's website for upcoming fun events, such as wine tasting the last Monday of every month. Bring Choice City Butcher & Deli to you—the shop has an extensive catering department ready to meet your needs. Their courteous staff is able to accommodate private parties on-site, bring a chef in your home or manage large events such as graduations or weddings. Plan a stop at Choice City Butcher & Deli, where the staff strives for excellence.

104 W Olive Street, Fort Collins CO (970)490-2489
www.choicecitybutcher.com

Big Dog Deli

Pete Walsh, owner of Big Dog Deli, was a schoolteacher before becoming a sandwich maker, so it is fitting that he named his shop after P.D. Eastman's classic children's story, *Go Dog Go*. The neighborhood sandwich shop has a steady stream of regulars who come in for the hearty subs made with freshly baked bread. Every sandwich is toasted and named after a breed of dog. You can try the stand-by Saint Bernard, which is made of turkey and Swiss, or the pleasing Pyrenees, filled with chicken salad and bacon. Every order is topped with mayonnaise, German brown mustard, hot peppers, vegetables and dill pickle. With favorites like the Big Dog, a prime rib sandwich, Big Dog Deli has earned the honor of Best Sandwich from the *Denver Post*. The sandwich makers at Big Dog Deli craft each sub thoughtfully by putting the toppings between the meat and cheese to create a melt when toasted and keep moisture away from the fresh bread. Salads come with bread and choice of nine dressings. The Southwestern salad with corn, red pepper, avocado, cucumber and tomato is a hit. A seasonal soup is served daily. Go, dog, go to Big Dog Deli and become Pete's newest regular.

300 Nickel Street #14, Broomfield CO (303) 460-1000

Hays Market

The Hays family has passed their grocery store legacy down through the past four generations. In the 1920s, Thurman and Louisa Hays moved from Indiana and opened the first Hays. In 1996, the family built a 25,000 square-foot store at Johnstown Center Drive, and in 2001, they expanded to a second location in Berthoud. No matter where they landed, the Hays brought their down-home wisdom with them. Along with offering first-rate products, they thrive on customer service. They cut their own meats and make their own sausage. The pristine deli, bakery and produce departments display fresh, varied and delicious products. You can select your groceries while your prescription is being filled at the pharmacy. Thurman and Louisa passed the store to their son Chet, who passed it along to his son Rick and wife Sally. Today, Rick and Sally's sons Ryan, Neal and Russell run the market. In almost 80 years, one thing has not changed. The Hays family is proud to offer the highest quality products available and deliver the friendliest service in town.

201 Johnstown Center Drive, Johnstown CO (970) 587-4658
919 Mountain Avenue, Berthoud CO (970) 532-0257
www.haysmarket.com

Loredana's

More than a decade ago, Loredana Ottoborgo went on an errand to the local farmers' market to pick up basil for her family's restaurant. A conversation with the basil farmer encouraged her to sell her pesto blends at the farmers' market. Loredana's was a hit. The Ottoborgos came from Northern Italy to Colorado, where they opened a restaurant in Dillon. True to Italian tradition, the whole family was involved. Loredana met Jay Sharpless, her husband, in the seventh grade at a North Denver grade school. They both worked together at the restaurant. Loredana created about 10 different flavors of pestos, ranging from layered pestos with sun-dried tomatoes and mascarpone cheese for appetizers to a light citrus pesto for fish. Loredana and Jay spent several years traveling the local farmers' market circuit. Along the way, they opened up a commercial kitchen and retail shop in Olde Town Arvada. Along with her original pestos, Loredana and Jay have created rare vinaigrettes, one-of-a-kind Italian marmalades, Italian olive tapenades and marinated Italian cheeses. You can still meet Loredana and Jay at the local farmers' markets. Soon their children will be helping out as well. To find out what farmers' markets and holiday shows they are at, visit the website. Loredana's is also available at Whole Foods, or order online and have it shipped anywhere in the United States or Canada. Develop a passion for Italian food at home using Loredana's specialty products. Buon Appetito!

7523 Grandview Avenue, (Olde Town) Arvada CO (303) 477-3900

Good Health Natural Grocers

Good Health Natural Grocers is the best place in town to buy health food. That's the verdict of the readers of the *Glenwood Post Independent,* who have consistently recognized the store in the Locals Choice Awards since it opened in 1997. The store was recently purchased by new owners Steve and Sandy Swanson, who have upheld the store's dedication to health, while also incorporating many more locally produced items. Steve has spent years doing non-profit community service and brings that sense of community to the shop. Sandy was raised in a home that advocated organic foods and vitamins and brings her expertise in those fields. From produce to dairy, everything here is natural and organic. The store specializes in items that were grown or created in Colorado. Good Health has many vitamins, herbs and supplements, as well as cosmetic and beauty aids that haven't been tested on animals. The friendly staff members will provide you with the information you need to make healthy choices. To feed your family and keep them healthy, make the natural choice at Good Health Natural Grocers.

722 Cooper Avenue, Glenwood Springs CO (970) 945-0235
www.goodhealthgrocery.com

Photo by Brian Boyer

Deli Italia

5280 magazine bestowed the award for Best Muffaletta in Colorado upon Deli Italia. Try it only if you are really hungry, because this gargantuan sandwich comes stuffed with ham, salami, capicolla and provolone. Then again, no matter what you order at this popular gathering place, you are going to be well fed. One of the subs even bears the name of Monster Veggie. Overall, the lengthy list of sandwiches offers everything from a straightforward roast beef with mayonnaise, lettuce and tomato to the complex Dante's Inferno— a stack of ham, salami and capicolla served with hot habanero paste, dressing and provolone. Pizzas and salads are also popular, along with lasagna, manicotti and spaghetti with meatballs. Deli Italia has been satisfying robust appetites since 1986. Owner Bernadette O'Dowd is especially proud of the homemade mozzarella, pointing out that Deli Italia was the first place in Colorado to make its own. The pastas, sauces and breads are also made fresh on site. With its full-service market, Deli Italia carries everything you need to prepare an Italian feast at home. The business also offers catering. Subdue a muffaletta or some other large monster on the menu at Deli Italia.

1990 Wadsworth Boulevard, Lakewood CO (303) 238-7815
www.deliitalia.com

8th Street Deli

Expect more from your deli—that's the philosophy that guides chef and owner Jason Higens at 8th Street Deli. He offers items and services that go beyond what you'd expect at your neighborhood deli. Jason started his culinary career in 1992 as a dishwasher at a five-star restaurant. He quickly moved up, mentored by chefs, as he trained in fine dining establishments in Glenwood and Snowmass Village. His mentors trained to bring his own touch to food, which he does at 8th Street Deli. If you're looking for a delicious, hot breakfast, you'll delight in the omelettes, quiches and breakfast sandwiches. Sumptuous sandwiches and soups are just the thing for lunch, along with fresh salads. Pick up a loaf of fresh bread to enjoy at home, along with a cookie for dessert. Those looking for a taste of elegance will be glad to learn that 8th Street Deli is a tasting room for local wines. You'll also find locally grown beef and fresh seafood, as well as imported cheeses, breads and cookies. The deli offers a full range of catering services, from American dishes to Greek, Mexican and even wild game if you like. For a taste of elegance and neighborhood deli charm, come to 8th Street Deli.

205 8ᵗʰ Street, Glenwood Springs CO (970) 945-5011
www.8thstreetdeli.com

Passion for Picnics

Romance on the river—biking in the mountains—music at the park. Heather Finley has thought of dozens of ways to enhance your picnic choices, because as she says, "Time moves slower, food tastes better when eating outdoors." Heather opened Passion for Picnics in Glenwood Meadows Center in 2006. She and her three kids are old hands at picnics, a tradition they started in Hawaii and carried with them to Colorado. Heather's products are popular year-round because Colorado likes to be outdoors year-round. You might take a wicker basket filled with crackers, cheese and lemonade out to your favorite swimming hole on a hot summer day or sweeten a cross-country ski or snowmobile outing with fondue, crusty French bread and a flask of sipping chocolate fitted in an insulated backpack. The store's gourmet baskets are particularly popular and can be themed to match a special occasion and shipped anywhere in the United States. The store sells waterproof blankets, wine accessories, table linens and supplies for a child's tea party. Whether you are planning a camp-out, a backyard barbecue or a hike, Heather knows how to enhance your day and make your feast a memorable one. Make the most of your time outdoors with a visit to Passion for Picnics.

25A Market Street, Glenwood Springs CO
(970) 947-9113
www.passionforpicnics.com

Salvador Deli

For Gabby and Blake Leavitt, a joyful life involves mixing healthy food, conversation, music and artwork. They used this formula to create Salvador Deli in 2006. The Greeley restaurant is known for its glorious sandwiches made with fresh, organic bread, organic fillings and house-made sauces, such as a raspberry chipotle sauce that adds a spark to grilled chicken. Best-sellers include the sundried tomato chicken with pesto and the Tantalizing Turkey Guacamole. You can order all-fruit smoothies or Colorado-roasted organic Fair Trade coffee. For a refreshing change of pace, try the bubble tea, an unusual, flavored tea textured with large tapioca pearls. Salvador Deli is open seven days a week for breakfast and lunch. It features occasional live jazz music and represents a different local artist each month. Gabby and Blake met at the local university and have thoroughly enjoyed creating an environment that's healthy and fun-filled for customers and employees. The pair are devoted recyclers and extend their earth-friendly philosophy to the restaurant's paper and cleaning products. They offer free wireless Internet and a space that will attract everyone you know. For wholesome living, plan a visit to Salvador Deli, Where the Sandwiches are Surreal.

800 9th Street, Greeley CO
(970) 353-1998
www.thesalvadordeli.com

The Truffle

Some foods are so fine that we save them for honored guests or to give as special gifts. These are the kinds of exotic foods you'll find at The Truffle. Artisan cheeses, cured meats, and of course, truffles, are among the tantalizing options at this gourmet and specialty cheese shop. Between 75 to 125 cheese varieties are on hand at any given time. The cheeses are from artisan producers from around the world, sample a Colorado goat cheese, a sheep's milk cheese made in a monastery in France or a raw milk cheddar from England. You'll also find French patés and cold cuts from Salumeria Biellese in New York City. You can purchase truffles, both the chocolate and the mushroom variety. Boulder's Breadworks supplies fresh bread. Special olive oils, honeys and tapenades will add pizzazz to otherwise humble foods. The owners sample everything in the shop to ensure quality. The Truffle even ships gift baskets worldwide so anyone can enjoy these delights. Owners Robert and Karin Lawler have extensive experience in the restaurant business, where Karin worked as a server, bar manager and wine buyer and Rob worked as a chef. Bring the products of small farms to your table with a visit to The Truffle.

2906 E 6th Street, Denver CO
(303) 322-7363
www.denvertruffle.com

Steve's Meat Market

Hunters know Steve's Meat Market well for its processing of deer, elk, antelope and other wild game. The staff makes steaks, roasts, burger and 20 different types of sausages, stix and jerky from as many as 100 animals on a typical day. Owners Steve and Karen Hein like to keep things hot in the retail part of the business with a jalapeno and cheddar sausage that will stoke your taste buds. Other piquant treats include chorizo and peppery jerky. Those who like it mild will enjoy the bratwurst and cheddar dogs. If you're looking for something to cook on the grill, Steve's sells thick and juicy steaks as well as beef, buffalo and elk burger. Steve's Meat Market operates out of an 1890s former livery stable and was named an Arvada Business of the Year in 2005. The business award honored the significant renovation of this historic building as well as commitment to the development of Olde Towne Arvada and community spirit. Discover the meat lovers' paradise that is Steve's Meat Market.

5751 Olde Wadsworth Boulevard, Arvada CO
(303) 422-3487
www.stevesmeatmarket.com

Belfiore Italian Sausage

As good as the sausage is at Belfiore Italian Sausage, the name of the business only tells part of the mouth-watering story. The same meats, cheeses and pastas that you would find at a village grocer in Italy can be found under the roof of this busy store. The prosciutto, mortadella and salami are, in fact, imported from Italy, as are many of the cheeses, including Parmigiano-Reggiano and Pecorino Romano. The foods are prepared right on the premises with the freshest and finest ingredients. These include ravioli, gnocchi, lasagna as well as Old World dried sausage and hand-rolled meatballs. The recipes have been handed down from generation to generation. Do you like your sausage mild or do you prefer a little heat? Belfiore carries to both. You can tell from his name that owner Gino Guiseppe Scarafiotti knows Italian food. A native of Colorado, Gino bought Belfiore Italian Sausage in 2006. The business has been a Denver destination for over 50 years. You are invited to shop for the makings of your Italian feast at Belfiore Italian Sausage.

5820 W 38th Avenue, Wheat Ridge CO (303) 455-4653

Life Source One

Before Life Source One, many people in Greeley faced mealtime with dismay. "If bread containing gluten makes you ill, where could you go?" asks Tracy Senstock, who teams up with her husband, Patrick, to run Greeley's first health food store. Life Source One caters to those with specific food allergies and dietary needs as well as those simply trying to follow a conscientious lifestyle. Tracy and Patrick conceived the store as a resource for treating our earth, spirit, mind and bodies with equal respect and wellness. Tracy has since acquired advanced training in endocrine functioning and nutrition. You'll find breakfast cereals, snacks, organic and natural meats and more, plus earth-friendly household products, such as cleansing detergents and toilet paper. The store also stocks vitamins, natural remedies, books and magazines. Stop in for a hot house/chi machine experience and a detoxifying ionic foot cleanse. Life Source One also offers products to pamper the body and spirit, such as aromatherapy, fountains, wind chimes, crystals, local art and more. The Healing Connection, LLC., operates alongside Life Source One, offering a staff of wellness practitioners who provide rolfing, massage, energy healing, yoga, psychological counseling and more. Discover the wonders of a healthful, natural lifestyle at Life Source One.

2961 W 29th Street, Greeley CO (970) 351-8083
www.lifesourceone.com

Spice Boys of the Rockies

A Chinese spice shop in Vancouver inspired Cal Smith and David Citizen to add some spice to Denver. The duo opened Spice Boys of the Rockies soon after their epiphany in Vancouver. Floor to ceiling shelves artfully display aromatic wares. The Boys create blends of delectably fragrant herbs and spices, suitable for every type of cuisine and capable of inspiring even the most timid chef to get creative in the kitchen. All of their spices are much fresher than those you can buy in a standard grocery outlet. You can definitely taste the difference. Kim Bremseth, chef and chocolatier, recently joined the team to add his spice-infused chocolates and new creations to the mix. Truffles take on new life when infused with flavors that range from spicy to sweet, chili to chai. The Spice Boys' oddly-shaped Boulders, rocks you drop in coffee, tea and hot chocolate, are made on the premises and sold in bags. Tea is sold by the cup and in packages. Colorado products find a home here as well—burritos from Longmont and Salsa Del Sol from Denver. You can have ice cream in a cone or dish. A journey to Spice Boys of the Rockies will stimulate your culinary spirit and make your mouth water. Take the trip.

309 W 11th Avenue, Denver CO (303) 595-0551
www.spiceboysrock.com

Restaurants & Cafés

Village Bistro

Wayne and Angela Palinckx of Westminster felt their community lacked something important. It needed a place to bring dates, to have business lunches, to gather with friends and family to enjoy quality food and service without having to drive downtown. In 2006, the Palinckxs created that place, naming it the Village Bistro to emphasize its central community role. The restaurant has turned out to be just that. High ceilings and stone accents create a comfortable, inviting atmosphere, complete with a fireplace and heated patio. The full bar is outfitted with 42-inch, high-definition televisions tuned to sports. The Palinckxs have also created a proud wine list, to pair with the menu. The American bistro-style menu offers soups and salads, steak and seafood and changes seasonally. Weekly specials include fresh fish and game and a crème brulée of the week. Start with one of the fabulous seafood appetizers, such as the calamari, which comes with an assortment of dipping sauces. The Guinness Lamb is a customer favorite, while Chef's Choice offers fresh catch-of-the-day with lobster mashed potatoes. Desserts include bananas foster and chocolate lava cake with ice cream. Village Bistro was open only one year when *Yellow Scene* named it the Best of the West 2007. Visit soon to find out how Westminster does gourmet.

2821 W 120th Avenue, #300, Westminster CO
(303) 410-2887
www.villagebistroonline.com

East West Grill

If you were to point randomly to a spot on the globe, chances are that the East West Grill has something on its menu from that part of the world. With over 70 choices, the menu spans Asia with shrimp spring rolls, sesame chop salad and masman curry chickin, and Russia with an egg noodle stroganoff sautéed in sherry sauce. A wealth of delicious pasta dishes represents Italy, including the superb Lobster Sensation Alfredo and chicken parmesan. For Tex-Mex, try the baja chicken wrap and chicken tortilla soup. The wild salmon caesar salad is a California-inspired favorite. Each dish is made fresh at the time of the order. The fast service at East West Grill appeals to the lunch crowd, while whole families show up for dinner to embark on their culinary tour of world. Adults can enjoy their meals with a glass of wine or beer while children can play at their popular kids area. Owners Felicia Mak and Chuck and James Hsu have collected hundreds of recipes over their decades in the restaurant industry, not neglecting the ever-popular macaroni and cheese and grilled chicken rice bowl. For a table that spans continents, take your taste buds traveling at the East West Grill.

408 4th Street, Alamosa CO
(719) 589-4600
1387 S Boulder Road, Louisville CO
(303) 604-9999
1873 S Pueblo Boulevard, Pueblo CO
(719) 566-8898
www.east-westgrill.com

CooperSmith's Pub & Brewing Co.

The menu at CooperSmith's Pub & Brewing Co. comes to you in the form of a four-page newspaper called the *Cooper Crier*. Which of the beers masterfully crafted on the premises will you deem worthy of bold headlines? The Punjabi Pale Ale features plenty of assertive hops, while the Poudre Pale Ale offers a lighter variation on the theme with a slight caramel flavor. Try the Albert Damm Bitter for brewer Dwight Hall's version of a British bitter, or the Horsetooth Stout for full-bodied flavor. Anaheim and Serrano chiles add zest to the light and crisp Sigda's Beer. The menu also presents many columns of newsworthy food choices. You won't be disappointed, whether your appetite demands something light like a garden salad, something smoky like brisket with garlic mashed potatoes or something fishy like the Sesame Seared Ahi Tuna. Pizzas from the wood-fired oven make a popular alternative to pub standards that include fish and chips, pot pie and bangers and mash. A favorite in Old Town Fort Collins since 1989, CooperSmith's operates out of a pair of buildings dating to the early 1900s that represent two sides to the CooperSmith personality. Pubside underscores the bar, while Poolside offers diners access to twelve tournament-size pool tables. Come by early to quaff a pint or later to enjoy a meal and play pool, darts or checkers at CooperSmith's Pub & Brewing Co.

5 Old Town Square, Fort Collins CO
(970) 498-0483
www.coopersmithspub.com

Imperial Chinese Restaurant

A Denver tradition, Imperial Chinese Restaurant has been serving first-rate Chinese cuisine since 1985. Readers of both the *Denver Post* and *Westword* have voted it the Best Chinese Restaurant in Denver for 13 consecutive years, and it was rated Top Chinese Restaurant by *Zagat Survey* from 2000 to 2002. Owner and founding chef Johnny Hsu came to Denver from Hong Kong in 1979, having attended culinary school there. He started with a casual restaurant in 1980, but by 1985, he felt the market was ready for an upscale Chinese restaurant. Johnny created the menu personally and continues to oversee his cooks, ensuring that they are specific to the recipes and each dish is consistent in its quality. He travels often to China looking for new ideas to refresh the menu, but many of the originals continue to be popular. Johnny was the first to introduce sesame chicken to the Denver area, a perennial favorite, along with the Peking duck. He was also the first to introduce lettuce wraps and whole fish, which Imperial serves with your choice of sauce: ginger, black bean or Szechwan. The full bar makes such exotic signature drinks as the Green Plum martini and a mean Mai Tai. The setting is beautiful, with dark woods, sculpture and tasteful lighting reflected by the plated ceiling. In 2004, Johnny was inducted into the Denver Restaurant Hall of Fame. An integral part of the community, he serves on the board of several local organizations. Visit Imperial Chinese Restaurant for lunch or dinner and the best service in town.

431 S Broadway, Denver CO
(303) 698-2800
www.imperialchinese.com

The Wayside Inn

When Jeremy Roush and his wife, Debbie Hermance, bought the Wayside Inn in 2006, they didn't just take over a Berthoud community icon. Jeremy, a graduate of the Culinary Institute of America, also assumed the responsibility of representing the entire tradition of American cuisine. If the pressure is getting to him, it doesn't show. A message at the top of the wine list encourages guests to have fun. Jeremy joyfully prepares such favorites as Colorado lamb, Iowa pork chop and local trout for the hungry crowds that gather in the pub and dining room. What could be more American than chicken noodle soup? Jeremy makes his from scratch with fresh chicken and egg noodles. The original Wayside classic, fried chicken, is served with a mound of buttermilk mashed potatoes, cream gravy and seasonal vegetables. Every dish that leaves the kitchen is a tribute to the hard work and contributions of the American farmer, rancher and producer. Even the lunch and pub menus reflect the restaurant's commitment to offering the best foods the nation has to offer. Because all meals are crafted at the time they are ordered, Jeremy can cater to the specific dietary requests of his customers. On the wine list, a fine selection of vintages appears under such headings as Zen and Zin, Arousing Reds and Full Figured Chardonnays. Taste American greatness at the Wayside Inn, a Berthoud fixture since 1923.

505 Mountain Avenue, Berthoud CO
(970) 532-2013
www.waysideinnrestaurant.com

Fish

At Fish, the "fish is so fresh that someone might get slapped," says owner Mike Reeves, who has the fish for his Fort Collins restaurant flown in three or four times a week. You can choose a live lobster right from the tank or try fish such as ahi, tilapia or trout. The sashimi, steamers and ahi egg rolls are some of the favorites at Fish, where you can enjoy an atmosphere Mike describes as Colorado casual along with a plate presentation you would expect from the finest dining establishments. Mike borrows from several traditions for his menu, which includes raw oysters, fisherman's stew, fish and chips and some East Asian-inspired entrées. You can also choose a fish for simple grilling. Sushi is a good choice for large and small catered events. The sushi is prepared right at the party. You will find a full bar and an excellent wine selection, including more choices of wine by the glass than there are seats in the house. Fish has won many awards since it opened in 2001, including a best presentation award from Taste of Fort Collins and accolades for Best Seafood from the *Rocky Mountain Chronicle* and other publications. Fish is a market as well as a restaurant, so you can purchase seafood to take home. Mike is a Colorado native with a degree from Colorado University at Boulder. He loves to fish, and he's been cooking since he was 15 (he once owned a Mexican restaurant in Canada). When it's fish you crave, come to Fish. You'll find fish on a whole new scale.

150 W Oak Street, Fort Collins CO
(970) 224-1188
www.fishmkt.com

Daily Bread

Daily Bread is the locals' favorite place to get their daily bread. That's the conclusion of the readers of the *Glenwood Post Independent,* who named the restaurant the Best Bakery in the Locals Choice awards. That's not a surprising result, given the dedication owner Mark Bartnik has to his hometown and customers. Mark grew up in Glenwood, but left to attend the Culinary Institute of America. After that, he went to Poland, where he met his wife, Joanna, who is also his business partner. The restaurant offers traditional American cuisine with a Polish flair. One lunch favorite that has earned Daily Bread great renown is its Polish pierogis, pasta pillows filled with ingredients that include meat, sauerkraut, spinach and other delectable treats. You'll also find delicious potato pancakes and *golabki,* a stuffed cabbage in a light tomato sauce. If you're looking for more traditional American fare, you'll delight in the array of burgers, sandwiches and soups. Daily Bread offers a full range of breakfast options, including omelettes, pancakes and Polish-style blintzes. The atmosphere is friendly and inviting, which explains why some people are such regular customers that if they don't come in, somebody calls them up to make sure they're OK. The bakery sells bread and coffee cake to bring home, and the restaurant provides a catering service. Get your daily bread this day at Daily Bread.

729 Grand Avenue, Glenwood Springs CO
(970) 945-6253

Café Gondolier

Café Gondolier has been a top choice for Italian food in Boulder since 1960. The recipes that restaurateur Gary Kugel learned from his Auntie Lou have stood the test of time. University students, famous for knowing all the great bargains, flock here on Tuesdays and Wednesdays for the all-you-can-eat spaghetti nights. Beloved also for its New York-style pizza, Café Gondolier is family-friendly any night of the week. Gary has passed Auntie Lou's recipes to his son, Nelson, who seems to tout a different dish every time someone asks him for a recommendation. Try the *cioppino,* he suggests, a fisherman's stew loaded with scallops, mussels, shrimp and calamari. Nelson also says that you can't go wrong with the spaghetti topped with the Mix, a combination of freshly chopped garlic, olive oil and marinara. He is partial to chicken dishes, too, such as the chicken and ziti and the *frittura picatta,* which comes with artichokes, tomatoes, lemon and capers. Gary retired in 2001, but he still keeps a hand in the business and bakes his delicious pastries daily. Long-time patrons are ready to nominate him for the Dessert Hall of Fame for his *crème brûlée* alone. After tasting it, one food critic paid the highest compliment by declaring, "I could have eaten three." For home-style Italian cooking and the ambience of a small-town restaurant, try Café Gondolier.

1738 Pearl Street, Boulder CO
(303) 443-5015
www.cafegondolier.com

Sundance Steak House & Saloon

At Sundance Steak House & Saloon, your introduction to the flavor of the West begins with steak dinner and often continues well into the night. In fact, owners Mike and Mimi Poppenwimer are fond of saying that the Fun Never Sets at their Old West restaurant and watering hole. Saddles and other cowboy gear make up the decór, as hearty appetites feast on the Sundance signature prime rib, served with baked potato, vegetables, salad and roll. Country line dancing is the main entertainment at Sundance, with as many as 600 people kicking up a storm on some nights. After a free lesson, you'll be right out there in the middle of the crowd. Arm-wrestling tournaments and tough-man competitions also occur from time to time. Several weekends a year, the restaurant hosts live bull-riding in its outdoor arena. Up to 40 riders at a time line up for the bone-jarring stomp around the ring on the back of a mean bull. Rodeo clowns compete for the attention of spectators. Sundance offers various specials throughout the week for ladies, college students and families. Local polls consistently rank this place as the best in Fort Collins for prime rib and for dancing. Wear your cowboy hat if you've got one, and head down to the Sundance Steak House & Saloon for a real western experience.

2716 E Mulberry Street, Fort Collins CO
(970) 484-1600
www.sundancesteakhouse.com

Annie's Café

Fresh, hand-patted burgers and breakfast served all day top the list of tantalizing comfort foods at Annie's Café, a Denver favorite since 1981. The extensive menu and retro décor evoke a time and place where everyone is welcome. *Zagat Survey* and *Parenting Magazine* rated Annie's as Excellent and named it one of the Best Family Travel Guide Restaurants in the nation. Enjoy breakfast, lunch, or dinner amid memorabilia of 1950s posters, tin lunch boxes and toys. Lunches offer one-third pound burgers, home-cut fries, malts, shakes and soda fountain fare. From the Mexican side of the menu, the green or red chili is so good you might want to take home a quart. Dinners will tempt you with meat loaf, chicken fried steak, and many other savory choices of entrees and salads, accompanied by your choice of beer or wine. Save room for dessert which features homemade gingerbread, cakes and brownies. A one-of-a-kind restaurant, Annie's has earned repeated local praise, having been named Best Breakfast and Best Retro Dining in *5280 Magazine* as well as receiving the nod for Best Hamburgers from the *Rocky Mountain News*. Don't forget to grab an old time favorite from the candy counter before you leave. Since Annie's is centrally located and easy to reach, we know you'll be back.

4012 E 8th Avenue, Denver CO
(303) 355-8197
www.annies-cafe.com

The Golden Burro Café & Lounge

A stop at the Golden Burro Café & Lounge is a must. This eatery has been a community favorite for nearly 70 years and has been a popular stopover for travelers almost as long. Its deep rooted history is embellished with Victorian furnishings and a multitude of old photos on the walls, documenting itself as Leadville's icon for friendly gatherings. Owners Dave and Jane Wright use fresh, quality products and hand-prepare almost everything on the menu, which is probably the most diverse in Lake County. The Golden Burro is famous for homemade green chili and meatloaf, roast beef and pork tenderloin roast dinners, as well as its old-fashioned country fried chicken dinner, which is deliciously crispy on the outside and melt-in-your mouth tender on the inside. From casual café style entrées to upper scale evening dinners like shrimp scampi, 14 ounce steaks, prime rib and lobster, the Golden Burro has something for every appetite and budget. The banquet room and full service lounge is the ideal place to host special family gatherings and corporate events. Large groups are welcome any time. Recognized repeatedly as the most friendly and professional service around, you'll also want to visit their website for information about summer entertainment and special events. Spend some time in the heart of the historical business district on Harrison Avenue with friends and family at the famous Golden Burro Café & Lounge.

710 Harrison Avenue, Leadville CO
(719) 486-1239
www.GoldenBurro.com

The Breakfast Club

If you are searching for a regular breakfast spot that is thoroughly satisfying, a little bit adventurous and very affordable, it's time you visited the Breakfast Club. Families, college students and retirees share a love for this restaurant, which opened in 1992. Owners Dave and Angela Hakes credit their staff, the community and their customers for creating the warm and friendly atmosphere at the Breakfast Club. Their excellent staff allowed them to open a Loveland branch of the Breakfast Club in 2002. The breakfast burrito, stuffed with pork, mild green chili, potatoes and cheese, gets big votes for breakfast or lunch. Omelettes combine your favorite flavors, while waffles, pancakes or French toast accompany some splendid bacon. Fans of eggs Benedict or biscuits and gravy are both well pleased. Lunch is equally worthy with such specialties as pork roast, meatloaf, lasagna and house-made soups. The Hakes buy from many food suppliers to guarantee that quality is never compromised in all areas of the business. The menu is tried and true, proven by 15 years of customer loyalty, but new daily specials add variety and excitement. The Breakfast Club offers a specially sized menu for seniors and recently eliminated trans fats from the menu. If you like the décor, the vintage tin signs on the walls are available for purchase. Prepare to join the gang at the Breakfast Club, satisfaction is guaranteed.

121 W Monroe Drive, Fort Collins CO
(970) 223-7193
1451 N Boise Avenue, Loveland CO
(970) 461-1261

The Silver Grill Café

The Silver Grill Café is the oldest restaurant in Northern Colorado, serving breakfast and lunch since 1933 and with roots going all the way back to 1912. Wooden floors, huge windows looking out on Old Town, and spacious booths and tables lend the place character. The Silver Grill's breakfasts are legendary. They have been named the best in all of Colorado by news stations and lauded by local publications. They are known for their gigantic homemade cinnamon rolls, made fresh daily and oozing with sweet sugary toppings. The breakfast fare includes blueberry pancakes with hot syrup and butter, steak and eggs, country-style biscuits and gravy, homemade granola, vegetarian huevos rancheros and even a tasty trout filet and eggs. The lunch menu is replete with time-tested delights. Homestyle blue plate lunch specials, juicy burgers, creative or classic deli sandwiches and salads prepared just the way you like them are a few of the options. The Silver Grill is also known for special evening events and private parties. John Arnolfo has owned the grill since 1979 and he has made it a family affair by enlisting sons Zach and Sam and mother, Frances. John, managing partner Carrie Hartwell, and their team have worked tirelessly to improve and develop the restaurant, expanding the original premise to include five buildings, 6,000 square feet and room for 150 patrons. Fifty more can dine on the sidewalk or airy back patio. For a meal that'll satisfy every member of the family, come to the Silver Grill Café.

218 Walnut Street, Fort Collins CO
(970) 484-4656
www.silvergrill.com

Johnny's Diner

Photo by J.M. Beck 2006

Customers on the run have been flocking to Johnny's Diner since 1985 for homemade food served in a flash. Doug and Joan Beck own and run the busy eatery, whose name comes from Doug's middle name, John. Johnny's Diner serves breakfast anytime, and some of the most popular options include huevos rancheros and numerous omelettes served with home fries and Texas toast. If you've got the appetite for it, you can't go wrong with the Big Bopper, a plate of cheese-covered fried potatoes topped with sausage, bacon and eggs. Pancakes, French toast and several types of breakfast burritos are popular all day long. Burgers come in many configurations, and all feature Johnny's secret sauce. If you've got a super-sized appetite, go for the Giant Burger; for a change of pace, consider the pastrami cheeseburger. Sandwiches include patty melts, BLTs and Coney Islands. For a small charge, you can add fries and an all-you-can-drink option to any sandwich or burger on the menu. Johnny's Diner offers both red and green hearty homemade chili, and the fact that Doug makes 30 to 35 gallons of chili each week attests to its popularity. Johnny's also whips up the ultimate thick, creamy milkshakes. Try a frosty Dreamsicle shake with a burrito, taco or stuffed cream cheese poppers. Chicken fried steak, kid's meals and an assortment of salads and sides complete the menu. For a flashback to yesteryear with nostalgic music plus fast and friendly service, take your appetite to Johnny's Diner.

2323 S Havana Street, Aurora CO
(303) 368-8307

Hot Cakes Diner

Since 1994, folks have been arriving sleepy at Hot Cakes Diner and leaving ready to face the day. Hearty breakfasts are the specialty at this popular Denver restaurant, which opens at six in the morning on weekdays and seven on weekends. The first ones in are often workers from St. Joe's Hospital, who are made welcome with menu items named after their professions. It might take more than one RN to eat the Hot Cakes Nurse, which features two huge buttermilk cakes with two eggs and a choice of meat. Here's your chance if you've never tried sweet potato waffles. They're delicious. For years, owner Tom Schumacher and his crew have ushered in fall by serving pumpkin pancakes that make some folks wish it would stay October for the whole year. If you're dropping by for lunch, the Reuben on marble rye is a great choice. The Mexican Hamburger, which comes in a tortilla, is for big appetites. Other Mexican treats include huevos rancheros and burritos. Sandwiches, skillet dishes and a tasty vegetarian chili round out the menu. Hot Cakes Diner is located right across from St. Joe's on 18th and Humboldt Streets. Visit Hot Cakes Diner for a meal that will make a good day even better.

1400 E 18th Street, Denver CO
(303) 832-4351

Beso de Arte

What's the buzz on Beso de Arte, downtown Morrison's upscale Latino bistro? Regulars rave about the spirited ambience, inventive martinis and delicious sea bass. Tender and flaky, the sea bass is served with the Chilean staple, *pebre*, a tomato, onion and pepper-vinegar relish. The extensive menu at Beso do Arte presents a tour of the Spanish-speaking world. The Caribbean salmon with mango relish evokes tropical beaches, while flavorful Tex-Mex fajitas bring sizzle and spice to your table. The Rojo al Molcajete, a slow-simmered pork dish in a red chili sauce, is served in a lava rock. Order a few tapas if you prefer nibbling. The crab and goat cheese wonton is marvelous. Wash your meal down with a strawberry margarita or cherry martini. The 1870s building boasts an Art Deco interior that pulses with life, especially when the Latin music cranks up. After dinner, enjoy salsa dancing on the patio by the miniature waterfall. Bring your appetite, your dancing shoes and your dates to Beso de Arte, where exciting cuisine meets romantic ambiance.

102 Market Street, Morrison CO
(303) 697-3377
www.besodearte.com

Eggcredible Café

Darek and Anna Zurek put their Polish pride into their breakfast and lunch spot, the Eggcredible Café. The décor is rich in Old World charm, including hand-crocheted curtains imported from Poland. Cute dolls dressed in folk garb smile at customers as they satisfy their hunger with a Diesel Omelet, large enough to feed a couple of truck drivers. Try the Flat Iron Omelet with salmon if you prefer fish, or go with the theme by ordering the pierogies, the crescent-shaped dumplings that are a staple of the Polish diet. A breakfast combo features pierogies stuffed with tiny blueberries, sweet strawberries and tangy farmer's cheese. At lunch, the three-meat pierogi is a crowd pleaser, as is the sauerkraut and mushroom version. Chef Maciek Wardak from Warsaw presents a menu loaded with cross-cultural delights, including whole wheat waffles, burritos and eggs Benedict with the chef's own hollandaise sauce. Located on the second floor of the Days Inn Hotel, which the Zureks own, the restaurant is popular throughout Boulder. Pop in for some pierogies and other reminders of Poland.

5397 S Boulder Road, Boulder CO
(303) 301-0005
www.eggcredible.com

Randy's Pub & Grill

The carefree days of malts and burger-stand food are brought back to life at Randy's Pub & Grill. A 50s-style diner with an eclectic western touch, Randy's offers the highest quality all-American food from the bee-bopping days of the past. It is far cry from the traditional chocolate-strawberry-vanilla malt shops and offers 65 different flavors of shakes and malts, as well as an extensive and inventive menu. Try a classic bacon cheeseburger or get adventurous with a specialty burger, such as the Brian Gary Burger, which simply needs to be seen to believe. Known to locals as one of the best places to satisfy a craving for a juicy cheesy grilled burger, Randy's holds its own in the restaurant industry. The *Greeley Tribune* named Randy's burgers the best in the county, while the *Denver Post* raves about the Cajun-battered fried cod. For appetizers, choose deep fried macaroni and cheese, mozzarella sticks and spicy pub pickles. If you're in the mood for a lighter dish, try a spicy chicken bacon salad or a pecan chicken salad. After your meal, feel free to sit in the pub and enjoy the full bar or one of the eight beers on tap while being entertained by live music. Also, don't forget to sample some of the outstanding spicy wings, often cited as the best in the county. Take a real vacation from the ordinary when you come to Randy's Pub & Grill and find that old-fashioned comfort food of days gone by.

708 31st Street, Evans CO
(970) 330-2985

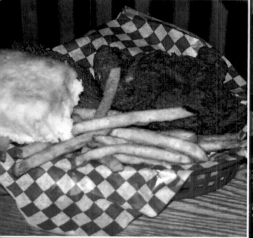

Charco Broiler

Since 1957, the Charco Broiler has served its customers terrific food at reasonable prices. Fort Collins' paper, *The Coloradoan*, has recognized the restaurant with the Best Steak in Town award for many years running. In addition to steaks cooked precisely to your liking, a wide selection of seafood is available, including favorites such as salmon, halibut and lobster. With 20 different burgers and an assortment of appetizers, you can't go wrong. For the lighter appetite, there are a dozen salads that hit the spot, plus lasagna, spaghetti and a number of fresh sandwiches. A variety of chicken dishes round out the entrées, providing tasty choices for everyone in your group. The restaurant also features a full service bar, a fine selection of wines, and beer from domestic and local breweries. The Charco Broiler serves breakfast, lunch and dinner to appreciative locals and visitors. This family-oriented establishment is a popular breakfast stop, with giant platters of meat, eggs, potatoes and toast, and a variety of omelettes. The restaurant has a laid-back, comfortable feel, with dark wood, comfortable booths and intimate lighting. Service is friendly and the staff members are knowledgeable. If you have room for dessert, the restaurant's homemade pies make a delicious end to a fine meal. Make it a point to dine at the Charco Broiler and see for yourself what the buzz is about.

1716 E Mulberry Street, Fort Collins CO
(970) 482-1472
www.charcobroiler.com

Up the Creek Restaurant

Enjoy a breathtaking view of Vail when you dine at Up the Creek Restaurant. Located right beside sparkling Gore Creek, Up the Creek is one of the best settings to sample some of Vail's best cuisine. Owner Peter Stadler knows that quality dishes keep people coming back. Peter and his executive chef Kyle Cowan make sure that the food is as fresh as possible. You won't find halibut on the menu in the winter because it isn't in season until spring. Fresh salmon is flown in from New Zealand until Alaska salmon is mature. Kyle is passionate about cooking simply and allowing food to retain its natural flavor. House specialties include local wild game such as buffalo, elk and caribou. Buffalo burgers are a hot item. The adventurous eater might want to try kangaroo or ostrich. Be sure to try the local favorite, lamb, which is deemed by many as the best around. In addition to tasty meat dishes, guests can enjoy pastas such as the roasted tomato with fresh mozzarella ravioli or the seafood fettuccine scampi. For a lighter meal, the summer lunch menu offers eight tantalizing salads, including the crisp buttermilk chicken or the grilled flat iron steak salads. Whether you're a summer hiker or here to ski the winter slopes, stop by Up the Creek Restaurant and enjoy a great view with a great meal.

223 Gore Creek Drive, Suite 103, Vail CO
(970) 476-8141
www.vailupthecreek.com

Ghin Asian Blend & Sushi

Asian blend is not Asian fusion. That distinction is clearly made at Ghin Asian Blend & Sushi, where the union of flavors, textures and colors are subtle and altogether agreeable. Ghin means to taste and to eat in the Thai language. Because taste is an integrated experience of all the senses, it is a simple, universal pleasure. Mildy Sundarapura grew up in the restaurant business with her family in Colorado. After receiving her culinary M.B.A. degree, she opened the Tuk Tuk Thai Bistro. The restaurant was warmly accepted by the community, so that there are now four Tuk Tuks as well as Ghin Asian Blend. The sushi and many other dishes are not what you will find at other restaurants. The creative combinations of flavors are carefully considered, each a defined and complete journey of taste. Popular dishes include a most satisfying chicken Adobo, a roasted salmon with cilantro mango sauce and curry puffs. Ghin Asian Blend is quickly becoming a local favorite and merits regular visits when you find yourself in Lakewood. As it says on the menu, at Ghin Asian Blend & Sushi each meal is a small work of art that is exclusively yours.

220 Union Boulevard, Lakewood CO
(303) 914-9999
www.ghinrocks.com
www.tuktukrocks.com

MiZuppa Frisco

One of Colorado's most unique restaurants, MiZuppa Frisco will certainly please and delight you no matter when you visit. The menu changes daily to reflect the season, the weather or the whim of a creative chef. As the name suggests, this casual diner lures customers looking for delicious soup. It also serves exotic wraps, fresh salads and panini sandwiches at reasonable prices. In 2006, the Best of Summit competition named the restaurant Best Lunch Site. You can try traditional chicken noodle or tomato basil soup. The flavorful seafood gumbo or potato and smoked gouda soup might catch your eye. Courageous epicures might be drawn to the high country elk stroganoff or the vegetable soup laced with ostrich or wild boar meat. MiZuppa uses the freshest natural ingredients, and vegetarians and vegans will be happy to find selections just for them. A delightful range of homemade breads and cookies complete your meal. Soup and sandwich combos make the perfect choice for an early evening supper. Doug Schwartz started MiZuppa years ago after traveling through Italy and France sampling the work of the great chefs of Europe. In 2002, he sold the thriving restaurant to George Schmitt, who developed it into a franchise. Today, Colorado has four MiZuppa restaurants and more are planned. MiZuppa Frisco co-owners Wayne Scyzgial and Diana Armstrong welcome you to enjoy the soup in their little corner of the world.

842 Summit Boulevard #38, Frisco CO
(970) 668-8138
www.mizuppa.com/mizuppa_restaurant_frisco.php

Basil Doc's Pizza

When it comes to superior taste and inventive menus, the doc is in. At Basil Doc's Pizza, you'll find all natural, hand-tossed pizzas with local and worldly flavors. The menu is sure to please even the pickiest eater, with choices ranging from the zesty Moab pizza with chicken, pineapple and jalapeño to the Italian-inspired pesto pizza with fresh basil, garlic and olive oil. If you're looking for the ultimate cheese experience, try the quattro formaggio, with four types of exotic cheeses. For a real pizza adventure, try one of the many regionally inspired pizzas: New Haven clam, the El Paso, the Taos or Cabo San Lucas, each with its own individual combination of ingredients. If you're not in the mood for pizza, Basil Doc's also offers fresh organic salads, specialty calzones and strombolis. Originally an offshoot of Pepe's Pizza adjacent to the Yale campus in Connecticut, Basil Doc's has evolved to what the *Denver Post* now calls the "best pizza in town." Don't forget to leave room for the gelato—delicious Italian ice cream—and finish off the perfect pizza with a sweet cool delicacy usually only available in Europe. Owner Mike Miller invites you to indulge your taste buds at Basil Doc's Pizza in the Denver area.

1481 South Holly Street, Denver CO
(303) 782-9900
www.basildocspizza.com

smashburger

A new contender for the title of best burger around attempts to win over burger lovers by using only Certified Black Angus Steak. Fresh, never frozen, the meat is smashed on the grill to sear the beef and seal in the flavor. The result is no ordinary burger, but a delicious smashburger, which can only be found at the place called smashburger. The menu offers tantalizing smashburger options such as spicy Baja and mushroom Swiss, but one of the beauties of this restaurant is that you can create your own masterpiece. After deciding between a half-pounder and a third-pounder, you can choose your bun, cheese, sauces and toppings. The freedom to build-your-own applies to the chicken sandwiches and salads as well. In a nod to tradition, you can complement your main choice with French fries, or else enjoy something different on the side, such as an onion blossom or veggie frites, flash-fried asparagus spears, carrot sticks and green beans. The breakfast smashburger comes with bacon, fried eggs and cheese. The complete morning menu also features such specialties as pancakes, platters and Benedicts. Priding itself on being quick and casual, smashburger is nevertheless not your typical fast-food joint. Those who are serious about their burgers claim that it takes just one bite to tell the difference. Meet a prime candidate for your new favorite burger at smashburger.

1120 S Colorado Boulevard, Glendale CO 3356 Youngfield Street, Wheat Ridge CO
www.mysmashburger.com

The Original Hard Rock Café

Happy hour is a four-hour event that starts at three in the afternoon at the Original Hard Rock Café in Empire. This café, not related to the chain restaurant, got its start in 1934 when Pop Goodell bought the old Empire restaurant for $50 with another $50 due later if he could make a go of it. Pop renamed the restaurant in honor of the area's hard rock mining operations. The Hard Rock has seen many owners since and was gutted by fire in 2000. Today, the historic structure looks better than ever with wood ceilings, floors and walls, two old-time ceiling fans and an outdoor patio. Owners Dave Johnson and Eric Rebo are executive chefs who've remained flexible with their menu, looking for what foods please their customers most. Their breakfast burrito, which comes smothered in the house green chili, is an all-time customer favorite, earning fans from a diverse clientele who stop on their way to Loveland and Winter Park ski resorts. Their equally famous sourdough bread crowns such lunchtime classics as the BLT. You can enjoy breakfast or lunch daily and dinner on the weekends. Local microbrews are on tap. The historic quality of the scene and the consistent quality of the meals and service inspire many happy customers to buy Hard Rock Café T-shirts. Prepare for straightforward good cookin' and pleasant surprises at the Original Hard Rock Café.

18 E Park Avenue, Empire CO
(303) 569-2618
www.menusfirst.com/empire/hardsrockcafe.htm

Bono's Italian Restaurant

Bono means *good* and good Italian food is what Bono's is all about. Owner Albert Bono is of Sicilian descent, where his repertoire of recipes gets their influence. Born in Boston, Massachesetts, Al grew up on the ethnic cuisines from Boston's North End and the culinary marvels of his mother's authentic homemade cooking. Bringing to Golden a traditional Sicilian cuisine with an East Coast spin on it, Bono's has established itself as a fixture in the community for over 16 years. The menu includes such items as shrimp scampi, six-cheese lasagna and chicken parmigiana. A full-service bar offers a wide variety of wines, beers and liquors. Dessert cannolis and tiramisu are made fresh, and the espresso, cappuccino, mochas and Italian sodas have been complimented as being as good as some European cafés. Bono's is also known for its hearty submarine sandwiches. *5280 Magazine* bestowed an Editor's Choice award upon Bono's for its cheese steak panini. This family business is also run by Al's wife, Susan, who has created a home-style atmosphere that turns a meal into a social experience as well as a culinary one. Bono's Pizza is second-to-none in Colorado. Whether it's a chicken scampi pizza, Hawaiian or just plain cheese, Al's attention to detail leaves no question that every bite is as good as the first. For a truly enjoyable and authentic Italian dining experience, try Bono's for lunch, dinner or take-out and you won't be disappointed.

14799 W 6th Avenue, Golden CO
(303) 278-1068

Shakespeare's Pub & Billiards

Three-time president of the United States Billiards Association Jerry Karsh has been around the game he loves since 1945. Today he owns Shakespeare's Pub & Billiards, where the whole family can enjoy the game in a clean and airy atmosphere. Jazz music on Sundays and a pub menu with literary aspirations turn playing a few games of eight ball into a downright urbane experience. With its four carom, one snooker and 16 pocket tables, this pool hall caters to billiards players of all stripes. The antique-style, European tables are bound to be among the handsomest you will ever try. The pub features 57 beers and such food favorites as the Hamlet pizza, which comes with the works, and the Julius Caesar Salad. Bite into the Tempest, a classic Reuben, and taste why this sandwich made the Best of *Westword* list. *USA Today* named Shakespeare's one of the top ten pool halls in the United States, a credit to both the excellent facilities and the classy atmosphere. Refer to Shakespeare's *Antony and Cleopatra* (Act 2, scene 5) for the quote, "Let us to billiards," which inspired Karsh to name his establishment after the Bard. Knock the eight ball in the side pocket while reciting your favorite soliloquy at Shakespeare's Pub & Billiards.

2620 Walnut Street, Denver CO (303) 433-6000

Cinos Coffee & News

For a quick vanilla latte, a tasty bite to eat or to catch up on the day's events, the place to go is Cinos Coffee & News. With hundreds of magazine titles, you can browse for hours while sipping your favorite beverage. The menu encompasses classic favorites such as lattes, mochas and blended coffee drinks as well as smoothies and milkshakes, so you're sure to find a new favorite at Cinos. Breakfast and lunch items include deli sandwiches, burritos, salads and hot, fresh soups. Owners Kristi and Hank Stephan have roots in Lafayette and take pride as a locally owned and operated company. They love the social aspects of their work and try hard to make each and every customer feel welcome. Several local groups meet here weekly to catch up and make new friends—an endorsement for the comfortable, welcoming atmosphere at the shop. With free wireless Internet access, Cinos is also a great place to conduct business, update your blog while you travel, or just browse the Web. To soak in the atmosphere of a true local gathering place, stop by Cinos Coffee & News. You can relax and stay awhile.

2770 Dagny Way, Lafayette CO
(303) 926-9565

Miller's Bar & Grill

When you want to be where the fun is, go to Miller's Bar & Grill. Owned by Carolyn Miller and her son, Brad, Miller's has a cozy, festive atmosphere. The neighborhood grill is family-friendly, offering a children's menu for the younger set, and the food is excellent. Miller's has won local awards for its burgers and its red chili. The grill also makes fantastic sandwiches, appetizers and pork tenderloins. There are eight beers on tap, more than 30 additional brews and a full bar. Miller's opens early on Sundays for breakfast. It is a sports bar, so televisions are always tuned to the current games and events. Miller's offers food and drink specials to accompany sporting events such as NFL games and NASCAR races. Events as big as the Superbowl feature major prize giveaways. In true community spirit, Miller's even organizes group outings to attend local sports events. The bar offers NTN trivia and video games and will sometimes bring in live music. Once a month, there is a comedy show and karaoke. Be part of a treasured gathering place at Miller's Bar & Grill.

3021 N Garfield Avenue, Loveland CO
(970) 962-9659

Liz's Luncheonette

At Liz's Luncheonette, Liz Roach designs sandwiches the way some people design rooms. She starts with a basic concept, and then she gets creative, ending up with something that is as surprising as it is tasty. For example, she jazzes up the standard turkey-provolone by sprinkling on dried cranberries and walnuts and topping everything with a layer of blue cheese and pesto. Another house specialty combines roast beef with mushrooms, horseradish sauce and provolone. Conformity makes Liz restless, so she substitutes turkey for the expected corned beef in her Reuben. Customers can even build their own sandwich, and wash it down with a latte or fruit smoothie. Bagels top the breakfast menu, available with melted cheese, cream cheese and a myriad of other fillings. As a rule of the house, the breakfast burritos are more than ample in size. Loyal customers say that Liz's cookies are not to be overlooked. In addition to serving at her café, Liz also delivers and caters. Try Liz's Luncheonette for something creative to eat.

1600 Specht Point Road, Fort Collins CO
(970) 490-1322

Kobe An
Japanese Cuisine and Sushi Bar

A seemingly endless list of sushi choices awaits you at Kobe An, the oldest Japanese restaurant in Colorado. Ownership never cuts corners, but uses the freshest fish available for its delicious nigiri and rolls, including mackerel, striped bass and various tunas. There's fine imported sake to complement your meal and a traditionally elegant atmosphere in which to enjoy it. Besides sushi, you'll find everything from tempura and noodle dishes to such house specialties as curry and Japanese-style steak. Established in 1979, this restaurant caters to groups with its sushi plates, combination dinners and the popular Treasure Boat Dinner—all of which encourage sharing. The latter drops anchor at your table loaded not only with crab legs, rolls and lobster baked with Kobe An's own dynamite sauce, but with teriyaki chicken, beef kushiyaki and fresh seasonal fruits as well. Head Sushi Chef Rex Aoki specializes in creative sushi with his own distinct sauces. Michelle Trujillo, who owns Kobe An with her husband, Marco, recalls that her mother, Kimie, started the restaurant because she missed the food of her hometown in Japan. It is a testament to the quality and service that Kobe An enjoys such a strong and loyal clientele while doing very little advertising. Enjoy lunch or dinner at Kobe An, and then spread the word around that its fine Japanese cuisine is second to none.

85 S Union Boulevard, Lakewood CO
(303) 989-5907
www.kobean.com

Paradise Bakery & Café

You'll feel right at home when you enter one of the 11 Colorado Paradise Bakery & Café branches, with their outstanding food, lively music and passion for excellence. All of the food is made from scratch daily. The menu is extensive. To help you decide on your meal, try some of the many delicious samples always on hand. Breakfast includes omelettes with both meat and vegan choices. The Belgian waffles are out of this world. Yogurt-granola parfait is a popular healthy breakfast choice. The chicken walnut and turkey cranberry sandwiches are lunch-time favorites. The cafés offer several soups, among them the famous fire-roasted garlic tomato soup. You'll find a delightful choice of pasta and garden salads, with a variety of combination plates. Healthy kids meals come in cute packages, with activity sheets and pages kids love. Snacks and desserts? Choose a brownie, bagel or cinnamon roll. You may buy any of the breads to take home. The Paradise does a booming business with its catering services as well as the popular box lunches for parties from one to 100. Don't miss the Paradise Bakery & Café, where everyone leaves with a cookie and a smile. See the website for a Colorado location near you.

1001 16ᵗʰ Street, Suite A130, Denver CO
(303) 436-1192
www.paradisebakery.com

La Piazza - An Italian Restaurant

The Rocky Mountain News has named La Piazza's meatball sandwich the best you can get two years in a row. The paper also describes La Piazza as the place East Coast transplants flock to when they want real thin crust pizza. Jeannie and Nevin Rudloff have created one of Colorado's best Italian eateries, a place that is comfortable and family friendly, with prices that are as easy to swallow as their award-winning cannoli. La Piazza features a menu full of Italian specialties, including antipasto, grilled panini, pasta, house specialties, and, of course, pizza and calzones. Everything about this restaurant, from the black-and-white photos of Italy and the chunky, homemade marinara to the heavenly Tiramisu, speak of quality and authenticity. If you're planning a party with up to 45 people, La Piazza can accommodate you. They'll serve you from the menu, or they'll come up with a special party buffet tailored to your taste. The next time you are in the mood for outstanding Italian food, head to Wheat Ridge and visit La Piazza. You don't have to be from the East Coast to know great food when you taste it.

10160 W 50ᵗʰ Avenue, Unit #8, Wheat Ridge CO
(303) 421-3311

Dos Gringos
Burritos & Café Olé

Some days, it seems like everybody in Carbondale is headed to this popular restaurant that celebrates the mountain lifestyle. "It's the people's place," say owners Julie and Nelson Oldham, who serve up delicious burritos, wraps and margaritas, while going out of their way to support the community. Hosting fundraisers for scores of local non-profits and staying open late after the local high school football games are just a few of the ways they support the community. The walls feature the work of many local artists and dozens of signed posters by the talented bands the restaurant has hosted over the years. Of course, if you are hungry, what you will like best is the food that is served quickly and is all completely homemade. The Oldhams had never owned a restaurant before they took a leap of faith in 2000 and took the town by storm. Their adjoining coffee bar, Café Olé, serves organic coffee and creative breakfast burritos, like Green Eggs & Ham. Just follow the caravan of caffeine addicts on their way to Aspen Mountain for a day fresh powder skiing. Try breakfast, lunch or dinner at Dos Gringos Burritos & Café Olé and feel like a Carbondale insider.

**588 Highway 133, La Fontana Plaza, Carbondale CO
(970) 704-0788**

Trail Head Tavern

With daily food and drink specials and an old-fashioned tavern atmosphere, the Trail Head Tavern is a great place to eat, drink and be merry with friends. Owner Eric Flashner is proud that the bar and grill, which opened in 1996, is an old-time gathering place rather than a trendy nightclub. The food is tasty, plentiful and inexpensive. The Trail Head serves fish and chips, tacos, salads and a variety of sandwiches and burgers. The Bacon Cheddar Trailburger is a particular favorite among the locals. Other favorites include the Trail Burger as well as wings, which people say are the best in town. In addition to the regular menu, you'll find daily specials such as Meatloaf Monday and Beer & Brat Saturday. The tavern has 14 beers on tap, the majority of them from local breweries. Happy Hour is every day from 11 am to 7 pm. The Trail Head is a great place to watch the Broncos or any other of your favorite teams play. Televisions are scattered throughout the bar, and there's one large projection screen. The Trail Head Tavern also offers pool and foosball tables. If you're looking for a great place to sit and enjoy food and drink with friends, come to the Trail Head Tavern.

148 W Mountain Avenue, Fort Collins CO
(970) 221-5757

Café Bluebird

Serving up fresh and delicious breakfasts, lunches and coffee with a smile, Café Bluebird has been Fort Collins' Coziest Cafe since the early 1980s. Proof that it is one of the friendliest places around is that two of its owners, Edie and William Dahlgren, met and married while working here. The two, along with Laurie Thebarge, purchased the restaurant in 2000. It is truly a partnership of labor, love and friendship. You'll see a lot of familiar, friendly faces at the café. Edie and William estimate that 70 percent of the customers are regulars. Combine that with the fact that there's little turnover among the staff, and you'll see why this is the kind of place where most everyone knows each other by name. It's the quality of the food and service that keeps them coming back, though. Breakfast options including crépes florentine, croissants, omelets and many other delectable dishes. The restaurant is especially renowned for its blueberry coffee cake with brown sugar, cinnamon and walnut topping. Lunch options range from salads to sandwiches, pasta dishes and the all-American burger with your choice of toppings. Come on in to Cafe Bluebird for the company of friends old and new while you enjoy a hearty meal.

524 W Laurel Street, Fort Collins CO
(970) 484-7755
www.cafebluebird.com

Suzette's Fine Southern Cooking

Chris Dill got a lot of exotic requests when he was a private chef in Hawaii for six years, an experience that made him long to fix an old-fashioned meatloaf sandwich with mushroom gravy and sweet potato fries. Celebrating the joy of Southern-style comfort food is what Suzette's Fine Southern Cooking is all about. Chris is not only the chef but the owner of the restaurant, where his goal is to give Southern cuisine an upscale twist while providing an experience that the whole family can enjoy and afford. Dinner at Suzette's includes first and second courses, followed by a choice of entrée and the dessert du jour. While you can't go wrong with any of the entrée choices, the blackened catfish filet has been particularly well-met. In addition to his stint as a private chef, Chris also cooked at the Four Seasons in Hawaii, proving that he could hold his own with any of the trendiest chefs out there. These days he's just having a blast making people happy with his chicken and dumpling soup, egg salad sandwiches and fried green tomatoes. He invites y'all to join him for lunch or dinner at Suzette's Fine Southern Cooking.

181 N College Avenue, Fort Collins CO
(970) 482-5150

Fin's Grille

Only dynamite food finds its way onto Fin's Grille menu, resulting in a loyal local following in the midst of the tourist town of Glenwood Springs. Donny Andre was given the nickname Fin when he was working as an oyster shucker in a Daytona Beach raw bar—he was consistently tipped with five dollar bills. Two decades later, Fin is still his name. Despite the casual atmosphere of relaxation and good times, Fin's is upscale fine dining with a riveting dinner menu and an extensive wine list. The beef steaks come from Amish-raised, grain-fed Black Angus, aged two to three weeks to achieve tender perfection. Any meal can be embellished with a garlic rub, blackening, blue cheese crumbles or sides such as broiled lobster tail or sautéed mushrooms. The ahi tuna appetizer is notable. Mussels and oysters are handpicked and scrutinized by Fin's expert eye. Two-room dining separates an intimate dining room from the frolicsome side, where live music plays Thursdays and Saturdays. Tuesday nights are ladies' nights; appetizers and drinks are two for the price of one. Fin's Grille hosts private dinners and provides catering services, and a cooking school is in the works. The classes will be taught by Fin's award-winning chefs. Fin's supports the community, hosting a charity fundraiser every year and sponsoring local scholarships. The motto at the restaurant is Living the Dream, and that is exactly what you will be doing when you sit back for a great meal at Fin's Grille, only steps away from the Colorado riverfront.

**710 Grand Avenue,
Glenwood Springs CO
(970) 945-4771**
www.finsgrille.com

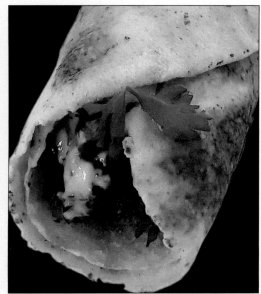

Photo by Stuart Spivack

The Pita Pit

The package makes all the difference at the Pita Pit, where your sandwich comes to you not between heavy slices of sourdough in a handy pouch of flatbread. The pita bread may be lightweight, but it can hold a lot of stuffing, making pitas a fast, satisfying and relatively low-calorie meal. The Greek gyro-style pita, featuring tasty strips of seasoned beef and lamb, is the most popular item on the menu. Try it with such traditional toppings as cucumber, black olives and Feta. The Pita Pit also offers many vegetarian options, including falafel, baba ganoush and hummus pitas. For an American bend on the tradition, try one of the inventive breakfast pitas with such fillings as eggs, avocado and sausage. Salads, soups and smoothies round out the menu at this perfect lunchtime dive. Owners Greg and Amber Krasnodebski point out that Fort Collins has the second highest number of restaurants per capita of any town in the United States, meaning cruel competition for any establishment below first-rate. The Pita Pit excels by offering a distinctive product and doing all the little things right. Drop by and taste for yourself why this lively place has been pleasing hungry crowds since 2002.

1232, W Elizabeth Street, Fort Collins CO
(970) 416-7600
www.pitapitusa.com

Pete's Place/Papa Frank's

Like the bustling kitchen of a big, Italian family, Pete's Place/Papa Frank's restaurant has something lively happening every night of the week. If you missed Team Trivia on Tuesday and Texas Hold'em on Wednesday, join in on Friday or Saturday for the mutual embarrassment of Karaoke. Through the week you can catch a bit of live music to delight your family as you enjoy your meal together. Tom Rizzi brought his successful Broomfield restaurant, Papa Frank's, to Frederick and melded it with the existing restaurant, Pete's Place. The combined restaurant makes in-house all the homemade Italian staples it serves up, including the hamburger and sausage. Some recipes are treasured culinary heirlooms from Tom's family. The spaghetti with sausage meat sauce has pleased thousands of hungry people over the years. In the summer months, seafood lovers delight in the all-you-can-eat Fresh Fest with selections of shrimp, mussels, calamari and crab. Pete's Place/Papa Frank's is a community-minded business that participates in special events such as Frank's Run, an annual motorcycle event raising funds for the Make a Wish Foundation. Bring your own lively family to Pete's Place/Papa Frank's any day of the week for a memorable night out.

201 5th Street, Frederick CO
(303) 833-2818

The Vault Tavern

Since 1999, customers looking for a fun night out with friends have been streaming to the Vault Tavern. The Fort Collins tavern began its life as a bank in 1907. Some of the original features are still there, including the large vault door that gives the tavern its name and the majestic 18-foot ceilings. The original old-fashioned fireplace gives guests a cozy place to warm up in the winter, while a patio out back is the perfect place to enjoy a warm summer night under the stars. Even on the busiest nights, there's plenty of room to move about and socialize. The walls are decorated with the works of local artists and the sounds of live music and poetry often fill the air. The Vault has 10 beers on tap, none of them domestic. It offers daily drink specials, with happy hour Monday through Friday, from 3 pm to 7 pm. A small food menu satisfies for those looking to grab a quick bite. Rick describes the Vault as a *Cheers* kind of place, where everybody, from the regular customers to the serving staff, knows your name. If you're looking for a friendly neighborhood tavern to enjoy a drink and some company, come to the Vault Tavern.

146 N College Avenue, Fort Collins CO
(970) 484-0995

Los Arcos

This restaurant has been serving up traditional Mexican food for nearly 30 years, since owners Ignacio and Adela Luevano moved here from Mexico. Now in its second generation of Luevano family operation, Ignacio and Adela's children, John and Sandra, help keep the hot plates steaming and the salsa spicy. While the margaritas are reason enough to stop in, you won't want to miss the zesty food made from century-old recipes. Be sure to try the green chile fajitas made entirely from scratch. The marinated steaks are enough to please even the hungriest visitor, while the cilantro-spiced quesadillas offer a cheesy piquant that wakes up the taste buds. For dessert, the famous Los Arcos cheesecake burrito is always a treat for new and returning customers. This deep-fried flour tortilla enfolds a creamy whipped cheesecake batter and is topped with ice cream and fresh strawberries. Perhaps the only thing better than the food is the family-oriented ambiance inside the restaurant. Whether you're a local regular or it's your first visit, you'll be welcomed in like one of the family. The attentive staff is happy to immediately seat you and serve fresh homemade salsa and warm chips as an appetizer to your meal. If you happen to stop by on a Friday, you'll be serenaded by the spunky sounds of a mariachi band fully decked out in traditional attire. For a fiesta in your mouth, make Los Arcos your next stop for authentic Mexican food.

4991 W 80th Avenue, Westminster CO (303) 426-8523
9045 Forsstrom Drive, Lone Tree CO (303) 858-8860
www.arcosrestaurant.com

Chicago Times

Chicago may have invented Chicago-style pizza, but the deep-dish, buttery-crusted temptation reaches perfection at Chicago Times in Loveland. Select from an array of enticing meats, such as Italian sausage and marinated chicken breast, to fill the mouth-watering crust. The wide variety of toppings and fillings include, artichokes, feta cheese and even French fries, so dive in and imagine yourself in the windy city. Many satisfied customers rave about the huge chunks of fresh veggies and the killer sauce. Remember, though, pizza is only part of the Chicago Times' menu. Experience another Chicago institution and try a Vienna hot dog, described as a hot dog that has been dragged through a garden, complete with onions, tomato wedges, pickles, a few peppers and a dash of celery salt. Chicago Times offers a comfortable, cozy eatery where you can scan the city coastline painted on the walls and watch Chicago sports teams on television while the kids enjoy video games. Take-and-bake selections and delivery to the entire city of Loveland will help you indulge your pizza and calzone cravings at home. Reasonable prices and comfortable surroundings make Chicago Times your kind of place.

115 E 29th Street, Loveland CO
(970) 461-0651

Richard's On 3rd

Nestled among homes in Old Town Longmont lies a delicious gem to those who come from near and far to dine on authentic Southwestern fare. The historic landmark building has a glorious outdoor garden complete with a water feature providing soothing background to conversation taking place under umbrella-covered tables. Inside, you will find a similar cozy atmosphere with café tables and chairs, old-fashioned lamp posts, slate floors and striped awnings. The atmosphere everywhere is local, warm and welcoming. The dining experience is extraordinary. Richard and his wife, Judy, relocated from Taos, New Mexico after having owned a well-known restaurant there. They brought the flavors of authentic Southwestern foods back with them and added a creative twist of their own. Award-winning margaritas are found at the top of the menu—truly outstanding. Enjoy these or any of their assorted beers, from Longmont or Mexico, or a glass of wine alongside freshly made guacamole or thick green chile salsa with chips. Now you move on to the main Southwestern entrées and house specials. Chile rellenos, enchiladas, burritos, tacos and quesadillas are popular dishes, but do not miss the award-winning Fresh Mango Blue Corn Green Chile Chicken Enchiladas or Smoked Mussels Rellenos. If you visit for lunch, enjoy these dishes,k or one of the gourmet salads or delicious creatively prepared sandwiches.

1283 3rd Avenue, Longmont CO
(303) 776-0985

Casey's Bistro & Pub

The luck o' the Irish is alive at Casey's Bistro & Pub—fine food, drink, fun and friends are guaranteed every time you go in. The owners, who identify themselves as "two Irishmen, an Aussie and an American," named their pub after the famed Irish playwright Sean O'Casey, whose portrayals of Irish life made him a hero of the Emerald Isle. It's that everyday life and friendship that's celebrated every day at Casey's. Patrons gather to celebrate, commiserate and generally enjoy each others' company in the welcoming atmosphere of the pub. And what better way to enjoy the company of friends than with good food and drink? You'll find a variety of American pub grub here, but if you want the authentic Irish experience, try such favorites as shepherd's pie, pot-steamed mussel, corned beef and cabbage or classic fish and chips. You'll raise your glass to the fine selection of European brews on tap here, as well as Colorado favorites including Coors and Fat Tire. Casey's is the local sponsor of the Colorado Rapids Major League Soccer team and hosts viewings of the away games at the pub. It also supports the local rugby team and raises funds for the local children's hospital, extending its sense of to the community. Here's a toast to the food, friends and fun you'll find at Casey's Bistro & Pub.

7301 E 29th Avenue, #100, Denver CO
(720) 974-7350
www.coloradopubcompany.com

Hoke's Genuine Pit BBQ & Catering Company

Darin (Hoke) Holcomb got his start in 1996 catering to businesses and parties. Today, Hoke's Genuine Pit BBQ & Catering Company continues to cater to parties of all sizes, but the restaurant is the big attraction. As soon as you step in, you'll smell the results of Hoke's passion for true Southern barbecue. Hoke's slow smokes all of its meat for many hours to give it that true taste of Texas. Home-grown sauces come on the side, mild and spicy. Try the beef brisket, Pappy's hickory-smoked prime rib or the deep-fried catfish dusted with cornmeal and served with rémoulade dip. The marinated cole slaw is a favorite side. All of the food is prepared daily and made fresh right in the kitchen to ensure a taste like no other. Hoke's prides itself on being a working man's place. The atmosphere is warm, the prices are fair and a buck will still buy you a beer. "We close when the meat runs out," Hoke says. The community has rallied behind the establishment from its opening day, and Hoke feels it's only fair to give back to the community. The company has supported Ronald McDonald House and the Susan G. Komen Foundation to fight breast cancer. Hoke's Genuine Pit BBQ has one mission—to keep it genuine. As the slogan says, where there's smoke, there's Hoke.

9134 W 88th Avenue, Westminster CO
(303) 424-QPIT (7748)
www.hokesbbq.com

Castillon's Mexican Restaurant

Castillon's Mexican Restaurant has brought the bright, spicy flavors of Mexico to Fort Collins for more than 10 years. Owner John Castillon has been a part of the tradition of excellence since 1973, when he got a job as a dishwasher there. The restaurant was then known as the El Dorado. John went on to enjoy a brief career as an accountant, but when the restaurant became available in 1997, he decided it was an opportunity he couldn't pass up. "I had to come back to a business I love," he said. He brought his whole family into the business, including his mom, sisters and brother. John's cooking incorporates some old favorite recipes from the El Dorado together with some of his mother's recipes, including her renowned pork tamales. The Mexican tradition of fresh food is alive and well here, with everything including chips and salsa made fresh daily. Castillon's is especially renowned for its fajitas, served sizzling and ready to eat. Castillon's is mindful of its place in the community, with 25 percent of sales every Thursday going to charity. If you're looking for a fun, family-oriented place to go for authentic Mexican food, try Castillon's Mexican Restaurant.

320 S Link Lane, Fort Collins CO
(970) 493-2739
www.castillons.com

Bumpa's Barbecue

If lip-smacking, mouthwatering ribs rate high on your list, you won't find a better spot than Bumpa's Barbecue. Co-owners Mike Lowry and Charles Ash have devised a process of smoking and barbecuing their meats in a way that can't be beat. Their secret? Alligator juniper and their own spicy rub. Alligator juniper is a hearty tree found in the mountain regions of the Southwest. It has a high heat output making it excellent for barbecuing. Bumpa's special rub, which took several years to develop, finds its way on all of the delectable meat served at this popular dining spot. Ribs are slow-cooked throughout the day; other meats are cooked for 12 hours. Bumpa's keeps the menu simple. Choose from baby back ribs, pulled pork sandwich, beef brisket or lime chicken. Add some baked beans, coleslaw or potato salad and you've got yourself a meal that satisfies. Eat at the restaurant or call in your order. Bumpa's creates custom packages to feed almost any size get-together. Barbecue sauce, Bumpa's rub and Bumpa's rib kit are sold separately. Be sure to grab some on your way out. Bumpa, by the way, is the name Lowry's grandkids gave him and it stuck.

13½ S Parish Avenue, Johnstown CO
(970) 744-4846
www.bumpasrub.com

Coral Room

What is filet mignon doing on the menu of an Asian and Pacific Rim restaurant? Perhaps it's there so chef/owner John Nadasdy can prove that his talents aren't limited by some prescribed notion of culinary boundaries. A contributor to *Citysearch Denver* declared the Coral Room's filet mignon "the best I've had in the country." John brings in the Asian influence by preparing his with ginger soy marinade. Korean lamb shank and coconut curry with chicken, shrimp or tofu are other highlights on a menu rich with flavorful delights. Known for attracting a hip, sociable crowd, the Coral Room features many specials throughout the week, including two-for-one appetizers every day during happy hour. On Monday nights, wines are half price by the bottle, though most are also available by the glass. Families enjoy the Reef Room, which includes a play area for kids. John and co-owner Nick Mystrom opened the first Coral Room in the Highlands in 2002 and followed with a second in Stapleton in 2005. Managers Sue Nelson in Highland and Jerry Hise in Stapleton invite you to be part of the thriving social scene and celebration of flavor at the Coral Room.

3489 W 32nd Avenue, Denver CO (Highlands)
(303) 433-2535
7352 E 29th Avenue, Denver CO (Stapleton)
(303) 321-WINE (9463)
www.coralroom.com

Buca di Beppo

Step inside Buca di Beppo restaurant and you'll be instantly transported to 1950s Little Italy. The scent of baking bread wafts from the ovens, mingling with the spicy aromas of garlic, homemade marinara and Alfredo sauces. Buca di Beppo is dedicated to delivering the flavors of old Italy in new, exciting combinations. Start by picking out an aged, imported wine to enjoy with your meal. The fresh artichoke spinach dip is a perfect appetizer for the menu ahead, made with asiago and Romano cheeses, garlic, black pepper and sage. Buca's famous pizzas are made in the Naples style, using specific imported ingredients and baked in a wood-burning oven. Naples is the origin of pizza, and connoisseurs still consider Naples pizza the finest in the world. Of course, the toppings at Buca di Beppo are full of modern zest. Try the Spicy Arrabbiata, with 4 cheeses, red onions, spicy sausage, pepperoni and toasted fennel seeds. Buca's wide selection of pasta dishes and entrées are inspired by old-world Sicilian recipes and made in large portions, so they can be shared among large groups or taken home as some of the tastiest leftovers. But don't fill up before you get some dessert. Buca makes tantalizing tiramisu, spumoni and chocolate cannoli. Indulge in the best of old and new Italian cuisine at Buca di Beppo.

1400 Market Street, Denver CO
(303) 595-EATS (3287)
www.bucadibeppo.com

Positano's Pizzeria

A transplant from the east coast who grew up in an Italian family moves to Colorado and suffers cuisine shock. How does he survive? "I found that if you wanted to eat Italian, you had to make it yourself," says Doug Blardo, who teamed with Biago Scotto, a 40-year veteran in the pizza business, to open Positano's Pizzeria. For more than 15 years, they have stayed competitive with the chain stores by hand-making their pizzas with the finest cheeses and ingredients while keeping their prices affordable. New York-style thin crust pizza is the specialty. For a monster of a pie made with love, try the Supreme. It comes with just about everything you can imagine going with tomato sauce and mozzarella, including three kinds of meat and a whole garden of vegetables. The Bianco, on the other hand, appeals to minimalists with fresh roma tomatoes marinated in olive oil, garlic and fresh basil on a bed of cheese. The menu includes many more gourmet pizzas, plus calzones, stromboli and five different pasta dishes. "Sure, there are many places to enjoy New York-style pizza in town," notes Amanda Koubek-Keller, restaurant reviewer for the *Coloradan*, "but not one place comes as close to the 'real deal' as Positano's." Drop by and experience why this pizzeria makes everyone feel like a New Yorker at heart.

3645 S College Avenue, Fort Collins CO
(970) 207-9935

Lemon Sisters Deli, Café and Food to Go

Established in 2000, the Lemon Sisters is well on its way to becoming the Denver institution that owner Claire Griffin envisions it being some day. The business has already earned recognition from *5280* magazine for having the Best Lunch Under $8 and from *Westword,* which named it Best Lunch-Delivery Service, praising its filling salads and homemade soups, particularly the Thai Pumpkin. Each day, the kitchen crew at Lemon Sisters starts before the sun to prepare fresh baked scones, cinnamon rolls and coffee cake for the breakfast crowd. The breakfast burritos are also very popular. Sandwiches stacked high with a quarter-pound of meat plus a choice of cheese and veggies make a hearty lunch. The menu also offers vegetarian and sugar-free selections. Works of a local artist co-op, T.A.G. (The Art Guild), adorn the café. Claire was once part of a touring comedy act known as the Lemon Sisters, a name that stuck when she shifted her focus to the food industry. Today, Claire teams with her mother, Myra Griffin, who has been helping restaurants run for more than 30 years. Grab a bite at Lemon Sisters, or have your breakfast or lunch delivered to you anywhere downtown at no extra charge.

617 22ⁿᵈ Street, Denver CO
(303) 825-4133
www.lemon-sisters.com

Historic Johnson's Corner

The Food Network featured Historic Johnson's Corner as one of the Five Top Truck Stops in the United States, but plenty of folks who have never driven anything larger than a minivan come every day to experience this celebrated American enterprise. Whether you are hauling cargo to California or hauling a hungry family to grandma's house, this full-service truck stop, restaurant and motel will replenish you for the journey ahead. There's no need to call ahead when that urge for chicken-fried steak, green chili or cinnamon rolls strikes, because Johnson's has not shut its doors since it opened in 1952. Back then, it was just a gas station in the middle of farmland. Today, Interstate 25 runs right past it. Located halfway between Denver and Cheyenne, Wyoming, and only an hour from Rocky Mountain National Park, its facilities include an RV campground and even a chapel. *Travel & Leisure* magazine once selected it as offering one of the ten Best Breakfasts in the World. In 1999, the 106th *Congressional Record* of the U.S. House of Representatives recognized Johnson's Corner for exemplifying "the industrious spirit and can-do attitude that have made America great." Take a break from the road at Historic Johnson's Corner.

2842 SE Frontage Road, Johnstown CO
(970) 667-2069
www.johnsonscorner.com

Jus Cookin's Restaurant

Jus Cookin's Restaurant in Lakewood was founded in 1988 on great food, friendly service and reasonable prices. After almost 20 years, it has earned the reputation as one of the best places in Colorado to enjoy home cooking. Family owned and operated by Steve and Char Modlich, the restaurant serves up old-fashioned comfort food made-from-scratch daily. Jus Cookin's is open for lunch and dinner, and the menu includes such favorites as fried chicken, meatloaf and chicken pot pies. Other familiar entrées include chicken fried steak, Yankee pot roast and liver and onions. Lunchtime finds patrons dining on open-faced turkey or meatloaf sandwiches and huge fresh salads. Soups are homemade and change daily. Summertime at Jus Cookin's means scrumptious fresh raspberry, blackberry and peach cobblers. Chef Steve uses about 10,000 pounds of Colorado peaches each summer for his peach cobbler. In March 2003, the fried chicken and roast turkey and stuffing at Jus Cookin's was named one of America's 75 Best Food Buys by *Food & Wine* magazine. Go where the locals go. Jus Cookin's is a comfortable place to bring your family, friends and out-of-town guests for some of the best home cooking you'll ever find in a restaurant.

Simms Street & 8th Place, Lakewood CO
(303) 205-0123
www.juscookins.com

Pete's Kitchen

Pete's Kitchen is Pete Contos' flagship restaurant, and of his eight restaurants, it serves the most varied clientele. The breakfast crowd arrives hungry and leaves satisfied after devouring breakfast burritos and such hearty all-American food as steak and eggs and stacks of pancakes. Burger lovers choose Pete's Kitchen for lunch or dinner, while those with a taste for Greek comfort food enjoy gyros and souvlaki. Pete's Kitchen also serves a number of Greek specialty dishes, including chicken ka-bobs and Greek-style baked chicken. Sources such as *5280 Magazine* and Citysearch Denver have repeatedly honored Pete's Kitchen with awards such as Best Breakfast Burrito, Best Hash Browns and Best Cheap Eats. Other accolades include Best Breakfast and Best Late Night Dining. If you enjoyed the party just a bit too much last night, you'll be glad to know that Pete's also ranks as Top Place to Nurse a Hangover. In short, you should think of Pete's Kitchen as your all-purpose diner, which stays open 24/7, 365 days of the year. What's more, the folks here and at the other Pete's restaurants look after your health by progressively eliminating all trans fat from the food they serve. Treat your appetite to a meal at Pete's Kitchen.

1962 E Colfax Avenue, Denver CO
(303) 321-3139
www.petesrestaurants.com

Pete's Restaurants

It's an inspiring story—how a man from a small town in Greece became a dean of Denver's Greek community and a member of the Colorado Food Service Hall of Fame. Pete Contos bought the first of his eight restaurants in 1962 with money he saved during seven years as a service industry employee. That venture, the Satire Lounge, is still going strong serving Mexican food at Colfax and Race Street. Pete's Kitchen soon opened nearby, and these days there seems to be a Pete's to fit every mood. If you seek fine Greek cuisine, try Pete's Central One Restaurant on South Pearl. Pete's Ice Cream satisfies snackers with Pete's own blend of gourmet coffee and Dreyer's ice cream. Expressing pride in their heritage, Pete and his friend Taki Dadiotis persuaded City Council in 1995 to designate a six-block stretch of Colfax Avenue as Greektown. Five of Pete's restaurants are located in this area, including the Bank Bar & Grill, the Gyros Place and Pete's Greek Town Café. If you're near the University of Denver in the south part of town, try Pete's University Park Café. All told, the businesses employ about 150 people, many of whom have worked for Pete for 20 and even 30 years and can't imagine working for anyone else. A local magazine writer summed up Pete's contribution to the Denver scene best: "We've all spent time in one of the eight restaurants he owns, surrounded by the good food, friendly service and comfortable buzz of activity." Make a visit to one of Pete's places a part of your Denver experience. Check Pete's website for more info on each of his places.

www.petesrestaurants.com

Lakewood Grill & Bar

Lakewood Grill & Bar offers an eclectic menu of tavern food, choice steaks and ethnic specialties in a vintage glass block and exposed brick building that has become a local landmark. The grill, in business since 1950, boasts the oldest continuous liquor license in Lakewood and offers great drink specials to complement outstanding food. You may spot owner Eleftherious "Larry" Cusulos driving up in his classic 1950 Buick Special, the same model that Howard Hughes owned. Once inside you'll have a hard time choosing from the tempting menu. Try the Paisano Pie, a deep-fried calzone, or The Postman, a breakfast plate that smothers a chile relleno, two eggs and home fries in green chile, jack and cheddar cheese. Still other favorites include El Gordo's Burrito, a super-stuffed burrito, and green chile by the cup or bowl. Appetizers, soups and salads, plus sandwiches, both specialty and classic, round out the menu. Another featured classic is Joanne the waitress, who's worked at the grill since 1981. Although Joanne won't tell her age, she's rumored to be near 80 and gave Larry her two-year notice three years ago. Lakewood Grill serves great live music as well, with blues jams, acoustic jams, classic rock 'n' roll and karaoke offered on various nights of the week. Come on over to the Lakewood Grill & Bar, where your favorite food and cocktails are always in style.

8100 W Colfax Avenue, Lakewood CO
(303) 237-8051

Jose O'Shea's Café & Cantina

Jim Hotchkiss has been in the restaurant business his whole life. With his finger on the pulse of the Lakewood community, he was looking for the next need to fill, along with the help of his son, Chad Hotchkiss, and wife, Cathy Hotchkiss. What they saw was a distinct need for New Mexican cuisine—a variation of Mexican cuisine characterized by frequent use of green chiles, cilantro and cumin. In 1978, Jim founded Jose O'Shea's Café & Cantina and teamed up with Victor Huff to design the restaurant as a festive homage to the traditional adobe villa with clay tile roofs. Chef Arturo Martinez presides at the restaurant with a menu full of specialty burritos. The popular Garbage Burrito weighs in at two-and-a-half pounds with everything but the kitchen sink in it. He makes 20 different sauces from scratch, including his grandma's hatch green chile sauce and a lip-smacking jalapeño cream cheese sauce, to enhance his dishes. Saturdays and Sundays feature a brunch menu, with live mariachi and harp music on Sundays. While the main floor of the restaurant offers a classic family atmosphere, the upper floor caters to the cantina crowd. Readers of *Westword* and the *Rocky Mountain News* both voted Jose O'Shea's for the Best Happy Hour in Colorado. It features a free taco bar and chicken wings with drinks. You're guaranteed a fun time when you visit Jose O'Shea's Café & Cantina.

385 Union Boulevard, Lakewood CO
(303) 988-7333
www.joseosheas.com

The Canyon Chop House

Since 2005, lovers of succulent steaks, fine wines and an elegant atmosphere have been having a grand time at the Canyon Chop House. The steakhouse is owned and operated by Chef Matt Schump and his wife, Maggie. Matt received his culinary training in Portland, Oregon, before working in fine restaurants in Washington, D.C., Lake Tahoe and Boulder. During that time he honed his skills and developed specialty in contemporary American cuisine. Matt determined that Fort Collins was in need of a fine steakhouse and decided to open one. At the Canyon, most everything is made from scratch from the freshest ingredients. Many of the ingredients, including the finely aged Coleman Beef and the delectable Walrus Ice Cream, are from Colorado suppliers. The steakhouse is renowned for its steaks, aged and grilled to perfection. You'll also find braised beef short ribs, coriander crusted tuna and a variety of other elegant favorites. The wine list has more than 180 selections and a full range of beer and liquor options, so you're guaranteed to find the perfect beverage to complement your meal. A grand dining experience awaits you at the Canyon Chop House.

211 Canyon Avenue, Fort Collins CO
(970) 493-9588
www.canyonchophouse.com

Virgilio's Pizzeria Napoletana

Virgilio's Pizzeria Napoletana holds a special place in the hearts of those who take pizza seriously. Virgilio's burst onto the scene in 2005 and in its first year, earned such coveted awards as Top 10 Best New Restaurants by *5280 Magazine*, Best of CitySearch 2006 and 2007, Best NY Style Pizza by the *Rocky Mountain News*, and Best in Denver by AOL's CityGuide. This authentic pizzeria is your passport to Italy. Owner Virgilio Urbano was born in Naples, Italy, and grew up close to the famed pizza epicenter, Wooster Street, in New Haven, Connecticut, less than an hour from New York City. Virgilio brings the best of Italy, New York and New Haven to Colorado. Rather than describe the pizza, or pies as they are called, here's what local food critics have said: "It was some of the best New York-style pizza I'd ever eaten," the *Rocky Mountain News* claimed. "I brought nonbelievers to Virgilio's and they left having been converted to the faith. They testified to the magic that happens when great crust, sauce, cheese and toppings meld into one." *5280 Magazine* said, "The verdict is in, thanks to our readers, and I have a new favorite spot for pizza—and garlic knots." The *Denver Post* said, "About the garlic knots: Under no circumstances should you walk out of Virgilio's without a big mess of them, either in your belly or in a to-go box." If it's your first time here, start with the garlic knots, an Italian beer and the amazing *verde* salad, and then hit the authentic Margherita pizza. Bring a big group (or appetite) and try the big Stromboli and the house favorite, a white pie loaded with ricotta, garlic, sausage, sun-dried tomatoes and spinach. Head to Virgilio's Pizzeria Napoletana and save the airfare to Italy.

7986-B W Alameda Avenue, Lakewood CO
(303) 985-2777
www.virgiliospizzeria.com

Santiago's Mexican Restaurant

The demand for really good Mexican street food seems to increase with every new customer to Santiago's Mexican Restaurant, and Santiago's just keeps growing. All 21 locations are managed by the same team: Carmen Morales, Eric and Martine Casados, Shawn and Rachel Wells, and Thomas and Suzzette Olguin. All continue to use the same family recipes that made the pilot restaurant in Brighten such a hit when it opened in 1990. Santiago's caters to families, keeping prices low and the atmosphere friendly. It's open for breakfast, lunch and dinner. It's renowned for its stuffed sopapillas, award-winning breakfast burritos and energetic, vivacious staff. *Denver Westword* recognized Santiago's as having the Best Cheap Breakfast in town. Top of the Rockies awarded it Best Green Chile in Colorado. Santiago's customers consume more than a million pounds of chile each year. The product is also sold in many Colorado supermarkets. Experience authentic Mexican cuisine and find a new home away from home at Santiago's Mexican Restaurant.

21 locations
www.eatatsantiagos.com

Florindo's Italian Cuisine

Florindo's Italian Cuisine serves authentic Italian dishes drawn from every region of Italy, not just one or two. Owner and Chef Florindo Gallacchio, a native of Italy, created the entire menu himself. His signature dish is the poached salmon, but the whole menu is a delight. Among the many choices you'll find baked rigatoni in parchment paper, homemade tiramisu and a variety of seafood and handmade pasta dishes. The exclusive wine list represents the best of Italy. The ambience is contemporary European. Word-of-mouth is Florindo's major form of advertising, and a usually packed house is evidence that the word is good. Gabby Gourmet featured Florindo's as one of the Top Restaurants in the Rocky Mountains and Zagat Survey gives it an excellent rating. Florindo came to New York from Italy in the 1970s. He worked at various restaurants before finding his permanent home in Glenwood Springs. Florindo and his wife, Roza, opened Florindo's Italian Cuisine together in 1988. The restaurant offers catering and takeout in addition to elegant celebrations. Sample Florindo's Italian Cuisine to survey the finest of traditional Italian fare.

721 Grand Avenue, Glenwood Springs
(970) 945-1245

Sacred Grounds
Coffeehouse & Delicatessen

It's the customers that are sacred at Sacred Grounds Coffeehouse & Delicatessen. Owners Joel and Liz Karr have made their restaurant a place where you'll be comfortable, happy and well-fed. Virtually everything at Sacred Grounds is made from scratch. The deli has fresh breads ranging from white to marble rye, as well as a broad selection of wraps and bagels. For breakfast, enjoy a variety of sandwiches and wraps, with ingredients such as eggs, bacon, lox, salsa and avocado. Lunch options include sandwiches, homemade soups and chili. Enjoy a delicious smoothie made from whole fruit or a steaming cup of espresso with coffee from a local roaster. For dessert, try a delectable homemade brownie or sticky bun. The atmosphere here is warm and friendly, with plenty to do. Sacred Grounds was the first restaurant in downtown Glenwood Springs to offer free Wi-Fi service. There's a free Foosball table for those looking for a little competition. Heavenly food, drink and atmosphere await you at Sacred Grounds Coffeehouse & Delicatessen, the restaurant with a heart.

725 Grand Avenue, Glenwood Springs CO
(970) 928-8804
www.sacredgrounds.biz

Clancy's Irish Pub

Clancy's, just a wee bit west of Kipling, has been a frequented stop since 1973. The pub was originally owned by Bob Murray, who built the business one handshake and one well-poured drink at a time. Joyce Wood and her family bought the pub and its traditions after Bob's death in 1997. To honor Bob and build on the already successful business, the Woods decided to begin offering fish and chips as served in many English pubs. Now their fish and chips is legendary—*Westword* magazine voted Clancy's the best fish and chips in Denver. Along with great spirits, Clancy's has a large variety of appetizers. Enjoy the traditional hot wings or the oysters on the half shell. For a bit o' the green, try one of the fresh and creative salads. The steak salad is marinated steak sliced thin served on a bed of fresh greens, peppers and onions. If you want something a bit different, try one of the awesome sandwiches. Many regulars love the Tipperary, a grilled chicken melt on rye topped with crispy bacon and cheddar. Or try one of the flavorful sausage sandwiches, such as the Clancy's Pride and Joy, smoked beef sausage steamed in beer and served open-faced on bread. Customers appreciate that all of the deli items are available by the pound. Visit Clancy's where the best o' food, the best o' spirits and the best o' people come together.

10117 W 37th Place, Wheat Ridge CO
(303) 424-2964
www.clancysipub.com

White House Pizza

White House Pizza celebrated their tenth anniversary in 2007. The pizza is half of the reason for their success—the other half is the atmosphere of fun and amazing specials. Besides pizza with an extensive choice of toppings, White House serves a mean barbecue and a variety of pasta, oven-baked sandwiches, appetizers, soup, salad and desserts. The restaurant has a full bar. Diners can choose to eat upstairs or out on the patio. They can also phone ahead and pick up their order or have it delivered. For groups and events, White House Pizza offers drop-off or full-service buffets. Regular specials include a Sunday glass of wine for a dollar with any pasta order and a free pint of beer with a barbecue entrée on Thursday. Live music plays every Wednesday. White House Pizza is a three-time winner of the Locals Choice award for Best Pizza and a three-time winner for Best Restaurant. The menu was developed by husband and wife team Kurt and Marla Korn, with a little help from nine-year-old Chally and eight-year-old Tanner. Kurt originally crafted his cuisine in Metro Denver, but the family was enamored with the beauty of Carbondale. Build it the way you want it and be part of the family at White House Pizza.

801 Main Court, Carbondale CO
(970) 704-9400
www.whitehousepizza.com

Juicy Lucy's Steakhouse

Located on the stunning riverfront of Glenwood Springs, Juicy Lucy's Steakhouse serves superior meals in a cozy atmosphere of warm-colored woods. When you try the Sterling Silver steak, which uses only the top 12 percent of quality wholesale beef, you'll understand why people stop in Glenwood Springs just to eat at Juicy Lucy's Steakhouse. In addition to quality meats, Juicy Lucy's Steakhouse serves two fresh fish specials daily, as well as organic vegetables and fruits sourced from local growers. For your salad course try the Seventh Street Salad, prepared with honey and poppy seed vinaigrette and served with strawberries, Gorgonzola cheese and spiced, honey-roasted walnuts. For an appetizer, a sure bet is the popular Elk in Fillo. This local delicacy is sautéed with spinach, pine nuts, goat cheese and mushrooms wrapped in a warm fillo purse. It is served with Shiraz bordelaise sauce. Offering over 200 fine wines, Juicy Lucy's Steakhouse has been awarded the *Wine Spectator* Award of Excellence. Owners David and Cece Zumwinkle serve as chef and dining room manager, respectively. They invite you to savor the rich flavors and original recipes at Juicy Lucy's Steakhouse.

308 7th Street, Glenwood Springs CO
(970) 945-4619

American Samurai

American Samurai Grill & Sushi Bar offers diners an intoxicating blend of American and Japanese flavors. Opened in 2004, this restaurant was Brighton's small business of the year in 2005. American Samurai wants everyone to know that Japanese food is much more than raw fish. Though the menu contains many of the most popular raw items, most of the sushi is cooked. You'll find everything from the familiar California roll to the more exotic Godzilla roll, freshwater eel and cucumber topped with avocado and strawberry. American Samurai's mouthwatering menu of hibachi-grilled items includes tuna steak, chicken teriyaki and shrimp. Looking for fusion cuisine? Try the Asian baby back ribs with plum barbecue sauce or the grilled strip steak with an Asian spice rub. Even the all-American cheeseburger shows up, with or without teriyaki sauce. More purely western items include prime rib and drinks such as espresso and cappuccino. Banana Spring Roll and green tea ice cream top the dessert menu, and a children's menu is available. Check the bar for your favorite alcoholic concoction. American Samurai offers quarterly wine tastings. The atmosphere is casual, with a sense of Japanese simplicity in the red and tan décor. Come to American Samurai, where delicious Eastern and Western flavors meet.

245 Pavilions Place, Brighton CO
(303) 659-2230
www.americansamuraigrill.com

Toast

Toast has always been a breakfast staple; now it's one of Littleton's best places to go out for breakfast or lunch. The restaurant serves all your good old American favorites, including pancakes, French toast, eggs Benedict and omelettes. It's the unique twist the chef has put on all these classics that makes Toast pop up above the competition. There are four different varieties of French toast here. Try it infused with chai tea and topped with clover honey, caramelized apples and vanilla ice cream. For a spicy variation, choose the Santa Fe French Toast, stuffed with egg, chorizo and green chiles and topped with queso anejo, salsa rojo and a smoked chili sour cream. Pancakes get a similar makeover, with varieties including Oreo cookies, strawberries and bananas and lemon and blueberry. Want a taste of all of them? Order the Pancake Flight platter and feed your whole table. For lunch, there's a variety of sandwiches, including the familiar BLT, loaded with crispy bacon. You'll also find more exotic varieties, including a grilled shrimp and bacon club and the restaurant's famous crab cake sandwich. The atmosphere is friendly and the service quick. Raise your glass to a breakfast-lunch menu that's fun and friendly to everyone.

2700 W Bowles Avenue, Unit B, Littleton CO
(303) 797-9543

Great Scott's Eatery

Great Scott's Eatery is like crazy, man. Burgers and shakes top the menu of classic all-American favorites at this restaurant with a 1950s theme. Begin the day with pancakes or show up later when the craving strikes for the quarter-pound bacon cheese burger or the half-pound Big Bopper. The chicken fried steak is popular as is the hot turkey dinner. Burritos, rellenos and enchiladas head the list of Mexican treats. Many folks cruise in just for dessert. If you're in the mood for homemade pie, we recommend apple for traditionalists and the Creamy French Silk Chocolate for the post-modern. The Jumbo Sundae comes with three scoops of French vanilla ice cream and a pantry full of choices for toppings. The tips that Justin Abrams made when he worked here bussing tables must have been fantastic, because he bought this fun place in 2000. He is proud to serve quality food in a family atmosphere at an affordable price. Preparing food for Meals on Wheels and participating in various fund-raising efforts are some of the ways that he gives back to the community. Sing "At the Hop" and "Love Me Tender" on your way to Great Scott's Eatery.

7510 W Highway 287, Broomfield CO
(303) 469-5291
1551 N Cortez Street, Denver CO
(303) 428-3558
www.greatscottseatery.com

The Gold Hill Inn

Folks in the know have long taken the winding trail up Boulder's Sunshine Canyon to eat at the Gold Hill Inn. Inside, the rustic log cabin has massive stone fireplaces, antique paintings and comfortable log chairs. Frank and Barbara Finn opened the restaurant in 1962. Sons Chris and Brian Finn are now managing operations and continue to serve their six course meals, with the menu reflecting the seasonal offerings of local markets. Homemade bread and soup is followed by salad and a creative appetizer, perhaps an avocado stuffed with smoked fish. For an entrée, savor roast pork loin with Robert sauce or fresh salmon with sorrel sauce. For dessert, enjoy sour cream apple pie or flourless chocolate torte. You'll finish with a fresh fruit and cheese platter. On Friday nights, the inn hosts local and touring blues and bluegrass bands. Bluebird Lodge, a renovated nine-room miner's hotel, is available for Murder Mystery dinners. Nine couples participate in the overnight Mysteries that include hors d'oeuvres, five-course dinner with wine, after-dinner brandy and breakfast at the inn. For an evening to remember, don't miss the Gold Hill Inn, which *Gourmet Magazine* has called one of the best restaurant values in America.

401 Main Street, Gold Hill CO
(303) 443-6461
www.goldhillinn.com

Strings

Strings is one of Denver's hippest restaurants. Great service and delicious New American cuisine have long attracted both visiting celebrities and loyal locals. Popular and bustling, Strings is lighthearted and casual, never stuffy. The bright and airy retro-modern interior features chrome chairs and contemporary art. Head Chef Ed Kent transforms the menu seasonally with dishes that dramatize fresh local ingredients. Popular appetizers include beef *carpaccio* and sautéed crab cakes. Duck confit ravioli and seafood risotto are among the pasta creations. Popular seafood entrees include cashew-crusted sea bass and Riesling-poached salmon. Beef, veal and chicken dishes are available as well. Owner Noel Cunningham, born in Ireland, followed his family into the culinary trade at age 14. He was a sous chef at London's famed Savoy Hotel by age 23, a notable feat. After service at top Los Angles-area restaurants, he came to Denver in 1986 to open Strings. Noel is well known locally for his philanthropy. Chef Ed Kent has been working in restaurants since he was 10, when the dance of the kitchen first mesmerized him. Strings offers full-service catering and private rooms for special parties. Turn your next dinner out into an enchanting experience at Strings. The staff will be delighted to see you.

1700 Humboldt Street, Denver CO
(303) 831-7310
www.stringsrestaurant.com

Sports Column

According to co-owner Mark Kinsey, the Sports Column is located exactly 96 steps from Coors Field, home of the Colorado Rockies. Closely tied to the club for which such heroes as Dante Bichette and Todd Helton played, this sports bar opened in 1995 on the eve of the team's inaugural season. After you spend some time soaking in the atmosphere and draining a mug of beer or two in one of its three big rooms, including an outdoor rooftop patio, you will be qualified to settle a friendly dispute. Was *Sports Illustrated* right in naming the Sports Column the 19th best sports bar in America, or is Mark's mom right in proclaiming it the best in the world? Fox Sports Network, *Top of the Rocky*, and Citysearch all agree that it is the best in Denver, at least. The food is as fun and as hearty as the fare sold at the ballpark, and includes the Rockie Dog—an all-beef kosher dog served with relish, onions and your choice of sides. Other signature selections include the hand-cut Iowa pork tenderloin and the chipotle chicken wrap. The weekday all-you-can-eat soup and salad bar makes the Sports Column a smart choice for lunch. The Sports Column doesn't exactly shut down when baseball is out of season. Folks pack the place to cheer for the Broncos and Nuggets and to follow sports from all over the world on the many television screens. Root, root, root for the home team at the Sports Column, the official sports bar of the Colorado Rockies.

1930 Blake Street, Denver CO
(303) 296-1930
www.denversportscolumn.com

The Hornet

Since 1995, the Hornet has established a reputation in Denver for pleasing everyone. Its fail-proof menu offers comfort foods with a twist. You can order a beer and burger or a creative entrée and martini and feel right at home at the restaurant. Its snazzy, contemporary design, with crayon-colored walls and crisp lines, makes for a trendy atmosphere. The outdoor patio is a hit in the sunny seasons. Always known for its burgers, the Hornet also serves a variety of soups and sandwiches, meat and pasta dishes. The Shells 'N' Cheddar, with lobster, pasta shells and cheese, has been noted as one of the best meals in town. Located in the historic Baker district and less than a block from the Mayan Theater, the Hornet is a great place to launch a date of dinner and a movie. The restaurant offers daily drink specials and stays open late for the after-movie crowd—the kitchen works until 12:00 and the doors don't close until 2:00. Saturdays feature a live music series from 10:00 until closing. Bring your friends, family and dates to the Hornet, where a good time is to be had for all.

76 Broadway, Denver CO
(303) 777-7676
www.hornetrestaurant.com

Café Europa

If the urge for a decadent pastry, a made-from-scratch panini sandwich or specialty coffee strikes any time between six am and midnight, you can find relief at Café Europa. This popular spot is considered by many to be Denver's coolest coffee house. Curiously, its story is tied to Hurricane Katrina. Exactly one year after that devastating natural disaster forced her to flee her home in New Orleans, Heidi Baltzer took over the ownership of Café Europa with the force of a tornado. She got rid of all artificial flavorings and anything else made from chemicals, canceled orders for pre-made sandwiches and brought a whole new attitude to coffee-making operations here. Nothing but a perfect pot every time pleases Heidi, who buys her coffee from three local roasters and offers 30 kinds. After running a much larger coffee house in New Orleans, she loves the smaller, neighborhood vibe at her new place. She improved the lighting and added wireless Internet access, making Café Europa a place where folks like to hang out. Word around here is that everything on the menu tastes good and fresh, but that the Hobo Potatoes are something really special. Drop by Café Europa as often as you can—a few times throughout the day works for some people.

76 S Pennsylvania Street, Denver CO
(303) 722-1024
www.cafeeuropadenver.com

Carlos Miguel's Mexican Bar & Grill

Carlos Sedano and Miguel Martin, owners of Carlos Miguel's Mexican Bar & Grill, invite you to discover what fresh, authentic Mexican food really tastes like. Everything is made fresh and to order, and many of the recipes were originally created from Sedano's grandmother's recipes. Don't forget to try her unique dessert, Enchiladas Dulces, crepes served warm with vanilla ice cream and drizzled with caramel sauce. For lunch or dinner, enjoy the flavorful Pollo Borracho, a chicken breast stuffed with poblano chiles, mushrooms, red bell pepper and cotija cheese. Top it with spicy habañaro sauce and get lost in the feast. Looking for a lighter dish? Try a tasty appetizer such as fried zucchini or a cheesy quesadilla. Carlos Miguel's prides itself on its creative cooks, who often go outside the box and feature a Chef's Creation. These may include Mexican-style salmon, shrimp or vegetarian dishes, each with its own special flair. Don't miss happy hour from 3:30 to 6:30 daily, when drinks, including the famously huge margarita, are $2.95 and appetizers are 50 percent off. Take your taste buds on a trip south of the border with a visit to Carlos Miguel's Mexican Bar & Grill.

740 N Summit Boulevard, Frisco CO
(970) 668-4900

Benny Blanco's Slice of the Bronx

The last delivery of the day at Benny Blanco's Slice of the Bronx could be someone's late snack or early breakfast. Orders go out all over Denver and the surrounding areas until 3 am at this authentic New York-style pizza joint. The New York pizza standard, of course, is all about the crust. You'll know as that first slice folds in your hand for the first bite that Benny Blanco's has mastered the art of the New York crust. Benny's makes pies up to 24 inches in diameter and offers as many as 20 different toppings. There's even a delicious thick-crusted Sicilian pizza. Benny's huge sub sandwiches are another menu favorite, along with chicken parmesan, manicotti and calzones. Regulars rave about the garlic knot appetizers. Eat in at Benny Blanco's Slice of the Bronx, order take out or have your meal delivered to your door, even as the rest of Denver is sleeping.

2009 Larimer Street, Denver CO
(303) 298-1476
www.bennyblancos.com

Hunter's Restaurant & Pub

Diners at Vijay Mehra's Hunter's Restaurant & Pub love the lively atmosphere, terrific food and superlative service they enjoy with each visit. Whether you seek a quick lunch, elegant dinner or just a stop-in with friends at the pub, Hunter's fills the bill. Fresh seafood and Angus beef are featured menu items that always satisfy. The curry walnut-crusted halibut is a signature dish, along with the Ahi tuna and the 12-ounce New York Angus steak. Angus beef burgers, dressed with portobello mushrooms, bacon and fancy cheeses are also popular. Appetizers of note include flash-fried golden calamari and phyllo crab triangles. The restaurant's set menus are famous—four-course meals of culinary delight. The well-rounded wine and spirits list nicely completes your dining experience. In the pub, you'll find munchies and entrees to complement your choice of beverage. Customers in the know bring their social and business gatherings to the restaurant's party room facilities. Treat yourself to a memorable dining experience at Hunter's Restaurant & Pub.

600 S Airport Road, Longmont CO
(303) 485-9980
www.huntersrestaurant.com

Appleridge Café

If you order the daily lunch or dinner special at Appleridge Café, you'll receive a free piece of pie with your meal. Owner Roy Jones and his staff want you to be pleased with every aspect of your visit to Appleridge, a Wheat Ridge tradition since 1979. They serve breakfast all day long and add a dose of friendliness that everybody, from regulars to far-flung travelers, appreciates. When a recent vacationing couple complimented the café's signature Breakfast Burrito, the hostess gifted them with cinnamon rolls, wishing them well on their travels. Everything at Appleridge is made from scratch, from the pies to a cream gravy recipe Roy got from his late mother. Employees peel 3,500 pounds of potatoes a week for a steady stream of hungry customers who frequent the café between 6 am and 8 pm Monday through Saturday. Friday night is steak night, with T-bone, rib eye or New York strip steaks at dazzling prices. Wednesday's lunch special is pork chops. Some of the cooks go back to the restaurant's earliest days. Bring your appetite to Appleridge Café.

3790 Kipling Street, Wheat Ridge CO
(303) 423-6800

Cherry Tomato

Chef Tom Felese's earliest memories are of his Italian-born grandmother lovingly preparing a delicious Sunday dinner for her family. At the Cherry Tomato, you'll get that same memorable Italian dinner experience. Tom honed his skills at the Culinary Institute of America, but his heart has always been in the handed-down recipes of his family. Tom and his staff prize the Italian tradition of using only the finest, freshest ingredients. "This is real Italian food cooked by a real Italian chef," Tom says. He notes with pride that when his mother is visiting from New York, she often helps out in the kitchen. You'll find all your favorite pasta dishes here, ranging from the familiar spaghetti and lasagna with slow-simmered sauce, to pasta puttanesca with capers, diced tomato and olives tossed with basil pesto, sundried tomatoes, garlic and olive oil. Those looking for heartier fare will delight in the chicken and veal parmigiana, breaded and baked to perfection. Seafood lovers will find plenty to please their palates, including frutte di mare (gems of the sea), with shrimp, clams, mussels and calamari with a choice of marinara, white wine or white cream sauce served over spaghetti. The wine list specializes in Italian vintages, organized by region, ensuring that you'll find the perfect wine to complement your meal. The casual Italian family dinner atmosphere is alive here, with a friendly staff that will see to your every need. Bring your friends and family to an authentic Italian family dinner at the Cherry Tomato.

4645 E 23rd Avenue, Denver CO
(303) 377-1914
www.cherrytomatodenver.com

Frasca Food and Wine

Frasca Food and Wine is the creation of co-owners Bobby Stuckey, master sommelier, and Lachlan Mackinnon-Patterson, chef. Their shared passion for the cuisine and fine wine of Friuli in northeast Italy is reflected in the exquisitely prepared fare and a comprehensive wine list boasting more than 200 varieties. The atmosphere is in the spirit of a traditional *frasca*, a friendly gathering place where farmers, friends and families could come and share a wonderful meal and plentiful wine. It is warm, welcoming and elegant but unpretentious. The food is classically Italian with a creative blend of herbs, spices and fruit. The menu changes to reflect the seasons and there is always something new to tempt you. Be sure to try the grilled, shaved Colorado leg of lamb or the butter-roasted Alaskan halibut. For dessert, don't miss the torte, seasonal fruit with chocolate cake and Valrhona dark chocolate gelato. Frasca's friendly and professional staff ensures a memorable evening with its attention to detail, expert wine pairing and extensive knowledge of the menu. Visit Frasca for impromptu gatherings, casual dinners, or special occasions. You are sure to have a wonderful time.

1738 Pearl Street, Boulder CO
(303) 442-6966
www.frascafoodandwine.com

Mi Casa Mexican Restaurant & Cantina

After a day on the slopes, enjoy a personal fajita buffet with tequila-marinated meat, caramelized onions and poblano chiles at Mi Casa Mexican Restaurant & Cantina. The restaurant has been satisfying hungry skiers and anyone else who appreciates Mexico's best culinary traditions since Alexandra Storm opened the restaurant in the 1970s. Dick Carleton became a partner in 1981, adding to a team that has sustained attention to detail throughout a long and exemplary tenure. At Mi Casa, Mexican food is a passionate undertaking that has involved some of the same managers for more than 20 years and resulted in long-time chefs and attentive servers. The restaurant is open daily for lunch and dinner and features a three-hour happy hour. You will find plentiful margarita choices and a selection of 80 tequilas. The tamales are made in-house, and signature dishes abound, including fish tacos and red trout encrusted with nuts. Black beans and Spanish rice accompany many dishes. Quesadillas, burritos, chimichangas, enchiladas—if you have a favorite Mexican food, Mi Casa probably serves it. Desserts include deep-fried ice cream, sopapillas and flan. Discover what 30 years of success means to you at Mi Casa Mexican Restaurant & Cantina.

600 S Park Avenue, Breckenridge CO
(970) 453-2071
www.stormrestaurants.com

Papa Frank's

In the 1970s, Frank Rizzi volunteered his family to supply a campaign dinner for Gary Hart, and they prepared an outstanding homemade spaghetti dinner for 375 people. This piece of family history set the wheels in motion for the creation of Papa Frank's Homemade Italian Food Restaurant, named in honor of the indomitable Frank Rizzi. His grandchildren, Dan Rizzi and Cindy Ritchey, own and operate the restaurant today, which continues to draw new customers with consistently tasty presentations of everyone's traditional favorites. Papa Frank's pasta is homemade on-site, and the meatballs come from a family recipe. There is a different special offered daily and all-you-can-eat spaghetti on Tuesdays and Sundays for one low price. Although spaghetti is the signature dish, everything is good. Breakfast is served until 11 am Saturday and noon on Sundays. When breakfast is over, lunch and dinner are both available. Papa Frank's is minutes from downtown Denver. If you don't have time to wait for a table, take advantage of Papa Frank's take-out service. Either way. Don't miss the opportunity to taste Papa Frank's famous spaghetti.

6570 W 120th Avenue, #C1, Broomfield CO
(303) 469-1401

Back Porch Café

For Mike Cooper, owner and chef of Back Porch Café, cooking is creating. Since 1983, customers have been enjoying the homespun specialties coming out of his kitchen that have made Back Porch Café one of their favorite destinations. Completely unassuming and unpretentious, this restaurant consistently presents fresh, quality food in the spirit of the Colorado outdoors. The bread and pies are homemade, and so are the chorizo and sausage. You'll find all of your favorites, made better. For breakfast you can choose a light meal such as quiche with fresh fruit or a full-on hearty breakfast. Or try one of the breakfast burritos—Mike began serving them 22 years ago, at a time when he was alone in offering such a treat. The large variety of lunch options includes delicious sandwiches on fresh, toasted, homemade bread. The many popular dinner choices include apple and smoked prime rib, house grilled salmon, and the house specialty, the Southwestern Chicken Burrito. Dine in or enjoy the beautiful Colorado views from the courtyard. Whichever you decide, the recipe for a great time is a helping of friends, mixed with the best micro-brews and great food at the Back Porch Café.

1101 E Lincoln Avenue, Fort Collins CO
(970) 224-2338
www.lambspun.com/BackPorch/bp.htm

Photo by Jeremy Hochhalter/Absinthe Photography

Holy Canoli
Italian Grill and Baked Goods

Holy Canoli Italian Grill and Baked Goods is an inviting place to linger in a warm and inviting atmosphere with views of the Rocky Mountains. Jim and Fran Worth and their three children opened the restaurant in 2007, but they started dreaming of it back in the 1990s. The whole family participates in the restaurant, which specializes in dishes that have been handed down from Fran's family. Sausage and meatball canolis are always popular. Pastas are freshly tossed, while spaghetti, lasagna, chicken parmesan and cheese-stuffed shells promise heavenly dining. The soups are made in-house as are the cookies. The grill carries gelato and sorbetto in 12 flavors. You can order an Italian soda, beer or wine to go with your meal and enjoy it in a spacious interior with three walls of windows or from a seat on the patio. For upbeat dining, visit Holy Canoli Italian Grill and Baked Goods.

2851 W 120th Avenue, #100, Westminster CO
(303) 465-HOLY (4659)
www.theholycanoli.com

Tuscato Ristorante Italiano

Visitors to Frisco find their way to Tuscato to savor authentic regional cuisine. Offering selections from several Italian regions, this popular restaurant challenges you to choose from an array of authentic dishes. Try Sicilian veal Marsala or osso buco, a delectable Northern Italian Milanese favorite consisting of braised veal prepared in a vegetable broth. You will face a tantalizing range of pasta dishes including Lasagna alla Bolognese, with béchamel sauce, parmesan and Bolognese meat sauce. The finest Italian cuisine demands fresh vegetables, so expect daily selections to change according to season. An impressively extensive wine list allows you to choose the perfect accompaniment to your meal. Top off your repast with chocolate caramel grande cake, four layers of rich chocolate cake with chocolate caramel frosting, or succumb to strawberry lace cheesecake. Daily specials often include a chef's choice, and full-service catering is available either at your location or at the restaurant. Owners Robert and Stephanie Kato are from Northern and Southern Italy and strive to represent all of Italy's foods here. Tuscato was voted Best Italian Restaurant in Summit County by *Summit Daily News*. Once you discover Tuscato, you won't have to fly to Florence or Rome to enjoy the delicious flavors of genuine Italian cuisine.

307 Main Street, Frisco CO
(970) 668-3644

La Tour Restaurant & Bar

La Tour Restaurant & Bar owner Paul Ferzacca is "the most innovative chef in Vail." That's what *Cooking Light* magazine had to say about the cuisine that has earned this restaurant the praises of *The Denver Post, Atlanta Tribune* and many other renowned critics. Paul's excellence comes from innate talent as a chef and a résumé that includes work at some of the most renowned restaurants in America, including the Ritz Carlton and Spiaggia restaurants in Chicago. At La Tour, visitors are treated to contemporary French cuisine in what one writer called "a chic and trendy setting." From a house salad with toasted goat cheese, to lobster bisque and escargot, the menu features a variety of elegant dishes to please your palate. Seafood lovers will delight in the options here, including seared ahi, citrus and fennel-crusted salmon and the ever-popular Dover sole. Certified Angus rib-eye steaks and a pan-roasted rack of lamb offer a hearty meal. The restaurant also features vegetarian options, including a roasted corn and shallot agnolotti. Be sure and save room for dessert, including the flaming créme brulée with berries. A certified somellier, Paul prides himself on the restaurant's extensive wine list, which has won the Award of Excellence from *Wine Spectator* magazine for seven years in a row. Come enjoy what *Ski Magazine* calls "one of the best culinary secrets in Vail" at La Tour Restaurant & Bar.

122 E Meadow Drive, Vail CO
(970) 476-4403
www.latour-vail.com

WaterCourse Foods

The greatest compliment owners Dan and Michelle Landes receive—and they receive it often—is that WaterCourse Foods has become a favorite restaurant for someone who previously thought he or she could not enjoy a vegetarian meal. A decade ago, WaterCourse started with breakfast and lunch five days a week. Today, it is open for all meals seven days a week and features its own bakery, which produces breads and pastries that are free of eggs, gluten and dairy products. The Landes' dedication to sustainable living and healthful, delicious food choices has earned their restaurant dozens of kudos, including Best Vegetarian Restaurant from *Citysearch*, *Westword* and the *Denver Post*. Choices are plentiful at WaterCourse, where you can order real maple syrup for the banana bread French toast and put soy, rice, whole or skim milk on the house-made granola. You can build your own salad with up to 40 fresh ingredients and order wine, beer or smoothies to go with your meal. Dinner specialties include BBQ Tofu, seitan steak and pasta. Michelle and Dan use biodegradable carryout containers and recycle whenever possible. Their 2006 remodel used recycled wood. Wake up and taste what's happened to vegetarian food in Middle America at Watercourse Foods.

837 E 17th Avenue, Denver CO
(303) 832-7313
www.watercoursefoods.com

Sweet Basil

A creative, modern American restaurant in the heart of the Vail village, Sweet Basil is Colorado's Most Popular Restaurant according to the prestigious Zagat Survey. A local favorite for more than 30 years, this restaurant has also won AAA's Four Diamond Award for providing "exceptional cuisine, great service and an elegant dining atmosphere" for the past two years. Owner Matt Morgan and his staff pride themselves on the dedication to quality that has earned them all those accolades—and after a meal here, you'll be joining the chorus of praise. Sweet Basil features a menu that changes with the seasons, ensuring that your food is made with the finest, freshest ingredients available. With elegant lunch options, including everything from a gourmet twist on the all-American burger to roasted leg of lamb salad, and dinner options ranging from prime rib-eye steak to North American venison, there's something on the menu for every taste. Save room for such delectable desserts as the sticky toffee pudding with rum caramel sauce. Pick the perfect wine to complement your meal from a list featuring more than 500 selections from around the world. Come savor the flavors of Sweet Basil.

193 E Gore Creek Drive, Vail CO
(970) 476-0125
www.sweetbasil-vail.com

The French Press

For an authentic French restaurant experience, the intimate bistro setting of the French Press restaurant is the perfect place for food and wine lovers. Stop in for breakfast and get a taste of real French toast, which can be prepared traditionally or stuffed with strawberry cream cheese and honey. For a breakfast on the spicier side, the French Press offers a specialty quiche of the day, and several other French, American and Mexican dishes. Lunch at the French Press may include any of a wide variety of fresh salads, zesty wraps and hearty sandwiches, such as the perfected French dip, served on a baguette with tender roast beef and warm au jus. Juan Cruz Anon, the Cordon Bleu-trained executive chef, outdoes himself at dinner at the French Press, and mouth-watering meals such as roasted Dijon chicken and grilled venison loin draw locals and visitors in by crowds. Enjoy one of the artisan cheese plates for an appetizer or dine like a Frenchman on Juan's Mussels a la Provençal, simmered in garlic and white wine. Stop in to the French Press today and see why this Colorado treasure is impressing people from all over the world.

34295 Highway 6 # C1B, Edwards CO
(970) 926-4740
www.thefrenchpress.net

D'Agostino's Mugg-n-Pye

If you love Italian food, then there's a very good reason why you would want to be in Frederick on a Wednesday, Thursday or Friday afternoon. That's when Dorothy D'Agostino serves her lunch buffet at D'Agostino's Mugg-n-Pye. You know there will be a couple of kinds of pizza. From the salad to the pasta, it's all you can eat. D'Agostino's is also open for dinner and offers delivery throughout the area. Dorothy and her crew make everything from scratch, including sausage, ravioli and the sauces. Over the years, the party room at the restaurant has been the site for many a big and boisterous Italian wedding. When things get too hot on the dance floor, you can step out onto the patio for a nice view of the city park and Miners Monument. D'Agostino's started out in the family in the 1970s. Dorothy has been running it since 1981, during which time she has formed solid ties to the community, helping out with functions all over town. She may be too modest to talk about it, but her employees can recite a detailed list of charities that she supports and contributions that she has made to numerous causes. For a business with a big heart, a huge party room and a lunch buffet for grand appetites, go to D'Agostino's Mugg-n-Pye.

141 5th Street, Frederick CO (303) 833-2270 www.dagostinosmuggnpye.com

Washington's Sports Bar and Grill

Claiming to serve the world's best burgers, Washington's Sports Bar and Grill is a must-do on any trip through Colorado. Our favorite is the Howlin' Coyote Bacon Burger, with homemade barbecue sauce. Providing classic bar and grill fare is what the folks at Washington's do best, whether it's poppers, wings, foot-long dogs or steak. You can also find less-common specialties such as the buffalo burger, the Rocky Mountain Oysters (don't ask) or the Peep (chicken smothered in fixings). Washington's has been around since 1978, making it a favorite among knowing locals, but it still brings in fresh faces daily with creative, delicious lunch specials. Once you're there, it's not just the food that will captivate your senses. The bar treats its patrons to poker games and trivia on a daily basis, DJs two nights a week and live cover bands each Friday. Megan Ingram and Shane Belcher, the personable hands-on owners, have decorated their establishment with kitschy farm equipment, aviation-themed objects and eccentric movie props that complement Washington's laid-back atmosphere. This is a bar with plenty of local history, and nearly everyone in Fort Collins has a story to tell about it. From 21st birthdays and engagements to raucous good times, Belcher and Ingram invite you to come make your own story.

132 Laporte Avenue, Fort Collins CO
(970) 484-3989
www.thewashbar.com

Mike O'Shay's Restaurant and Ale House

Enjoy a hearty and delicious meal perfectly prepared from fresh, quality ingredients and served with a smile at Mike O'Shay's Restaurant and Ale House, where owner Mike Shea has been serving the community of Longmont for more than 25 years. This popular eatery is the city's longest running, independently owned restaurant and features a diverse menu of delicious dishes from home and abroad, such as traditional Irish corned beef with cabbage and the restaurant's original Texas Cheese Chicken. Mike, a New Jersey native, started his culinary career at the age of 19 with a job in Bermuda, eventually returning to his home state. In 1977, he relocated permanently to Colorado, where he and his wife, Nania, opened Mike O'Shay's in 1981. Mike and Nania are sticklers for fine ingredients and carefully create their dishes from scratch. This attention to quality and impeccable service give this family-owned restaurant its charm. Mike O'Shay's stocks 15 different wine vintages and keeps 11 varied beers on tap. Finish your meal with such desserts as homemade apple crisp or Philly-style cheesecake and a choice of delicious coffee blends, including O'Shay's famous Irish coffee. Gather with friends and family or impress your colleagues while dining on a repast fit for kings at Mike O'Shay's Restaurant and Ale House.

512 Main Street, Longmont CO (303) 772-0252
www.mikeoshays.com

Shopping & Gifts

Nepal Tibet Imports

Clothing and accessories top the list of merchandise at Nepal Tibet Imports, where walking through the door feels like stepping into another country. Since 1993, owners Pranesh and Mina Maskey, both from Nepal, have been serving as cultural ambassadors, using their store as an uplifting place where people can come not only to shop but to appreciate the arts, crafts and dress of a distant land. Pranesh doesn't work through wholesalers; he travels to Nepal to purchase his merchandise. Shirts, scarves and handbags in every color of the rainbow brighten the store and are sure to lend vibrancy to your wardrobe. In addition, Nepal Tibet Imports carries artwork that Pranesh has selected from the markets of his home country. He buys metal work in Kathmandu, woodwork in Patan and stonework in Bhaktapur. You will find statues of Buddha and of Hindu gods and goddesses, pieces to turn a corner of your home or garden into a sanctuary. You will also find handmade paper journals as well as meditation materials, including incense, candles and music. Nepal Tibet Imports and a second shop, Thamel Imports Gift Shop, are located in the heart of the campus and business districts of Fort Collins, making them popular with students and tourists as well as with people throughout the area who embrace the cultural and religious aspects of Nepal, Tibet and India. For some cultural immersion to go along with your shopping, travel into Nepal Tibet Imports or Thamel Imports Gift Shop soon.

**129 S College Avenue, Fort Collins CO
(Nepal Tibet Imports) (970) 482-8681
19 Old Town Square, Suite 138, Fort Collins
(Thamel Imports Gift Shop) (970) 224-1000**
www.nepaltibet.com

A & J Antique Mall

Some years ago, Joann Malara caught the treasure-hunting bug from her sister. By the early 1990s, Joann owned too many antiques and collectibles to fit into her own home. That's when she decided to become a dealer, opening A & J Antique Mall in 2001. "Once you get into it, it never leaves you. There's no 12-step program for this affliction," says Joann, who loves to meet the people and hear the stories behind their finds. A & J Antique Mall belongs to Ft. Collin's Antique Row, a string of flea markets and antique malls at the south end of the city. More than 90 dealers sell at the 13,000-square-foot mall, which draws its clientele from throughout the United States and countries as far away as Japan, New Zealand and Italy. Enjoy complimentary coffee and tea as you tour the impressive assortment that earned A & J the 2006 Best Antique Store designation from the *Coloradoan*. You might find a military artifact, Native American artwork or the perfect Shabby Chic décor item. The mall's impressive collection of estate jewelry is popular with young people shopping for weddings. Prices at the store range from $1 to $10,000. Prepare to catch treasure-hunting fever at A & J Antique Mall, open seven days a week.

**6012 S College Avenue, Ft. Collins CO
(970) 226-6070**

Lipstick Ranch

KC Willis captures the Old West in fiber art collages that look like they came from a covered wagon. She's been selling her Lipstick Ranch collection to stores around the country for several years and her works are featured in a national catalog. In 2007, she opened the Lipstick Ranch shop in Longmont that also functions as her studio. Her favorite subjects are cowgirls of the Wild West, who she calls "the strongest women who ever lived." Her collages tell stories about such characters as Annie Oakley and Calamity Jane. The work usually includes a quotation and sepia-toned photo that KC scans and transfers to fabric. She frames this core with scraps of torn lace and vintage or artificially aged fabric, then finishes pieces with buttons or ribbon. Some collages are framed; others come affixed to furniture that KC's husband Logan Smith refurbishes for the shop. Lipstick Ranch art appears on clothing and journals, as well as on pillows. The store also carries work by other Colorado artists and gift items such as soaps, candles, gourmet tea and jewelry. You will find new Lipstick Ranch fine art greeting cards by Leanin' Tree with their combination of KC's Western imagery and touching, sometimes funny, words. Discover Interiors with Attitude at Lipstick Ranch, open Monday through Saturday.

525 3ʳᵈ Avenue, Longmont CO (303) 776-2505
www.lipstickranch.com

Earth Star

The spiritual journey of Earth Star owner Elizabeth Carroll enlivens the merchandise you will find at this Fort Collins store. Much of the clothing found here is imported from India, Nepal and Indonesia. The books, CDs, and DVDs are based on spiritual and Native

American teachings. The loss of family and friends in the early 1990s led Elizabeth on a spiritual journey that brought her to a Lakota/Dakota chief with whom she has worked closely for almost 10 years. Her store has become a vehicle for presenting the culture and traditional ceremonies of Native Americans and other indigenous peoples from around the world. You will find books on spirituality here plus VHS and DVD recordings covering yoga, feng shui and other paths for spiritual growth. Earth Star carries the complete series of spiritual DVDs by Chief Golden Light Eagle. Native American herbs are also available for ceremonies. Crystal massage wands and stars, incense, and aromatherapy oils offer ways to change you consciousness, while a sarong, a velvet Renaissance-style cloak or a beaded purse add exotic touches to your wardrobe. Earth Star participates in many outreach programs and has established a foundation for the benefit of the indigenous people of North America. Heighten your own sensibilities while honoring indigenous cultures around the world with a visit to Earth Star.

619 S College Avenue, Suite 1, Fort Collins CO (970) 472-0224 or (800) 801-9207
www.earthstar-store.com

Green Logic

Logic will tell you that it makes sense to buy products that are environmentally responsible. However, finding an array of earth-friendly goods under one roof can be difficult, unless you happen to be passing through Fort Collins. That's where you will find Green Logic, a

store devoted to sensible thinking. Folks bring their diverse shopping lists here, where recycled glassware and clothing made from organic fibers are some of the most popular items. Where else can you find bed sheets, jewelry and compost products all together in one place? Owners Colleen Barricklow and Jason Cohencious won't carry it if it's not organic, recycled or sustainable. They await the day when the merchandise they sell is as common as anything that you can get at a big box store. Until then, they are proud to provide Green Logic as a means of letting people buy goods that impact the world in a positive way. As much a concept as a store, Green Logic opened in 2005 and has been received warmly by locals and visitors alike. Colleen and Jason are "painting the town green," enthused the *Fort Collins Weekly*. Do something wise for the planet by shopping at Green Logic.

261 Linden Street, Fort Collins CO (970) 484-1740
www.green-logic.net

The Great Outdoors R.V. Co.

"We are committed to offering the best value in Northern Colorado," says Jeremy Heberer, owner of the Great Outdoors R.V. Co. His business partner, Billy Williams, puts it more bluntly: "We believe you should get the best price." All of this is music to the ears of anyone dreaming of hitting the highways and back roads of America in search of adventure. The Great Outdoors R.V. Co. can set you up in style and comfort, whether you are seeking a pop-up tent camper, a 40-foot full-time fifth wheel or something in between. A large selection of fifth wheels and travel trailers fills the outdoor lot and indoor showroom, including both new and used choices from Cedar Creek, Rockwood, Wildcat and Cherokee, as well as Wolf Pack toy haulers—companies known for their quality and for backing their products with excellent warranties. The Great Outdoors R.V. Co. is a full-service RV center featuring parts, supplies and service in addition to sales. The owners believe that they have one of the top service technicians in the business in Doug Malcolm, who is master tech certified by the National RV Dealers Association. A third-party tracking agency finds that customers are so satisfied with their experience at the Great Outdoors R.V. Co. that they consistently return to do repeat business, enthusiastically referring friends and family members. Check out the Great Outdoors R.V. Co. when you are ready to experience the great outdoors. You'll be the envy of the campground with your top-of-the-line RV of unbeatable value.

3511 W Service Road, Evans CO
(970) 339-1997 or (866) 912-0340
www.thegreatoutdoorsrv.com

Palma Cigar Co.

Barber Clay Carlton followed his heart and learned how to roll cigars. The Palma Cigar Co. displays his craftsmanship; high-end aromatic cigars are expertly wrapped in premium leaves. Clay is the only cigar roller in Colorado and regularly shows off his talent at private events. The Palma Cigar Co. is not the only flower in Clay's garden. Carlton is also the man behind Cigars for the Troops, a project that began when he sent a box of cigars to a soldier in Iraq in response to a letter in a magazine. Word of mouth and press reports led to more cigars for the troops. People began making donations, and in 2006 Cigars for the Troops became a non-profit organization with the goal of bringing a touch of luxury to soldiers living in a harsh environment far from home. Clay also owns Timberline Sports Barbers in Vail, and his cigars are available there too. If you enjoy tobacco, taste the handiwork of the extraordinary Clay Carlton in an outstanding cigar from the Palma Cigar Co.

Palma Cigar Co.: 1309 22ⁿᵈ Street, Denver CO
(303) 297-3244
Timberline Sports Barbers: 2161 N Frontage Road, Vail CO
(970) 476-0502
www.palmacigars.com

Front Range Antique Mall

Treasures abound at the Front Range Antique Mall, where 50 experienced dealers offer superior American antiques and collectibles from the 19ᵗʰ century to the present.. Regulars know the inventory changes quickly at Front Range and make weekly forays to comb the store for recent additions. At 11,000 square feet, the bright, clean and airy space is coveted by dealers, most of whom have been at the mall for a minimum of five years. Owner Karen Stockley started out as a dealer at Front Range and purchased the store when it became available in 2006. Karen has lived in Colorado for 40 years and learned to love antiques from her mother. It was the love of the hunt that originally attracted her to the antiques business and caused her to concentrate her business on rare, quality pieces. Over the years, she has collected prints, china and, presently, Victorian clothing. Karen offers complimentary coffee and cookies at the mall, which is open seven days a week. Leave the dusty attics to the dealers, and take your hunt for fine American furnishings, accessories and collectibles to the Front Range Antique Mall.

6108 S College Avenue, Ft. Collins CO (970) 282-1808
www.frontrangeantiques.com

White Balcony

Make sure you visit White Balcony, one of the newest and most refreshing additions to Fort Collins. Located in the heart of historic Old Town, this store offers a little something for everyone at prices that won't break the bank. White Balcony stocks an extensive mix of gifts, cards, home décor, accessories and whimsy. Fresh and innovative merchandising, along with ever-changing products, makes for a fun and one-of-a-kind shopping experience. Owner Justine Reed, a graduate of business school at Yale University, founded her shop in 2003 and it was soon voted Coolest Store Hands Down in the annual *Vail Daily Reader's Poll*. Since moving her store from Vail to Fort Collins in 2005, Justine has relied largely on word-of-mouth publicity and has rapidly gained a reputation for offering creative products and friendly service. Find the gifts, décor and styles that are just for you at White Balcony, where the locals love to shop.

146 S College Avenue, Fort Collins CO (970) 493-3310
www.whitebalcony.com

Checkpoint Racing

Guys love cars. That is nearly a universal truth. Checkpoint Racing is heaven for guys who love cars. Owner Mitch Williams outgrew his previous location and opened the doors of his contemporary-styled shop in January of 2007. It's filled with hundreds of items displayed on galvanized walls and racks made of metal pipe. Checkpoint Racing specializes in race equipment, tuning, electronics and composites for all types of auto racing, and carries trusted brands. Sparco, Momo, OMP, DMS, SPA Design and Pyrotec are just a few of the hundreds of brands in stock. All equipment is approved for racing by the FIA (Formula 1) and SFI. Supplying safety gear for European, rally, circuit and road racing, Checkpoint has your intake, header, clutch, harness, and helmet. Every motorhead will find what they crave in seats, race suits, shoes, gloves and performance parts in the shop and at the web site. Come in to try on clothing by Dickie's Girl, Piloti and Hat Version. Checkpoint Racing's boutique of racing items includes DVDs, key chains and books. The comprehensive inventory even includes house wares by Auto Art, such as dishes and clocks. Come to Checkpoint for vintage pin striping for any kind of vehicle. Mitch enjoys bringing an entire inventory of goods to your racing event. If you love cars, race to Checkpoint Racing and fulfill your need for speed.

3434 Brighton Boulevard, Denver CO
(303)296-3030
www.checkpoint-racing.com

The Moose's Caboose

When George and Candi Knox opened The Moose's Caboose gift shop in 1964, they didn't know it would end up as one of the most popular stores in the Vail area. Today, The Moose's Caboose is a fun, trendy shop offering all kinds of gifts including handmade jewelry, candles and a variety of accessories. Complete your country cabin with one of the popular trail signs, or find the perfect gift to take home in the jewelry section, which houses more than 3,000 sets of earrings. If you're visiting in the area, let the Moose's Caboose be your first stop for distinctive Colorado gifts. From rustic home décor to sharp-looking leather belts, you're sure to find something to suit your personal style. In addition to gifts with local flavor, enjoy browsing the work of local artists. The Moose's Caboose is home to some of the most creative handmade jewelry, pottery and Vail-themed ornaments around. Winter visitors will enjoy the easy Christmas shopping, and more often than not, they leave with much more than they had planned. Women will love the selection of bags and purses at the Moose's Caboose, as well as the cool sunglasses. One of the shop's biggest draws is its large selection of Brighton leather. These high-quality leather goods come in a variety of styles and colors, ranging from chic and modern to classic and elegant. To find some of the most diverse and original gifts in the area, visit the Moose's Caboose.

291 Bridge Street, Vail CO
(970) 476-5403

Edward's Pipe & Tobacco

A relaxing smoke can help keep stress at bay. So says tobacconist Armando Monge, owner of Edward's Pipe & Tobacco, who lives by the motto: "The more I puff, the less I fume." With its two smoking lounges, his business is a haven for cigar and pipe enthusiasts. One lounge is open to all adults, while a downstairs lounge featuring pool and poker tables, plush chairs and a big screen television, is exclusively for members. Edward's boasts one of the largest humidors in the state, holding about 1,500 cigars for sale. Monge also sells and repairs pipes. He offers pipe buffers for shining and 75 blends of tobacco to sample. Folks enjoy in-store discounts when they become members or when they rent one of the humidified lockers available for cigar storage. A brother store to the original Edward's in Tampa, Florida, this smoke shop has thrived in Fort Collins since 1972. Monge keeps the radio dialed to the jazz and blues station, so kick back in the lounge and blow a few smoke rings while enjoying the relaxing atmosphere at Edward's Pipe & Tobacco.

111 W Prospect Road, #D, Fort Collins, CO (970) 226-5311
www.edwardsfc.com

RV World

The ultimate camping experience starts at RV World. The adventure of camping and travel creates an unparalleled bond between family and friends. There is nothing quite like rising with the sun and going wherever the road takes you, enjoying the true beauty of nature along the way. RV World in Fort Collins is your personal headquarters for all your RV needs. Not only will customers find a wide range of new and used units, they'll be pleasantly surprised at the relaxed buying atmosphere and the knowledgeable and hospitable nature of every salesperson. RV World is a family business currently run by Kim Donjon and her brother, Tyler Gesick. They both take pride in employing salespeople that have a sincere desire to help and to find the exact unit to fit a customers' needs. RV World has an extensive inventory of new and used units, hybrids, pop-ups and 5th wheels. With the largest parts and service department in the region, you can feel secure that your unit will always get top-notch care. RV World also has a nice rental selection, from pop-ups to motor homes, it has you covered. Before getting behind the wheel of your new rig, be sure to get the lowdown on the must-do activities in the area. Kim and her staff at RV World would be honored to help you plan your RV adventure.

4401 E Prospect Road, Fort Collins CO
(970) 493-5400 or (888) 4Your RV (496-8778)
www.rvworldllc.com

Woody's Newsstand

Although Woody's Newsstand carries more than 4,000 magazine titles, many long-time Greeley residents still call it a cigar store. That's how the business started back in the 1940s, and old notions have a way of hanging on. Woody's holds the high honor of being a member of the Arturo Fuente Connoisseur Club, proof that it still does a good business in cigars. However, its current customers are a diverse bunch, drawn to the store for many reasons. In addition to the smokes and the magazines, Woody's carries books and gift items. It is a bookstore that stays at the forefront of the local literary scene by sponsoring many book signings. Its coffee bar/café is well known for its homemade soups, sandwiches, and salads, for the cookies and other baked treats, and for granola. The Health Department has awarded the business a Smart Meal designation for featuring healthful choices on its menu. Regular customers earn benefits by belonging to the store's book club, magazine club and coffee club. With so many great things rolled into one business, you'll want to drop by Woody's Newsstand.

942 9th Avenue, Greeley CO (970) 352-8117

Double B R Alpaca Ranch
The Alpaca Store...& More!

Bette Rittinger didn't even know what an alpaca looked like when, in 2000, she saw the name emblazoned on a passing trailer. Three years later, she was the proud owner of the Double B R Alpaca Ranch and the Alpaca Store...& More! As soon as she met these friendly, fluffy South American cousins of the camel, Bette fell in love with their adorable faces, mild manners and cloud-soft fleece. She also learned that they are relatively inexpensive to raise and that their fleece, spun into yarn, is superior to wool in almost every way: it is twice as warm, non-allergenic and doesn't pull. Bette first opened the Alpaca Store...& More! as an extension of her ranch, selling fleece and yarn from her own herd as well as sweaters, vests, hats, gloves and mittens of alpaca fleece. The ranch serves as an educational center, showcasing the process of raising alpacas and the products they produce. Families and school groups love to visit the alpacas almost as much as the alpacas enjoy the children. The alpaca store has expanded to include an assortment of Peruvian and Bolivian imports, including a dazzling display of artwork by famous Peruvian artists. The store has works by local artists as well. To help spread the word about alpacas, Bette participates in an annual Alpaca Elegance fashion show to benefit Peruvian children. Discover the irresistible world of alpacas at the Double B R Alpaca Ranch and the Alpaca Store...& More!

30 W Boulder Street, Nederland CO (303) 258-1400
www.alpacabbrilliance.com

bliss, llc

A holistic philosophy and commitment to Fair Trade principles characterize the lives and business of Raquel and Eric Koch. These Glenwood Springs residents opened bliss, llc to provide a convenient shopping place for local and Fair Trade merchandise. (Fair Trade promotes standards for international labor, environmentalism, and social policy to prevent exploitation of the producer and to bring original products to the consumer.) Gentle music plays as visitors look through the clothing, jewelry, glass art and home décor items at bliss, llc. The shop offers organic body products, incense, crystals and prayer flags to help create a sanctuary in your own home. Gift wrap, greeting cards and stationery are available as well. Raquel and Eric's daughter, Alana, helps to maintain a positive influence and a child-friendly spirit in the store. The goal of the enterprise is to create a space that imparts a productive energy, so that people leave feeling happier than when they arrived. The Kochs wish to travel the world and experience different cultures as part of their work toward the greatest good of all involved. You are what you eat, drink and wear, so shop with a clear conscience at bliss, llc, where the work of finding eco-friendly merchandise has been done for you.

6810 Highway 82, Glenwood Springs CO (970) 928-0907

El Loro Jewelry & Clog Co.

El Loro Jewelry & Clog Co. retails sterling silver jewelry with semi-precious gemstones, clogs, moccasins and gifts from around the world, such as you might see while traveling. This is no accident, because traveling was the inspiration for El Loro. Originally the venture of four teachers who traveled extensively, the store is solely owned and operated by one of the four original travelers. Owner Patricia Follendorf spends a lot of time in the shop and has a solid knowledge of the products she sells. The eclectic assortment of merchandise includes metaphysical items, inspirational icons for all faiths, home décor and clothing accessories. Customers can get creative and design their own clogs with the help of the El Loro staff. The store also proudly displays the work of local artists. El Loro has been an integral part of Boulder's famous downtown Pearl Street Mall for three decades, opening in May 1977. El Loro's name translates as a type of South American parrot, an image suggestive of exotic places. Make an excursion to El Loro Jewelry & Clog Co. to bring home unique gifts for all.

1416 Pearl Street, Boulder CO (303) 449-3162

Confetti Design

Sue Sharpe, owner of Confetti Design, has spent her life immersed in clothing and textile design. When she began selling her original clothing, she never dreamed she'd be the successful designer and shop owner that she is today. Named after one of Sue's T-shirt designs, Confetti Design opened in 1990 and thrives today as one of the most popular shops in the Glenwood Springs area. An eclectic selection of casual wear, trendy handbags, accessories and gifts sets the store apart. Individualized service and one-on-one consultations keep customers coming back. Sue travels all over the country to hand-pick her wide and varied inventory. She makes sure that all of her clothes are functional and comfortable as well as stylish. Sue prides herself on presenting fashionable options for women of the real world. She'll help you find the perfect outfit for a special occasion or update your wardrobe for a new era in your fashion life. Stop in to peruse the jewelry collection and see her latest designs. Experience a new way of looking at fashion when you visit Confetti Design.

731 Grand Avenue, Glenwood Springs CO (970) 945-8830

Through the Looking Glass

Alice in Wonderland is a tale of curiosity and wonder, and that is one of its attractions for Sharon Graves. Sharon and John Graves are the owners of Through the Looking Glass, a bookstore that focuses much of its inventory on children's books. Sharon became interested in children's books while raising her own children and later volunteering in schools. She opened the bookstore to share her passion for books with others and especially to encourage children to explore new worlds the way Alice does. A theme runs throughout the store inspired by the namesake story. There are pictures, toys and clocks that run backwards. The shop stocks audiobooks, greeting cards and gifts and often hosts book signings by local and national authors. If you remember the first book you fell in love with as a child, you'll understand Through the Looking Glass. Bring your children or come by yourself to explore Through the Looking Glass and encourage a lifelong passion for reading.

816 Grand Avenue, Glenwood Springs CO
(970) 945-5931

Peak-a-Boo Toys

Peak-a-Boo Toys offer both locals and tourists the latest and greatest in playthings. Owner Jeff Boyd wants you to know that his old-fashioned, independent store differs from the big-box mega stores. First of all, there's the extensive selection for kids of all ages. Second, Boyd allows customers to play with the toys in the playroom section of the store. "Tourists always ask what there is to do in Breckenridge besides ski," he reports. Peak-a-Boo is one answer. Bestsellers include board games from Thinkfun, play vehicles by Bruder and slot car racing sets by Carerra. For the younger set, stuffed animals from Gund and Douglas cuddle toys provide plenty of opportunities for hugging. Webkinz by Ganz toys allow kids to adopt and care for an adorable dog or cat, all online. Little Einsteins will love Scientific Explorer and Be Amazing, two science lines that lead to fun and discovery. A complete section of Klutz books teach tweeners and teens how to braid their hair 15 different ways, make their own candy or learn how to play the harmonica in half a day. Complimentary wrapping makes gift-giving easy. Next time you visit Breckenridge, plan to stop awhile at Peak-a-Boo Toys. It's a great place for youngsters and for the young at heart.

117 S Main Street, Breckenridge CO
(970) 453-4910 or (888) 440-4910

European Antiques

It's hard to walk through historic Carbondale without stopping at European Antiques, a favorite local shop. Opened in 2004, the shop is filled with European treasures and personally selected linens, furniture and home décor from the markets of France, Belgium and Italy. Sidney and Bernard Poncelet had never considered going into the antique business before Bernard, a native of Belgium, had the idea to sell some family heirlooms. That notion set them on a marvelous and unexpected journey into the world of international antiques. You'd never know, looking at the grand furniture collection, vibrant linens, wall hangings and vintage artwork that fill the store that European Antiques began with just a few hand-picked items. Sidney, with her natural flair for entertaining, places each item to flatter the next. Browse through an ornate chest spilling table runners and napkins from the south of France, or consider a hand-crafted wrought-iron doorknocker to make an artistic statement. Look for that perfect antique farmer's table to set off your kitchen décor. Sidney and Bernard invite you to visit European Antiques for classic European styles and artifacts.

358 Main Street, Carbondale CO (970) 963-4438

China Coast

It is possible to infuse your home with the flavor of old Shanghai, thanks to the unusual furnishings at China Coast in Boulder. Owner Susan Gallagher loves China and fills her shop with affordable 18th and 19th century Chinese furniture and collectibles. Susan founded the shop following six years spent studying the Chinese language and Asian literature and art. She lived in Asia for seven years. For her, collecting objects from the Orient is a passion. "I love the people, their culture, languages and art," says Susan. "China is truly an enchanting world, and it is the desire of my heart to share this with the world." Susan travels to China with her husband, Michael, three times each year to personally select the items for her warehouse, a combination of antique furniture plus porcelain, sculpture, jewelry and other specialty items. She's spent the last 20 years in the United States as an importer, and uses her expertise to find quality antiques for her customers. Her inventory offers collectors access to the work of master artisans, as well as pieces from out-of-the-way shops in the Chinese countryside. You may find blue and white pottery, small lacquered boxes, apothecary bureaus studded with dozens of small drawers and tiny embroidered children's shoes here. Susan and Michael invite you to view their collected treasures at China Coast's warehouse showroom.

1930 Central Avenue, Suite H, Boulder CO (720) 406-1628
www.china-coast.com

Sévya

Sévya is more than just a place to shop. It's a forum dedicated to preserving the indigenous art forms of India. Appropriately, the meaning of the name is *caring through service*. Owners and managers Kovida Das and Joan Rasch support artisans who uphold ancient

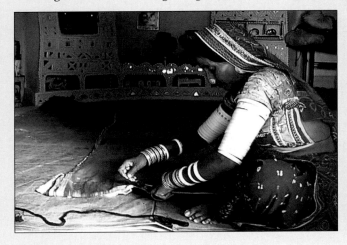

handcrafting traditions. Sévya's wide selection of items is made using the finest natural fibers and materials. The shop offers jewelry, handbags and scarves. A variety of art forms are on display, including Dhokra metal casting, ahimsa silk spinning, block printing and more. You'll find greeting cards, toys, quilts, home furnishings and other gift items that are both beautiful and meaningful. The revenue earned through the sale of these handicrafts is used for need-based development programs throughout India, under the auspices of the All India Movement for Seva. The shop is also a member of the Fair Trade Federation and is committed to Fair Trade principles. Become a part of something bigger while discovering treasures you'll adore for years to come with a trip to Sévya, a little shop that makes a world of difference.

2009 13th Street, Boulder CO (303) 440-4900
www.sevya.com
www.aimforseva.org

Noble Treasures

At Noble Treasures you'll find more than 30 antique and collectibles vendors creatively filling the spacious 100-year-old building. The shop is located in historic Old Town Lafayette, which boasts a comfortable, pedestrian-friendly vibe in an area known for high quality antique shops. Cindy Noble originally opened her antique store in 2004, and when Noble Treasures started outgrowing the space after only seven months, they moved into a much larger building. Martha Belsky then became co-owner, combining with Cindy to create a strong Noble Treasures business team. They share a common focus: to offer customers great value in honestly represented antiques at fair prices, not to mention good old-fashioned service. It's a place where when you walk in you are greeted with a smile and they probably even know your name. The shop overflows with variety. You'll find beautiful antique furniture, primitives large and small, vintage items ranging from furniture to kitchen gadgets, antique and costume jewelry, a large selection of old books, depression, carnival and crystal glassware, and collectibles of all kinds. A visit here reveals treasures in every nook and cranny. For a huge selection of authentic antiques, come browse in comfortable surroundings at Noble Treasures.

409 S Public Road, Lafayette CO (303) 926-4060
www.nobletreasuresantiques.com

Ginger & Pickles

Ginger & Pickles was named for the charming children's story that reflects an era when toys were made to stimulate the imagination, not overload it. Ginger & Pickles calls itself a General Store for Children because it is so much more than a toy store. The selection includes costumes and dolls that encourage role-playing, along with building sets, science and magic kits and many other interactive toys that encourage open-ended play. What you won't find is elaborate electronics or television-inspired toys. "We are a toy store in the European tradition, dedicated to values, aesthetics and the simple joy of play," owner Mary Baker-Blades explains. Her collection comes from around the world, and you are guaranteed to find more than one brainteaser or game that you've never seen before. *Westwood* magazine has honored Ginger & Pickles with its Best of Denver award. Mary writes *EdPlay Magazine's* "Buy the Book" column. Come and explore this fascinating store and let your imagination run wild. Visit Ginger & Pickles, because childhood is precious.

2632 Broadway, Boulder CO (303) 444-0294

The World Renowned Chile Hut & Southwest Trading Co.

There's nothing wrong with ketchup, but if you're ready to broaden your horizons, the folks at The World Renowned Chile Hut & Southwest Trading Co. are ready to help you. The selection of salsas and hot sauces at the Chile Hut numbers in the hundreds. Owner David Miller uses the Scoville heat index to justify calling his place the hottest little store in Colorado. The pungency of a typical jalapeno pepper registers about 10,000 units on the Scoville scale. David carries plenty of sauces at the Chile Hut that would make jalapenos taste like ice water, including one called the Source, which registers 7.1 million Scoville units. Needless to say, if you're new to gourmet sauces, you would want to avoid the Source or any item with the word Insanity or Inferno in its name. David can turn you on to something mild and sweet instead. Late July through August is a particularly exciting time at the Chile Hut, because that's the season for fresh green chilies from Hatch, New Mexico. The aroma of the chilies fills the air as they simmer in the roaster outside the store. Bring some home in a bag. David will provide you with recipes to make your own salsas. Also shop for Southwest rugs, blankets and jewelry at the World Renowned Chile Hut & Southwest Trading Co., your destination for alternatives to ketchup.

940 Main Street, Louisville CO (303) 664-9040
www.chilehut.com

Spanish Flea Antiques

Spanish Flea Antiques specializes in the treasures of Colorado's gaudy and wild mining past. One look through the high glass windows will intrigue any passerby. The building, which from 1904 to 1934 housed the Leadville Grocery, now overflows with antique bottles, mining collectibles and railroad memorabilia. Each treasure has a story to tell. Owners Tangereé Gillette, Michael Bridwell, and Kathy

Gillette have owned the business since 1970, when the Spanish Flea started out as a second-hand store and flea market. Owing to these beginnings, vintage and second-hand clothing are still featured in the store. Spanish Flea also offers a wide variety of costumes, which are popular for renting during Leadville's Boom Days. Boom Days, held annually in August, commemorate the town's rollicking Gold Rush days. With help from Spanish Flea Antiques, you can dress like a gunslinger, mountain man, saloon girl or Victorian lady. Kathy encourages folks to make costume reservations early for Boom Days. Other seasonal costumes can be ordered and delivered year round. Kathy, Tangereé and Michael are happy to buy, sell or barter antiques or collectibles. Touch the treasures of Colorado's mining past at Spanish Flea Antiques.

201 E 5th Street, Leadville CO (719) 486-1496

East West Imports - A Cultural Experience Center

The Asian arts are alive and well at East West Imports - A Cultural Experience Center. Owner Choko Oshima can find you almost anything you need to serve tea, sake or sushi. Choko, who opened the Fort Collins shop in 1969, fills it with Asian imports. Likewise, she fills the hearts of her customers with love and respect for the traditions of Japan and other East Asian countries. She can teach you how to speak Japanese or how

to cook like the Japanese. The shop offers classes in such age-old arts as *cha-no-yu* (Japanese tea ceremony), origami (paper folding) and *shodo* (calligraphy). You will find Asian tea sets and utensils here in addition to clothing, home décor and jewelry. If you don't find the product you seek, Choko can probably special order it or have it custom-made just for you. Whether you seek ingredients for your next sushi party, wish to prepare for your trip to Asia or even if you find yourself homesick for the East, you can make your life richer with a visit to East West Imports - A Cultural Experience Center.

203 W Myrtle Street, Fort Collins CO
(970) 493-0808
www.eastwestimportsllc.com

My Favorite Things

Since opening in 2005, My Favorite Things has been gaining momentum. "It seems to be growing daily," says owner Denise, who now features items from 50 consignors in her eclectic shop. Vendors are keeping the shop supplied with a large assortment of unburied treasure and—more recently—estate sale items. As a result, the store is an increasingly interesting place, and Denise's customers have found it a reliable source for all sorts of collectibles. Customers frequently say things like, "You've got a little of everything in here." You can find furniture, wind chimes, pewter, children's toys, clothes and gift cards. The bright, welcoming shop just makes folks feel good, which is exactly what Denise was hoping would happen. Whether you are looking for something in particular or just enjoy browsing, My Favorite Things offers Monday through Saturday hours for you to enjoy yourself among items that indeed just might become your favorite things. Denise admits to learning a great deal about merchandise values and the importance of holding onto treasures until the right buyer comes along. With so much constantly changing merchandise, you owe it to yourself to visit My Favorite Things as often as you can.

414 Main Street, Windsor CO
(970) 686-2822

The Light Connection

Shauna Barrow's aspirations for her business were small enough to fit in a kiosk at a shopping center at first. She wasn't sure whether there was enough of a metaphysical community in Louisville to support anything larger. She opened her store, the Light Connection, in 2003 when it became obvious that the demand for what she sold was considerable. "Everything I sell has a bit of magic in it," says Shauna. "Everything here is for the purpose of bringing you to a higher state of consciousness, of helping you connect to yourself." Metaphysical books, ritual crystals and aromatherapy oils are just a few of the things that you will find at the Light Connection. Native American dream catchers top a list of handcrafted items that also include angels, faeries and wizards as represented in paintings and sculptures. As a community gathering place for seekers, the Light Connection hosts workshops and psychic readings. Shauna has an open attitude to all seekers regardless of their path. As for skeptics, she pledges that if they are willing to try to connect with the metaphysical, she will help get them there. Let your journey to self-discovery include a stop at the Light Connection.

706 Front Street, Louisville CO
(720) 887-2788 or (866) 327-2788
www.light-connection.com

Photo by Lightdance Studio

Decorables & Antiques

The heirlooms and collectibles at Decorables & Antiques seem suspended in time. Most are as fresh as the day they were created, while some wear their age gracefully with a fine patina. Since 1988, Decorables & Antiques has been acquiring some of the best-quality antiques in the Denver area. Customers will find a large selection of bronzes, porcelains, paintings and furnishings spanning the Classic, Victorian, Art Nouveau and Art Deco periods. All items are in excellent condition, either carefully preserved or restored by the repair department at Decorables & Antiques. Owners Bob Leach and Chuck High invite you to bring in your own heirlooms for some expert freshening. If you'd like a professional opinion of what your antique might be worth, they would be happy to provide it free of charge or refer you to a professional appraiser. Above all, Decorables & Antiques strives to offer a rewarding shopping experience. Whether you are searching for an addition to a prized collection, a distinctive painting or a beautiful keepsake, drop by Decorables & Antiques.

6035 E Colfax Avenue, Denver CO (303)
399-8643
www.decorables.net

Town Center Booksellers

All any book lover asks of a bookstore is that it have an intriguing selection of genres and authors. Town Center Booksellers passes that test with flying colors, while offering plenty of charming atmosphere. With its leather chairs, pretty lamps and fireplace, the store might remind you of the parlor in your favorite bed and breakfast. Browse the shelves until you find a book that stirs your interest, relax in one of the chairs and read a few pages to decide if this volume is as good as the author's last. Complimentary tea and coffee prove that the owners seriously want you to feel at home and linger awhile. Clay and Louise Bennet opened Town Center Booksellers in 2004, feeling that it would fill a need in the community. Although they are proud of their store's independent status, they offer many features of a major chain, such as consistent, year-round hours and direct ordering from their website. Also, they gladly handle about 200 special orders a week. Theirs is a general bookstore with strengths in fiction, non-fiction, children's and regional. Spend an unhurried part of your day picking out a good book or two at Town Center Booksellers, located under the clock tower in the heart of Old Town Basalt.

211 Midland Avenue, Basalt CO
(970) 927-BOOK (2665)
www.towncenterbooksellers.com

Photo by Stephen Collector

Eads News & Smoke Shop

While the world has changed profoundly since 1913, Eads News & Smoke Shop proves that there are some constants in life. Eads has been the place in Boulder to find a good smoke and an interesting magazine since Woodrow Wilson was president. Its walk-in humidor is considered hallowed ground by the legions of cigar aficionados who drop by Eads regularly. Mike Johnson and Marg Parkhurst, the senior members of the staff, have been fixtures at Eads since Ronald Reagan's first term, while others have been greeting the same customers at this friendly shop for upwards of 15 years. Regulars at Eads are a well-informed bunch, thanks to the huge selection of newspapers and magazines available at the store. The number of free newspapers alone is staggering. What's more, you can name any topic under the sun and there's a good chance that you will find a magazine on the racks that covers it. Take care of your smoking and reading needs at Eads News & Smoke Shop, a business with definite community presence.

1715 28th Street, Boulder CO
(303) 442-5900
www.eadsnews.com

Englewood Camera

Offering a picture-perfect camera-buying experience has been the tradition at Englewood Camera for more than four decades. Owners Les and Bryce Cole are proud to offer everything from antique cameras and equipment to the most modern digital gear. More than one shopper has commented on the store's old-fashioned looks and service. The store buys, sells and trades used photographic equipment, making it the only store in town to offer older-style film cameras and antiques from the pre-color era that are still functional. If you're looking for the latest in digital photography equipment, you'll be delighted in the variety here, including well-known brands such as Canon, Pentax and Nikon, as well as lesser-known, high-end brands such as Leica, Gitzo and Hasselblad. You can come to Englewood Camera for repair services as well as film processing and digital video transfers. The staff is made up of trained photographers who can answer all your questions expertly and help you pick the right gear for you. Come to Englewood Camera for everything you need to put your world in focus.

5855 S Broadway, Littleton CO (303) 797-0700
www.englewoodcamera.com

Lolly's Hallmark Shop

The Colorado presence is evident throughout Lolly's Hallmark Shop in Greeley, with many locally made specialty products that are as fun to give as to receive. Little Mismatched socks come in sets of three unmatched socks to mix and match as you please. Boulder Candy—mountain-sized rock candy—will appease your sweet tooth, while clean-burning WoodWick soy candles and heavenly-scented Yankee candles will fill your home with delicious ambiance. Make it a celebration with hand-painted Lolita wine and martini glasses from Lolly's. Finish your day with luxurious Goldleaf bath salts and lotions or Lollia bath products, which come in attractive gifts sets that have been recommended by Oprah. You can also browse a variety of specialty picture frames that will keep your memories present and alive in your home. You'll have to visit Lolly's to truly appreciate the selection, which includes a full line of Hallmark cards and products from as many as 400 different companies. Find out why *Greeley Tribune* readers voted Lolly's Hallmark Shop the Best Gift Shop in town.

2030 35th Avenue #E, Greeley CO (970) 356-3929
www.lollysgifts.com

Tewksbury & Company

Few stores fill their niche as neatly as Tewksbury & Company. Dave Tewksbury's shop, known as Downtown Denver's Lifestyle Store, has made a hit by understanding its clientele and its product inside-out. The store is all about enjoying Colorado. You'll find fly-fishing supplies, premium cigars, award-winning Colorado wines and various collectibles. Dave personally leads guided fly-fishing trips and has spent 30 years in the Colorado wine industry. He offers wine tasting daily at the shop. His hand-picked staff are all expert fly-fisherman and equally versed in cigars and wines, so you'll find exceptional person-to-person assistance when you come to browse the selection at Tewksbury. If you're a cigar aficionado, you'll love the authentic, limited-edition cigar store Indians—collectible wooden statues like those that traditionally advertised cigar shops. They're handmade from American hardwood and range from 4 to 6 feet high. You'll also see beautiful replica totem poles. Tewksbury offers a cigar-of-the-month club to feature prime picks from its more than 300 cigars. Find exceptional selection and service at Tewksbury & Company, a local legend.

1512 Larimer Street, Denver CO
(303) 825-1880
www.tewksburycompany.com

Paper Doll

Paper Doll is a whimsical shop that will put a smile on your face and a spring in your step. This charming card and gift store is owned Troy and Angela Rivington whose good taste and artistic style lets them create eye-catching vignettes that display the latest trinkets and treasures. Paper Doll has an ever-changing inventory of hand-selected jewelry, candles, paper products, gifts, seasonal items, toys and fun accessories for the home or office. Troy and Angela's goal is to provide a pleasing environment where people enjoy shopping for any occasion or just dropping in to say hello and see what's new. Fresh, subtle aromas waft off the natural products, and a cool musical beat adds just the right backdrop to the shop's cheerful ambience. Customers often express their delight in the store's beauty and wide selection, and they are equally charmed by the sensational service they receive. From elegant photo frames to funky gift-wrap, you can find it at Paper Doll, where it's all about the experience.

1141 Pearl Street, Boulder CO (303) 449-1661

Adorn Home and Gift Gallery

At Adorn Home and Gift Gallery, the adornments for you, your house, your kids and your pets are so unusual and change so frequently that some Longmont residents stop by twice a week to see what's new. Scott and Sharald Church opened the shop in 2006. They travel throughout the country to find their inventory and represent about 50 local and national vendors. Scott, who is an artist, contributes to the store's products with cards, wrapping paper and wall art. He is just one of the local artists represented in the shop. You will find nostalgic wall clocks, candleholders, vases and other colorful home accents along with such personal accessories as handbags, hats and jewelry. Shoppers enjoy light and airy surroundings. The welcoming space contributes to a developing downtown shopping scene. The Churches used their retail experience and art background to find a fit for getting out on their own in the business world. Their shop is open Monday through Saturday. Start your search for a gift, a wardrobe accessory or home décor with a visit to Adorn Home and Gift Gallery.

668 4ᵗʰ Avenue, Longmont CO (303) 651-6933

Jax Mercantile

Jax Mercantile has been Ft. Collins' source for outdoor gear since 1956. Two Jax stores serve the area—one devoted to outdoor recreation; the other, to farming and ranching. Whether you work outdoors or play there, these two stores have your needs in mind. Owners Jim and Nanette Quinlan take great pride in their sales people who have helped to build both the outdoor and farm store. The employees here are buyers as well as sellers with interests that match your own. If you are looking for hunting or fishing gear, you can count on a salesman who is a hunter or fisherman. If you are buying tack, tools or fencing, you'll find a farmer or rancher with

personal knowledge of the products you require. That knowledge has earned Jax letter after letter from satisfied customers. Boating, archery, climbing, camping, paintball—Jax knows what you need to get into the Colorado outdoor scene. An optics department offers cameras, binoculars and telescopes as well as radios and GPS units. A coffee bar lets you savor an espresso in between checking out military surplus or trying on boots. The farm store caters to your pets, your livestock, your home and garden. You will even find a gourmet kitchen section with locally produced foods, small appliances, dishes and cookware. Prepare for your outdoor work or play with a visit to Jax Mercantile.

1200 N College Avenue, Ft. Collins CO (outdoor store) (970) 221-0544
www.jaxoutdoor.com
1000 N Highway 287, Ft. Collins CO (farm store) (970) 484-2221
www.jaxfarmandranch.com

The Heart of the Earth

The Heart of the Earth anchors the eastern end of the downtown Loveland shopping district by offering an eclectic assortment of metaphysical supplies. Proprietor Gloria Ross opened the store in 2001 to provide the community a resource for crystals, books, music, gifts and Feng Shui supplies. By offering the necessary information and tools, Gloria enables her customers to explore alternative holistic life choices. Gloria began exploring other options in beliefs and practices in the 1960s and developed her spirituality over the years based on what worked for her. The Heart of the Earth enables her customers to research their own alternative choices. Customers feel the caring, relaxed atmosphere from the moment they step into the store, which is located in a delightful cottage. The Heart of the Earth is noted for its expansive array of stones, crystals and minerals that harness energy and hold many healing properties. You'll find a full line of aromatherapy supplies including an exclusive line of essential oils. Gift selections range from magical fairies, delicate angels, to all manner of chimes, candles, incense and jewelry. No matter what you are seeking, let Gloria's passion for personal growth and spirituality help you on your way. Stop in and check out what The Heart of the Earth has to offer you.

447 E 4ᵗʰ Street, Loveland CO (970) 461-7970

Momma Style

Momma Style in Loveland stands out as a delightful boutique nestled in the heart of Historic Downtown Loveland. Owner Sarah Sailer and her husband Jeremiah, originally from Santa Cruz California, moved to Loveland to raise their family. Once settled, Sarah's entrepreneurial spirit quickly led her to look for an outlet to once again sell the baby items she had produced and sold in California. A friendship with a local mom who produced custom maternity-wear spurred her on to create this momma boutique, a dream that seemed to blossom overnight. After extensive renovations to a space in an old 1920's building, and countless hours sewing, planning and painting, Momma Style opened for business on July 22, 2005. This boutique offers one-of-a-kind gift items, many of them handmade and designed by Sarah, including chenille blankets, retro-inspired onesies and custom bedding. In addition to luxurious nursing bras and other Momma essentials, Momma Style carries one of the best selections of classic wood and nostalgic tin toys in the area. You'll be reminded of your childhood when you see a Jack-in-the-box, a tin top or wooden Tinkertoys on the shelves. Consider pampering a Momma-to-be with the cranberry sugar scrub, or pick up the wooden sushi playset with velcro chopsticks for the budding sushi lover in the family. Whether you come to Momma Style to pick up a gift for a baby or child, a shower gift for a Momma-to-be, or some classic toys for your own collection, you'll be glad you didn't pass up this little treasure.

238 E 4th Street, Loveland CO
(970) 461-4780
www.mommastyle.com

Weddings, Events & Photographers

Jordan's Floral Gardens

Flowers are always attractive, but the length and brilliance of their display has a lot to do with the varieties you choose and how you grow them. Warren and Beth Jordan, of Jordan's Floral Gardens, have been taking the guesswork out of spectacular blooming combinations since 1979. Jordan's Floral Gardens grows flowers and sells them both cut and in containers. The Jordans create about 4,000 hanging baskets each year using 30 flower varieties. No time to pick out the best annuals and arrange them for long-lasting bloom and eye-popping color? Let Jordan's do the growing for you. You simply take home potted containers that will fill your patio with gracious good locks all summer. Not sure how many geraniums to plant or what to do with those cascading petunia-like Million Bells? Jordan's gets it right, so all you have to do is care for your purchase. Jordan's cut flowers offer similar satisfactions. Warren and Beth grow many of their flowers on the two-acre site and pick them at just the right moment to assure maximum longevity. Brides prize these blooms, and Jordan's obliges by handling the flowers for more than 70 weddings each year. Warren and Beth estimate that in the last 27 years they have raised 40 million cut flowers. You'll find their specialty bedding plants in nurseries from Casper to Colorado Springs. Stop by Jordan's Floral Gardens soon and brighten your day.

900 N Taft Hill Road, Ft. Collins CO
(970) 482-4471

Lionsgate Event Centers

Lionsgate Event Centers can help you throw the event of the year, be it a wedding or other event. Since 1990, owner Marie and Tom Jenkinson and their gracious team of professionals have helped families and companies create perfect scenarios for every occasion. The Lionsgate Event Centers are three venues elegantly outfitted with antiques and sophisticated touches throughout. The Gate House, which dates to 1910, was originally a dairy farm, and is ideal for groups of 150 to 500 or more. The Dove House was built in 1927 by

renowned architect William Bowman. It is appropriate for somewhat smaller gatherings of up to175. Overnight accommodations are available at the Suites at Gallery Ranch, two romantic retreats well suited for a wedding night or other special occasion. Lionsgate makes event customization easy by including a wide spectrum of rental items and services as part of its standard package. It also works with a large number of local vendors, including caterers, photographers and officiates. With the help of the company's expert organizers, you can quickly plan every aspect of your special day and then proceed, secure in the knowledge that Lionsgate will execute each step of the plan flawlessly. Learn what it is like to throw a relaxing event with the help of Lionsgate Event Centers.

1055 S Highway 287, Lafayette CO
(303) 665-6525
www.lionsgatecenter.com

Contemporary Studios

Stan Kerns, whose sharp eye and artistic sense have been creating beautiful photographs since 1978, practices his profession with a real grasp of the history of photography and the fine arts. After all, he has studied with some of the greats, including Ansel Adams. "I got a chance to pick his brain many times," says Stan. His workload shows that, after nearly 30 years of running Contemporary Studios in Greeley, his enthusiasm for his craft has not waned a bit. He still does about 30 weddings a year in addition to the innumerable   portraits he shoots of high school seniors and families. He never loses sight of the fact that he is dealing with people who have entrusted him with creating a permanent record of an important moment in their lives. It's Stan's philosophy that when someone looks at one of his photographs, that viewer should not feel that he or she is gazing at a picture but at a person. His time spent studying with the masters has deepened his understanding that a photograph is not only a reflection of the person being portrayed but of the photographer as well. Therefore, Stan strives to put his best into every project he undertakes. To have your portrait by a skilled photographer who is also a thoughtful spokesperson for his profession, contact Stan at Contemporary Studios.

1522 11ᵗʰ Avenue, Greeley CO
(970) 352-0301
http://web.mac.com/stankerns

Who's Got Thyme Catering

Whether you are looking for a formal wedding dinner, a buffet sandwich spread for a corporate function or hors d'oeuvres for an intimate party, Who's Got Thyme Catering is ready to serve you. Jennifer Burchett worked as the company's event designer for three years before taking over as owner in 2006. Her desire to get to know her clients results in creative, customized events and lasting friendships. The company handles 65 to 85 weddings a year as well as other functions. Along with the menu of Executive Chef Max Humbrecht and the services of trained bar tenders, servers and on-site chefs, Jennifer is always glad to recommend event locations, photographers, floral designers and other professionals. "It doesn't matter what the event is, I just try to make it as simple and easy for my client as possible," says Jennifer, whose versatility has made her the runner-up for Best Boulder County Caterer two years in a row. What Who's Got Thyme lacks in size, it makes up for in quality and attention to detail. Want a dinner with a Tuscan, New Orleans or New Mexico theme? Planning a brunch, luncheon or barbecue? Start your entertainment plans with a consultation at Who's Got Thyme Catering.

345 Main Street, Longmont CO
(303) 772-5669
www.whosgotthyme.com

De Croce Photography

Edward De Croce has been using photographs to capture moments in time for more than 40 years. He introduces unique insights and perspectives into every project he accepts. Through De Croce Photography, Edward offers a full range of personal and corporate photographic services. He takes creative and engaging pictures of weddings, individuals and anything that may catch his inspired eye. Gracious as well as artistic, Edward truly connects with his clients, and this helps him create distinctive images that capture the imagination. Each of Edward's photographs has a life of its own and can instantly transport the viewer back to that special time and place. Edward's parents, Edward A. and Singe De Croce, founded the studio in 1960, making him the second generation Edward at De Croce Photography. Edward has been at the helm of De Croce Photography for 20 years. He has traveled across the country and the globe in pursuit of his passion and has captured countless images of children and families, lovers and actors, each suspended forever in a portrait that future generations will cherish. Edward's stunning photographs of the ballet have graced the pages of *Dance* magazine. He has photographed judges, politicians and popes, as well as parents with their blissful children. Ensure that your wedding album, personal portrait or other important photography is the best it can be by relying on De Croce Photography.

Denver CO *(303) 388-6353 www.decrocephotography.com*

Photo Element

Photo Element captures special moments with its artistic, professional photography. Partners Tait DeBaca and Julie Luehrs founded their studio in 2004 and quickly earned a large and loyal following of clients who are enamored with the duo's talent and skill. Julie holds a degree in fine art, and Tait has an extensive photojournalism background. Together, they offer their own special perspective into the world of photography. The result is striking photographs that capture a viewer's imagination. Photo Element is a full-service photography studio that offers an array of on- and off-site services. The studio can handle commercial work, senior photos, wedding photography, inventive family portraits and any other special photographs that you might desire. All photos are digital. Both Julie and Tait are happy to use your suggestions about a particular shot, which guarantees that you will end up with pictures you truly want. Photo Element hosts a website where you can view and select your photographs for purchase. Turn your family's memories into works of art with Photo Element's creative, professional services.

1501 Boulder Street, Denver CO
(303) 433-0267
www.photoelementstudio.com

Lyric Ensemble

Adding music to your special event can assure its success by creating a comfortable atmosphere infused with balance, unity and continuity. The Lyric Ensemble understands that the great composers infused their music with these same elements and works with you to present the sound that will fit your event. Cellist Kimberlee Hanto created the Lyric Ensemble in 1987 and now acts as manager for the group. She loves playing chamber music and has a natural instinct for business. She also holds degrees from the Cleveland Institute of Music and the University of Colorado. For 20 years, the Lyric Ensemble has established a reputation of excellence with private performances of the master composers held throughout the Rocky Mountain region. The 12 professional musicians that comprise the Lyric Ensemble can perform as a quartet, trio or duo. Depending on the ensemble you choose for your event, the musical selections can include traditional wedding music, as well as popular, jazz or classical standards. The Lyric Ensemble is quite flexible and has played indoors or outdoors at such events as weddings, corporate parties and receptions. The ensemble's website allows you to listen to audio demos and view sample contracts and repertoire lists. Let the Lyric Ensemble bring the music of the masters to your special event with a call to Kimberlee.

3156 9th Street, Boulder CO
(303) 442-2025
www.lyricensemble.com

SongBird Flowers

Even before she became a professional florist, Nancy Anderson had an eye for floral arrangement. She has always been something of a naturalist, and would often gather bouquets of flowers and grasses for friends and family while walking in the mountains. Nancy honed her natural ability with formal training, and in 2003 opened SongBird Flowers in Bailey. Nancy's fresh approach to floral design earned her the 2006 People's Choice Award from the local newspaper as Best Florist. Nancy is a multi-talented designer who creates arrangements for affairs ranging from formal events to everyday occasions. She designs European-style plant baskets, and creates a wide variety of wreaths, including herb wreaths, bird seed wreaths and holiday wreaths. Nancy also carries high-end silk florals. "I believe a gift of flowers is unlike any other to create lasting memories and make people, both givers and receivers, feel special," she says. Think of Nancy as your neighborhood mountain florist. Call SongBird Flowers for floral arrangements that are as spirited as a bird's song.

Bailey CO
(303) 816-0065 or (800) 964-1059
www.songbirdflowers.com

Capelli Floral

If you are planning a wedding, you will appreciate knowing that one name will take care of both your flowers and photography. Capelli is the name. Denise Capelli owns Capelli Floral, and John Capelli is a professional photographer specializing in weddings. Flower shops are everywhere, but Denise cites several reasons why Capelli Floral enjoys such tremendous customer loyalty and word-of-mouth referrals. She is one of only 17 florists in Colorado certified by the American Institute of Floral Designers. This guarantees that folks who are looking for something extraordinary will find it here. Also, the selection of flowers at Capelli Floral transcends the every day and includes exquisite orchids and calla lilies. In addition to adding beauty and elegance to weddings, Denise's arrangements show up as centerpieces at many corporate events. Gift baskets are another specialty. Denise's shop is a showcase for contemporary photography and sculpture from around the world. Combine this with the beauty and fragrance of the flowers, and you might find yourself lingering for a while. Consider Capelli Floral and John Capelli when planning your wedding. Now if only they did cakes as well!

11 E Louisiana Avenue, Denver CO
(720) 570-1307
www.capellifloral.com

Westminster Flowers & Gifts

At Westminster Flowers & Gifts, the goal of creating long-term customer relationships is a top commitment. The family owned and operated business was an anniversary present from Donald Clark to his wife, Marie. Both were mourning the loss of their daughter, Delores, who had been killed in an automobile accident. Delores had loved bringing her mother flowers and missed the presence of both the flowers and her beloved child. Donald enrolled Marie into a local floral design school and upon graduation bought her the flower shop as a surprise. As he handed her the keys he said, "This is your sandbox." Donald passed away shortly after purchasing the shop, but 21 years later Marie still celebrates life and her memories by working as the senior floral designer here. Travis Bromley-Lujan owns the shop today, and fosters a fresh and creative approach to floral design. The shop's long stemmed roses, imported from Ecuador, are long lasting with large flower heads that hold their true red color. The roses are cut under water to prolong their freshness. Westminster Flowers & Gifts specializes in weddings. The experts here also can help you choose appropriate flowers for any occasion based on the principles of aromatherapy. The gift shop stresses quality, so you're sure to find something to please a special person here. For fresh blooms, thoughtful gifts and caring service, call or visit Westminster Flowers & Gifts.

8000 N Federal Boulevard, Westminster CO
(303) 427-3933 or (800) 745-3941
www.westminsterflowersandgifts.com

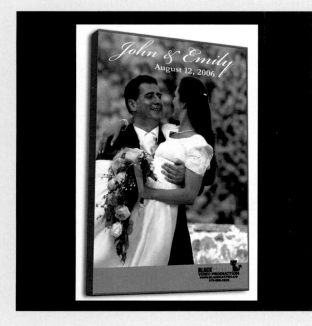

Black Cat Pro Video

Whether it's a wedding video, corporate production or television advertisement, Black Cat Pro Video has the talent and equipment to make a video production a hit. Owner David Himot and the staff at the Fort Collins video production house have been wowing their customers with fine wedding videos since 2005. Each one-of-a-kind storybook DVD is hand crafted, and brides choose the music that will accompany this record of their special day. Black Cat Pro shoots and edits the videos to produce a big emotional impact that brings the viewer back to those precious moments. Each video is professionally produced, with menus, scene selection and an image gallery. The company also produces a weekly television show called *Your Wedding TV*, which provides brides and grooms with information about the latest trends, fashions and wedding ideas. Black Cat Pro also produces exciting corporate videos, providing an essential resource for corporate communication. If you're looking to advertise on television, Black Cat Pro can bring its expertise to bear by creating ads that will appeal to viewers. For high impact video production, bring your projects to Black Cat Pro Video.

(970) 556-3525
www.blackcatpro.us

Blumen Plants & Flowers

Located in the heart of Nederland is a flower shop that encapsulates the quality lifestyle of the Colorado Mountains. Blumen Plants & Flowers, the premier boutique for flowers, serving Nederland and the surrounding mountain communities since 1986, offers a wide selection of quality flowers and products at prices often less than Boulder. Proprietor Kristen Barnett always puts her magic touch on bouquets, floral arrangements, corsages, boutonnieres and everything else she creates. She delights in being a part of organized events such as weddings, proms and formals, as well as interacting with each individual whether they are picking up a dozen roses for a sweetheart or just browsing the beautiful gifts throughout the store. The selection of products available at Blumen Plants & Flowers are as colorful and varied as the fresh-cut flowers and potted plants Kristen carries. Hand-blown glass vases by Raindance Glass, Moon Gulch medicinal products and one-of-a-kind greeting cards from Art by Sky make this boutique a must-see when you are in Nederland.

176 Highway 119 S, Nederland CO
(303) 258-3707
www.blumens.com

Suzanne Shaff Photography Worldwide

It is a passing moment, but its essence is timeless. Fabric flutters; glass clinks; a pair of eyes look up—and a camera clicks. Capturing the spirit of a relationship in a stolen moment is one of the specialties of Suzanne Shaff Photography Worldwide. Known particularly for wedding work, portraits and pet photography, Suzanne brings a photojournalist's love of the spontaneous to even the most formal of occasions. Her delight is to show off what people are all about. Whether the setting is elegant or everyday, her subjects emerge with a freshness and immediacy that seems to convey their very thoughts. Pets, comfortable in their own environments or with their owners, display the personalities that their families love. Wedding portraits convey both grand scope and personal intimacy. Black and white photos are a particular specialty of Suzanne's, and she includes some in every photo package. "Black and white pictures are so timeless and romantic," she says. "Black and white captures emotions that are universal: love, joy." Though her home base is in Denver, Suzanne travels extensively, photographing wedding ceremonies, engagement portraits, families and individuals at work and at play. Suzanne also shoots for corporations and not-for-profit organizations, both locally and internationally. She pursues special projects and photographic essays, for example, a four-year study in Aguascalientas, Mexico. To see samples of Suzanne's striking work, come to Suzanne Shaff Photography Worldwide.

1321 E 12th Avenue, Denver CO
(303) 332-7115
www.shaffphotography.com

Tim Zandee Photography

In the fast-paced society we live in, Tim Zandee's photographs are an antidote. Patience is perhaps the most important component of Tim's work. Specializing in natural scenes, he will wait for days if necessary for the perfect lighting, the right moment to click the shutter and produce a once-in-a-lifetime image. Zandee shoots medium format slides for their rich color and resolution. He specializes in four-by-five-foot and even six-and-a-half-foot, wood-mounted works. These standing pictures capture with true-to-life impact of that magical moment when light and presence came together in just the right way. Some of Tim's work has taken him to Hawaii, Oregon, Utah, Colorado, Montana, Alaska, the Southwest, Mexico, Germany and Italy. His images of the Southwest, Colorado and Mexico are especially popular. Tim's work is exhibited in art shows across the United States. Although Zandee is recognized worldwide, he will still take the time to meet with clients at their home, by appointment, to help place their purchase. Check the website for an event near you and to view the magnificence of our world as seen through Tim Zandee Photography.

11526 Harlan Street, Broomfield CO
(720) 887-6049
www.tzimages.com

Carlson's Barbeque Specialties

Chuck Carlson has been in the barbecuing business for more than 30 years, and it shows in the way he prepares each piece of meat. He and his wife, Charlotte, began Carlson's Barbeque Specialties as a way to give back to the community and promote their own livestock and meats. They started by catering a few special events, and found that not only did they love their new occupation, they were exceedingly good at it. The Carlsons can cater any event with any type of meat prepared any way imaginable, from prime cuts of beef and legs of lamb to roasts, turkeys, chickens and even whole hogs. Whether it's a corporate gathering of 3,000 people or an intimate get-together, the pair will always provide top cuts of meat to every customer. Carlson's Barbeque Specialties specializes in giving all clients exactly what they want, and to that end they offer a plethora of side dishes. A rainbow of salads, vegetables and potatoes are prepared any way the customer likes. There's a reason why customers keep coming back to Carlson's Barbecue Specialties—by raising animals the old-fashioned way and using recipes passed down through the generations, the Carlsons make a truly memorable meal. For barbecue that'll you'll remember, pay a visit to Carlson's Barbecue Specialties.

340 East C Street, Greeley CO
(970) 353-8095

Joanna B. Pinneo Photography

Pulitzer Prize nominee Joanna B. Pinneo is a photographic artist who knows how to respond to opportunities. Joanna doesn't believe so much in posing her subjects as she does in letting them be themselves and wait for the photographic opportunities to find her. This strategy has put her on the cover of *National Geographic Magazine* and the book titled *Women Photographers at National Geographic*, as well in a variety of other notable publications. Joanna is also the winner of the Alfred Eisenstaedt Award for Best Photography and the Nikon Sabbatical Award, which she earned for her photo essays that document teen-aged girls coming of age. Joanna has worked in 65 countries across the world and will happily travel for her clients. While Joanna B. Pinneo Photography can meet all of your photographic needs, the company specializes in documentary-style wedding and family journals that will allow you recapture events decades after the camera's click captures the moment. Let Joanna turn your special days and honored events into photographic essays that capture the true essence of every moment. Make a call to Joanna B. Pinneo Photography.

Longmont CO
(303) 485-2341
www.joannabpinneo.com

A Spice of Life
Event Centers and Catering Services

A Spice of Life Event Centers and Catering Services offers a fresh approach to any memorable occasion. Owners David Rubin and Dan Bruckner and their team have been earning a reputation for excellence since they first opened their catering business in 1987. A Spice of Life specializes in elegant weddings, corporate events, and social events including bar and bat mitzvah ceremonies, holiday parties and rehearsal dinners. *Modern Bride* and *Brides* have featured the enterprise. The *Boulder County Business Report* ranks it the number-one caterer in the county. Rick Yale, a third generation classically trained chef, brings over 30 years of experience to the kitchen. Whether it's an eight-course meal for 10 or a buffet for 800, Rick's team will not disappoint. You can have your event at A Spice of Life Event Center, a spacious yet intimate venue at the Flatirons Golf Course that can accommodate up to 300. A second location at East Lake can host up to 175 for a sit-down dinner and offers spectacular views. A Spice of Life can also cater at the location of your choice. The company is dedicated to giving back to the community and donates generously each year to many organizations. Make your event memorable with food and services from A Spice of Life Event Centers and Catering Services.

(303) 443-4049
www.aspiceoflife.com

Sable Landing Event Center

Sable Landing Event Center in Firestone is elegance in the country, whether you are looking for a small group or an outdoor setting for up to 200. Romance is in the air at Sable Landing, because they love weddings; however, this event center has also been the site for many bar mitzvah's, birthday parties and other group functions. Settings for beautiful wedding photos abound in the half acre Wedding Park. Have your photos taken by the gazebo or beside the waterfall with mountain stream amid the lush landscaping and foliage. The Sable Landing staff is available to coordinate your event and will make every endeavor to make your stay a success. Only one event is scheduled per day, so guests can use the facility from 11 am to 11 pm. Groups provide their own catering and beverages. Also available is the Inclusive Package, for smaller weddings of 30, which takes place in the indoor chapel and includes an intimate ceremony, flowers, cake and champagne toast. Call for a personal tour when you are ready to consider Sable Landing Event Center for your next special occasion.

5691 Sable Avenue, Firestone CO
(303) 651-6427
www.sablelandinginc.com

11:11 Productions

"Everyone we've shown them to says they are unlike any wedding photos they've ever seen." That's how one customer expressed her satisfaction to Barbara Colombo, whose artistic spirit touches every picture that she takes for her clients at 11:11 Productions. For Barbara, there is no greater compliment than to be told that she has captured something distinctive with her lens, whether it's a natural moment of intimacy or a sudden outburst of joy. Her approach to photography stems from her background in fine art. She believes that wedding photographs should record the essence of the occasion, illuminating the unique spirit and emotions of the celebration. A storyteller as much as a photographer, Barbara finds that black and white photography is best suited to weaving the artistic element of light together with the human elements of affinity and emotion. While her specialty is black and white, she does marvelous color photography as well. A professional photographer since 1990, Barbara brings an abundance of energy and creativity to every wedding she shoots, as well as family portraits and baby pictures. Her wedding images have been featured in the *Knot Wedding Pages*, *Wedding Bells Magazine* and *Colorado Bride Magazine*. Why hire just anyone to take photographs of your wedding, when you could have an artist create a visual story album that you will cherish forever? For details on packages and a consultation, contact Barbara Colombo at 11:11 Productions.

Boulder CO
(303) 258-8118 or (303) 570-2581
www.11-11productions.com

Tara's Ark Floral & Design Studio

Tara's Ark Floral & Design Studio is much more than a full-service florist. Owner Tara Martin has stocked the shop with home décor items, such as pottery and glassware, worthy of any special gift-giving occasion. You'll also find many imaginative Western-themed lighting ideas, including lamps and a wagon-wheel light fixture. Tara's Ark Floral & Design Studio has a special collection of unusual baby gifts and clothing items, with plenty of toys thrown into the mix. Wagons, rocking horses and other Western-style toys are among customer favorites. Tara satisfies everyone's sweet tooth with an awesome range of chocolates. Truffles, pecan clusters, caramels and chocolate assortments are just a few of your choices. The shop also carries the limited edition Mill Creek statues, with the selection emphasizing whimsical animal designs. Tara's huge assortment of lovely water fountains for both garden and home is legendary. Another of Tara's specialties is wedding consultation and the associated rental equipment you may need, such as gazebos or arches. For your floral needs, Tara's Ark offers arrangements for every occasion, including the popular trademarked It's Your Day Bouquet in its own attractive glass vase. Wow your friends and family with this floral beauty to let them know that any day is a great day to celebrate how wonderful they are. As a full-service florist, the shop has all wire services available. When in Greeley, you'll want to stop in and browse at Tara's Ark Floral & Design Studio.

2914 67th Avenue, Suite 100, Greeley CO (970) 339-5545 or (800) 339-5311
www.tarasarkfloral.com

Captured by Anet

Anet Chavez-Winston conducts her personalized mobile photography venture almost entirely by referral. Since 2004, Captured by Anet has specialized in portraits and special events, including marriages and civil unions. Her portfolio shows a particular knack for capturing the personality and flair of the gay/lesbian/bi-sexual/transgender (GLBT) community. Anet is also the personal

photographer for Nordstrom in Denver and takes their employee portrait and special event photos. Her recently published portrait studies have received national recognition. Anet discovered photography as a teenager, when she inherited the role of photographer for her school newspaper. Since then, she and her camera have been virtually inseparable. Although she thrives on the intimacy of portraiture, she also captures candid moments at various public events and offers these images for sale on her website. Anet works exclusively in a high-quality digital format, which ensures that her images are both affordable and adaptable to a wide range of purposes. She also employs a cleverly designed e-commerce website to advertise and provide personalized client access to ongoing project imagery. Call to have your personality Captured by Anet.

Denver CO
(303) 522-6330
www.capturedbyanet.com

5280 Mobile DJ Services

If you love music, you might think that Cameron Trainor of 5280 Mobile DJ Services has the perfect job. This DJ-for-hire travels from one party to another, casting the spell that gets people on their feet and dancing. Consider, though, the pressure that such a mood-setter and icebreaker faces. What if the dance floor should remain empty? Fortunately, choosing the perfect tunes for each audience is an art that Cameron has mastered. Although he specializes in weddings, Cameron knows how to move any event along, from college revels to corporate events, high school reunions to Bar Mitzvahs. Most of his business comes from referrals, and not just from satisfied customers. Caterers, florists, photographers and other vendors with whom Cameron has shared events have spread the word about his song selection and professional attitude. 5280 Mobile DJ Services caters the entire Denver metro area as well as the Front Range and mountain areas. Invite Cameron to your next party and let the master bring it to life.

6379 S Oldhammer Way, Aurora CO
(303) 594-1771
www.5280mobiledj.wordpress.com

Joe Diamo—Musician
Drummer/Pianist/Band Leader

Joe Diamo is as comfortable setting the tempo with his Big Band as he is playing north Indian Classical music with a tabla player. Since the age of eight, Joe's life has revolved around music. Currently, he is working on a number of creative concert projects involving the interfacing of Jazz/Blues with indigenous music from around the world. In addition, Joe teaches drums and piano from his studio in Lafeyette, and music-related classes through local continuing educational organizations. If you are looking for a collaborator for your

musical project, especially if it is innovative and improvisational, Joe is interested in talking to you. Joe has studied with a number of world-class musicians, (see Joediamo.com). He was such an accomplished student that he was touring Europe with an all city Jazz band, along with his friend Marion Meadows, by the time he was in junior high school. At the age of 16, he became the protégé of the legendary big band leader Ray McKinley. Getting a Masters Degree in Buddhist and Western Psychology at Naropa University and serious study of the esoteric traditions of the world convinced Joe that the making of music can be a profound act; a spiritual excercise and transmission. "Music and spirituality go together like the two wings of a bird," Joe says. Hire Joe Diamo M.A. musician extraordinaire for your special ocassion, catch him in concert or contact him for lessons, inspiration and collaboration.

2020 Timon Circle, Lafayette CO
(720) 890-7208
www.joediamo.com

Jon Sheppard Photography

If you're looking at a mountain through the window of a ghost town ruin or a field brimming with alpine flowers, but you just can't seem to capture the moment on film, come to Jon Sheppard. A seasoned traveler, adventurer and masterful photographer, Jon can teach you to describe your adventures with artistic photography. In the tropics, he excelled at underwater photography, scuba diving and boat charters. In Nashville, he played drums and was a cameraman for television productions. Today, his adventures center around his home in the Colorado high country and extend to tours in the West and overseas. He will take up to 12 people on a photo safari, combining adventure and excellent accommodations with insight into the hows and whys of photography. You provide your own camera equipment for the trip. You will be in the hands of an expert adventurer who has guided raft trips, gone skydiving and taught rock climbing and kayaking. He set a world record for skiing 18 Colorado resorts in one day and has raised more than $20,000 in a day for the U.S. Disabled Ski Team. Jon enjoys people and takes pleasure capturing moments at weddings and corporate events plus taking senior class pictures and family portraits. His adventures and his talents as a writer and photographer have led to the production of award winning books, including *Someday in a Place Out West, Always Colorado* and *Cowboys, Cowgirls and Wide Open Spaces*. For photography that captures the important moments in your life, call Jon Sheppard Photography.

Avon CO
(970) 949-9131
www.jonsheppardphotography.com

The Food Guy Catering

The Food Guy Catering can handle your needs for any event, from a small business lunch to a large wedding. Since 1997, owner Tom Harper and his staff have dedicated themselves to providing every one of their customers with service suited for their specific needs. For that reason, the Food Guy has no pre-set menu. Instead of choosing from a limited range of options put forward by the caterer, at the Food Guy, you'll sit down with staff professionals and plan out your vision for your event. Whether you're looking for Mediterranean dishes, high French cuisine or just good old-fashioned finger-lickin' barbecue, they can do it. In fact, staff members can even recreate a favorite family recipe of your choosing. The Food Guy can generate menus suited to special dietary needs, including diabetic and vegetarian menus. In addition to providing the food, the Food Guy can help you with flowers, wedding cakes, photography, videography and music through its network of wedding experts. The Food Guy will work within any budget. For food specially suited to your next event, see the Food Guy Catering.

Lakewood CO (303) 727-9200 *www.thefoodguy.net*

Authentic Denver BBQ

Want your guests to have a finger-lickin' good time at your next get-together? Whether it's a small gathering of friends and family, a grand wedding or a corporate function, Authentic Denver BBQ provides just what its name implies—some of the tastiest barbecue this side of the Rockies. If you're looking to cater a small, casual get-together, try the firm's grill cart, which offers a baked potato bar, hamburgers, hot dogs and fresh-sliced watermelon. Whether you're serving 15 or more than 3,000, Authentic Denver BBQ's buffet is always popular with guests. It provides grilled chicken breast, link sausage, baby back ribs and many other alternatives, along with potato salad, baked beans and all your favorite side dishes. If you're looking for something a little more fancy, you can spring for rib eye steaks, crab legs, maple-glazed pork chops and much else. Those with tastes for south-of-the-border cuisine will enjoy the fresh grilled marinated fajitas with green chile. For dessert, there's ice cream with all your favorite toppings. In addition to food, Authentic Denver BBQ can supply service staff, table linens and even help you find décor, photography and videography services and other essentials. For food that will put an authentic smile on your guests' faces, contact Authentic Denver BBQ.

Smoked salmon platter with snacks

Pig roast

Fruit, veggie and cheese mirror

AUTHENTIC Denver BBQ
Be the *HERO* of any occasion!

Denver CO (303) 232-4038
www.authenticdenverbbq.com

Bouquet Boutique Florist

Like a beautiful vine, Bouquet Boutique Florist has woven through owner Sue Sutton's life. Sue's parents opened the Broomfield shop in 1972, instilling her from an early age with the importance of fine flowers and customer service. After joining the family business at age 15, Sue knew flowers would be her life. She and her husband, Dennis, bought the store in 1984. Today she is an award-winning designer of wedding, funeral and high-style designs. The store stocks a wide variety of flowers and plants, including tropical and unusual flowers such as orchids and birds of paradise. You'll also find English dish gardens, silk and dried arrangements. Bouquet Boutique's selection and customer service have earned recognition from the local chamber of commerce and several other organizations. If you're in need of a fail-proof gift, the florist stocks an extensive line, along with gourmet food and fruit baskets, candles and greeting cards. A fully equipped Teleflora florist, Bouquet Boutique can deliver flowers and gifts anywhere around the world. For the kind of talent and service that's in the genes, visit Bouquet Boutique Florist.

290 Nickel Street, Broomfield CO
(303) 466-1251
www.bouquetboutiqueinc.com

Express Yourself

You want the people on your guest list to know, as soon as they glance at the invitation, that your party promises to be the event of the season. Helping to get that impression across is the business of Express Yourself. Calling their store a note-ably unique boutique, sisters Amy Forsey and Erin Jones offer an array of smart stationery for everything from wedding invitations and birth announcements to corporate galas and holiday events. Customers may choose from what the owners have in stock, or browse their many design books for ideas. Weddings are a specialty. Place cards and menus, even tuxedo rentals, are all part of what Express Yourself can bring to your big day. Personalized stationery for lawyers, accountants or just folks who enjoy writing letters is also in demand. In addition, the store offers a fine selection of gifts arranged by section: office, party, wedding, baby and kids. Amy and Erin took over this business in 2003, buying it from the family friend who founded it 1992. Serving an area that stretches from Glenwood to Aspen, they enjoy working one-on-one with individuals and professional event planners alike. Invite the whole neighborhood to your next party, and let Express Yourself help you get the word out.

214 Midland Avenue, Basalt CO
(970) 927-2533
www.expressyourselfbasalt.com

The Floral Boutique

When you walk into The Floral Boutique, you may just think you've stepped into a floral paradise. Abounding with color and lush greenery, the shop has a cozy country feel. Browse the artistic flower arrangements and enjoy the great customer service. Owners Lori Haroutunian and Wenonah Recio offer personalized arrangements to brighten any occasion. Wenonah has been designing high-style arrangements in the Roaring Fork Valley for over 12 years. Lori found her heart in this creative industry after leaving the corporate world to pursue her passion. The shop was purchased by Lori and Wenonah in 2004, however it has been in Carbondale since 1989. Lori and Wenonah specialize in making smiles by the dozen with their original arrangements and special eye for detail. They offer fresh and dried flower arrangements, whimsical garden décor and assorted gifts for all occasions. Find the perfect wedding centerpiece in your custom colors, or something different and unique. Stop into The Floral Boutique to find a beautiful way to brighten someone's day.

453 Main Street, Carbondale CO
(970) 963-0866
www.floralb.com

BodyPhotage

Countless artists throughout the ages have found the human body to be the most wonderful landscape. Darrell Pierson follows in their footsteps. He offers fine art nude photography at his BodyPhotage studio in Lone Tree. His images, primarily in black-and-white, are a celebration of the human form. "It is really about people being able to express themselves as the work of art they are from their own perspective and capturing it artistically on film," says Darrell. His clients are sometimes pregnant moms and are often women seeking a truly romantic gift to give to their husband or boyfriend. Some shots are of couples. In business since 1993, Darrell understands that trust and confidence are an important part of the collaborative process of figure photography. At his no-obligation consultations, he shows potential clients samples of his work, listens to their concerns and shares ideas. Whatever nervousness clients may experience before the shoot typically fades within minutes, and the joy they experience by the end makes it all worth it. Darrell's wife, Sherry, attends the photo sessions. Her discerning eye allows her to offer advice to both Darrell and the model. A typical bodyscape session lasts from 90 minutes to two hours. Darrell does all processing in-house using the finest print materials available. Sherry does the framing. Let BodyPhotage help you express your beauty.

Lone Tree, CO
(303) 790-9335
www.bodyphotage.com

Photo by Lisa Ann Loubiere

Sturtz & Copeland

Since 1929, Sturtz & Copeland has provided Boulder customers with high-quality products for all their flower and garden needs. Owner Carol Riggs and her staff are known for their beautiful flower arrangements and tropical plants for any occasion, including weddings, baby showers, parties, proms or funerals. The shop also offers stationery and custom and stock paper goods to complement the floral designs. Sturtz & Copeland takes pleasure in serving the wedding market with stunning arrangements and coordinated announcements, invitations and thank-you notes. The shop's enormous selection of greeting cards provides choices for any celebration. The Stutz & Copeland greenhouse is the oldest and largest in Boulder County, and the Boulder *Daily Camera* has honored the company as Best Garden Center and Best Florist for many years running. Carol employs a staff of master gardeners and horticulture experts to oversee the operations of the greenhouse, which specializes in orchids and other tropical plants. In the spring and summer months you'll also find French-style container gardens and a fine selection of annuals, perennials, vegetables and rose bushes. For celebrations large and small, come to Sturtz & Copeland's shop and tropical gardens.

2851 Valmont Road, Boulder CO
(303) 442-6663
www.sturzandcopeland.com

Wines, Brews & Spirits

Reserve List

If you enjoy wine but are intimidated by the mystery and pretentiousness surrounding it, then you will appreciate the approach at Reserve List. A clear, concise coding system makes shopping for wine a cinch. That's right, the days of having to learn French place names are over, because the wines at Reserve List are not organized by region or variety, but by flavor. The six flavor categories are color coded to simplify finding them. Plus, all Reserve List selections come with tasting notes, food pairings and reviews that can be taken home with you. For example, the Full Bodied Whites are coded by a dark yellow color with notes describing their character as developed and opulent. The wines, you are told, feature the taste of lush, rich fruit with a long lingering finish. New World Chardonnay can be paired with cream and buttery sauces, lobster, salmon, chicken and pork. Wasn't that easy? If you need more information or advice, there are three certified sommeliers on hand, who pride themselves on being friendly and approachable. What's more, shopping here is easy on your wallet, because the majority of the wines are priced under $25. Most are from small boutique wineries. Be sure to check the schedule of wine classes, tastings and special wine dinners when you drop by, and find out how you can join the Wine Club and Rewards Club. Experience the ease of wine shopping at Reserve List.

1886 S Pearl Street, Denver CO
(303) 722-LIST (5478)
www.reservelist.com

Frisco Wine Merchant and Foodies

Specializing in small and family-owned brands, the Frisco Wine Merchant carries a selection of wines that you usually won't find together in one place. Owner Susanne Johnston and her staff taste everything they stock. It's one of the perks of running a wine shop. Plus, it's the only reliable way that they can help customers choose for quality and value. Public wine tastings are frequent and are usually focused around a theme or region. Foodies, which shares a location and ownership with the wine market, fills a similar niche. This is the place to go for artisan cheeses, specialty meats, vinegars and olive oils. Other items include marinades, grilling sauces and teas. The staff is always ready with ideas for pairing cheeses with their perfect wine partners. They recommend goat cheese with Sauvignon Blanc or Semillon; for a hard cheese such as Parmesan or Asiago, try a Gewürztraminer, Riesling or even sherry. You can mix and match items from the two businesses to create a wonderful gift basket. Foodies also offers party trays and picnic goodies to go. Bring your taste for the exceptional to Frisco Wine Merchant and Foodies, two business striving to bring anything but the ordinary to Summit County.

721 Granite Street, Frisco CO
(970) 668-3153 (Frisco Wine Merchant)
(970) 668-3163 (Foodies)
www.friscowine.com

Wines Off Wynkoop

When you buy a bottle of wine at Wines Off Wynkoop, the transaction is only just beginning. It's fulfilled when you return next time and tell owner Jed Rulon-Miller that his recommendation was right on target. Jed considers himself a partner in wine to the downtown clientele that he serves, a matchmaker of sorts who thrives on uniting customers with the wine that they desire. Ask him or an employee for a good ten-dollar red, and you'll activate some internal mechanism that quickly scans the knowledge stored in his brain to identify a few prime choices. During the decade he's spent in this store, Jed has noticed that customers have become more knowledgeable, and he likes to think that he's helped in educating them. After all, Wines Off Wynkoop was the pioneering wine merchant in Lower Downtown. Jed's twelve years in the restaurant business were critical to his own wine education. At his shop, there's always a new wine discovery on the horizon for himself, his employees and his customers. Stop in for advice, or you're your favorite delivered for free throughout the downtown area. Meet your perfect match of a wine at Wines Off Wynkoop.

1610 16th Street, Denver CO
(303) 571-1012
www.winesoffwynkoop.com

Turquoise Mesa Winery

For more than 15 years, husband-and-wife team Tom and Mary Joan Bueb have enjoyed sharing their passion for winemaking with friends and family. As the quality of each successive batch improved, friends began to tell them that their wines were among their favorites and encouraged them to go commercial. Taking a giant leap of faith, Tom and Mary Joan opened Turquoise Mesa Winery in 2004. The tiny-but-mighty winery, as they call it, emphasizes quality of product over quantity. Tom and Mary Joan create seven varieties of wines in the Old World way, by hand. They use only Colorado grapes, most of which are grown in the Palisade area. Stop by for a free tasting of their excellent Chardonnay, Merlot or Cabernet Sauvignon, or take a behind-the-scenes tour. The winery is open on Saturdays and by appointment the rest of the week. Find out what the Bueb's friends have been raving about for years at the Turquoise Mesa Winery.

555 Burbank Street #Q, Broomfield CO
(303) 653-3822
www.turquoisemesawinery.com

Spero Winery

For the Spero Family, fine wine making is a generations-old tradition that has culminated in the creation of a fabulous urban winery, conveniently located in the popular city of Denver. Clyde and June Spero have a two-and-one-half acre vineyard that was planted in 1996 in Denver, where Cabernet Sauvignon and Merlot are grown. The family owned and operated Spero Winery uses grapes from its own vineyard. However, due to limited growing space, it also imports grapes from Colorado's Western Slope and from Lodi, California, where some of the grapes come from a vineyard owned by June's cousin. Spero Winery has a fabulous selection of wines, each aged in oak barrels for two years before bottling, including vintages such as Muscat, Chardonnay and Sangiovese, along with Zinfandel and its own Colorado Cabernet Sauvignon. It additionally vints a wonderful Merlot and a delightful Cabernet Franc, as well as two fabulous fruity dessert wines made from plums and cherries respectively. Spero Winery hosts a wine tasting each Saturday, which includes a tour of the winery, and it is also happy to arrange for a private tasting with advance reservations. The Speros further offer a wonderful assortment of gift baskets filled with great wines and favored Italian treats. Enjoy fine wine, good friends and time-honored traditions at Spero Winery.

3316 W 64ᵗʰ Avenue, Denver CO
(720) 519-1506

DaveCo Liquors

Sporting 102,000 square feet of merchandise, DaveCo Liquors is the largest liquor store in Colorado, and possibly even the largest in the world. Owner Henry Sawaged opened DaveCo's doors last November to over 3,000 customers. With a local band, a drawing for a brand-new car and a 20 dollar coupon, this crowd-pleasing day was a hit. Now, the store averages about 1,000 customers a day and it's no wonder why. With 250 imported beers and over 650 microbrews, beer aficionados can find their old favorites and discover new ones. In addition to the extensive stock of beer, DaveCo has myriad other amenities. A 1,000-bottle chilled wine cooler, 7,500-bottle humidity controlled wine cellar, a cigar humidor and a 500-square-foot wine tasting room put this store in a class all its own. Henry's goal is to change the image of liquor stores being beer-heavy with nearly three quarters of his store being devoted to wine. Henry has also seen consumer interest rise in flavored vodkas, so his 2,000-shelf stock is a popular place in the store. DaveCo Liquors has many events to keep customers' interests peaked in the beverage industry. On-site wine tasting events take place every Friday and Saturday as well as wine-pairing demonstrations. Henry is also planning a wine dinner series to benefit local charities. Above all else, Henry knows that customer satisfaction is the key to his success. Connecting with customers on a personal level is important to him, and although he supplies the largest selection of spirits in the state, he still knows his customers by name when they come in. Stop in to DaveCo Liquors yourself for a totally new experience in liquor and wine shopping.

16434 N Washington Street, Thornton CO
(303) 951-3820
www.davecoliquors.com

KaCee's Wine & Spirits

KaCee's Wine & Spirits aims to lift customers' spirits by offering a warm, comfortable place to buy fine wine. Owners Carol and Kerry Walsh created their store's name by merging their names, along with that of Kerry's six-year-old son Keegan. You'll find around 1,500 wines here, each of them hand-picked by the store's sommeliers, which include Carol and Kerry. They taste and evaluate between 30 and 40 samples from vendors each week, keeping their supply varied and up-to-date. Unlike most stores, where wines are arranged by price or by country of origin, KaCee's wines are arranged by varietal. "KaCee's is about drinking what you like, regardless of where it comes from or how much it costs," the owners say. The wine is attractively displayed at eye level on beautiful wooden wine racks made by a local furniture maker. You'll also find a large selection of microbrew and German beers, as well as 600 different varieties of high-end spirits. KaCee's Wedding & Event Planner Program can calculate just the right amount of beer, wine and spirits you'll need for your special ceremony, in just a 15-minute appointment. The store offers free delivery, accepts returns, and will work within any budget. Come by the store for twice-weekly tastings on Wednesdays and Saturdays. Whether you're looking for a glass of wine to enjoy in the evening or something to celebrate with, KaCee's Wine & Spirits will have you raising your glass.

13640 Orchard Parkway, Suite 100, Westminster, CO
(303) 254-WINE (9463)

Photos by Michael Baker/www.inlightphotography.com

Odell Brewing Company

At Odell Brewing Company, its not just owners Doug, Wynne and Corkie Odell who take pride in the beers they create, but the 36 employees who work together to bring their award winning product to you. Doug opened the Ft. Collins brewery in 1989 with his flagship beer, 90 Shilling, a light version of a traditional Scottish ale that won him this first medal at the 1991 Great American Beer Festival. Today, Odell's five mainstay beers are all distinguished award winners with a loyal following. Look for Easy Street Wheat, 5 Barrel Pale Ale, Levity Ale and Cutthroat Porter. You'll find seasonal beers, too, such as Isolation Ale, which celebrates the joys of getting snowed in with your favorite beer on hand. Doug loves beer, but he also loves the environment that makes Ft. Collins such a desirable place to work and live. Realizing that breweries can be a drain on the environment, Odell's recycles everything from shrink wrap and office ink to spent grain and water. The company supports Bike-To-Work day and avoids using energy during peak demand times. Odell's is also completely wind powered. People are equally important at Odell's, where a minimum of $1 per barrel goes to charity. The Odells have earned the loyalty of their employees with an open company style that honors workers as extended family. Visit Odell Brewing Company and find out how a company can produce great beer by caring about so much more.

800 E Lincoln Avenue, Fort Collins CO
(970) 498-9070 or (888) 887-2797
www.odellbrewing.com

New Belgium Brewing

A bicycle trip through Belgium in the 1980s inspired home brewer Jeff Lebesch to experiment with Belgian-style beers. In 1991, he was ready to launch New Belgium Brewing with the help of his wife, Kim Jordan. The beers have been a hit, and are now distributed in 16 Western states and as far east as Chicago. Jeff and Kim have established an idealistic business model that shares ownership with employees. The best known of their beers is Fat Tire amber ale. It attains a Belgian-style balance with a light flash of hops to tame the malt. It's one of six beers produced throughout the year—New Belgium Brewing also produces seasonal and experimental brews. Integrity underlies all phases of the New Belgium product, beginning with the plant itself, which is 100 percent wind powered and uses a variety of energy efficient technologies. The company recycles everything it can, water included. Every year, about 100,000 visitors stop by to taste the beers and enjoy the electrifying atmosphere. New Belgium shares its success with the states where it sells its beer by donating $1 per barrel to local charities. The company sponsors Tour de Fat, a costumed cycling circus that supports good causes. New Belgium Brewing invites you to live by its slogan: Follow your Folly; Ours is Beer.

500 Linden Street, Ft. Collins CO
(970) 221-0524 or (888) NBB-4044
www.newbelgium.com